The Army Gets an Air Force

The Army Gets an Air Force

TACTICS OF INSURGENT BUREAUCRATIC POLITICS

Frederic A. Bergerson

THE JOHNS HOPKINS UNIVERSITY PRESS
Baltimore and London

Recipient of the 1978 Leonard D. White Award

Copyright © 1980 by The Johns Hopkins University Press
All rights reserved. No part of this book may be reproduced or transmitted in any form or by any means, electronic or mechanical, including photocopying, recording, xerography, or any information storage and retrieval system, without permission in writing from the publisher. Manufactured in the United States of America

The Johns Hopkins University Press, Baltimore, Maryland 21218
The Johns Hopkins Press Ltd., London

Library of Congress Catalog Card Number 79-18191
ISBN 0-8018-2205-X
Library of Congress Cataloging in Publication data will be found on the last printed page of this book.

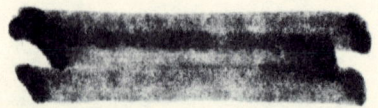

To Irene

Her children rise up and call her happy;
her husband also, and he praiseth her, saying:
"Many daughters have done worthily,
but thou excellest them all."—Proverbs 31

CONTENTS

Preface   xi

Chapter 1 / INTRODUCTION   1
Conflict and Combat   1
Soldiers as Public Officials   3
Roles and Missions   3
Compliance and Noncompliance   6
Historical Examples of Noncompliance   7
Bureaucratic Politics   15
Thematic Approach and Method of Analysis   17

Chapter 2 / AVIATION AND THE DEVELOPMENT OF THE ARMY'S MISSION: THE ARMY ACQUIRES, THEN VIRTUALLY LOSES, AN AIR ARM   20
Men at the Top   25
Lower-Level Participants   29
Armed Combat and Mission Discordances   33
Linking the Lower- and Higher-Level Participants   35
Mission: The Bomb   37

Chapter 3 / DOMAIN CONTROVERSY IN A TURBULENT ENVIRONMENT: EXTERNAL PRESSURES ON THE ARMY   39
International Setting Upset   41
Military Reorganization   43

Chapter 4 / HELICOPTER TECHNOLOGY: POLITICAL IMPERATIVE OR OPPORTUNITY?   62

Psychology of Technology   62
Technology and Doctrine   64
Technology and Procurement   66
Technology and Budgeting   67
Technology and Invention   68
Innovation and Invention   78

Chapter 5 / THE DYNAMICS OF INSURGENCY   82

Social Movements and Army Aviation   84
Mission: Who Decides?   87
Mission and Missionaries   88
Roles and Missions in a Bureaucratic Setting   89

Chapter 6 / ARMY AVIATION IN TOP POLITICS   121

Close Air Support   124
Top-Politics Rivalry   128
Procurement Politics   132
Hearings Politics   133
Trends in the Technopolitical Environment   138
The Future of the Army   141

Chapter 7 / ANALYTIC RECAPITULATION   143

The Model   151

Appendix 1. Selected Major Events in the History of Army Aviation   159
Appendix 2. Selected Aircraft Significant in the Development of Army Aviation   161

Notes   165
Bibliography   195
Index   209

TABLES

1. Perception of Organizational Legitimacy and Attitudes toward Organizational Goals   83
2. Categorization of Insurgents   84
3. Categorization of Insurgent Persisters   85

ix / Contents

FIGURES

1. Selected Postures Regarding Army Control of Army Air Support: World War II, 1941-1945 — 94
2. Selected Postures Regarding Army Control of Army Air Support: Fragmentation and Reorganization, 1946-1950 — 97
3. Selected Postures Regarding Army Control of Army Air Support: Preamble, 1951-1955 — 103
4. Selected Postures Regarding Army Control of Army Air Support: Amalgamation, 1956-1960 — 109
5. Selected Postures Regarding Army Control of Army Air Support: Envoys, 1961-1965 — 115
6. Selected Postures Regarding Army Control of Army Air Support: Comity, 1966-1970 — 119

PREFACE

Many political phenomena are not readily discerned by inquiring political scientists. The models and the techniques we use help us see more clearly those areas already perceived, but may not reduce our blind spots. This work is an attempt to come to grips with an elusive aspect of political reality—insurgent bureaucratic politics. My approach hopefully blends the behavioral detachment of the political scientist with the engaged quality of the political essayist. As such, its roots are implanted in the soil of paradox, and its fruits resist simple classification.

Two challenges stimulated my attempt: First, I sought to comprehend more fully the complexities of bureaucratic politics. I wished to learn how men in the middle of the military bureaucracy pursue a goal over time and to gauge the significance of circumventions of formal rules in such pursuits. In particular, I wanted to explain how the very nature of bureaucracy had been used to promote the cause of those members one might expect to be restricted by bureaucratic constraints. In addition, while realizing the importance of material incentives, I have stressed the nonmaterial component in motivation and have tried to show that political skill, leadership, and dedication are still important variables.

There was also a second source of motivation: I was a soldier in Vietnam. I observed the practical effects of Army aviation as a member of the 1st Air Cavalry Division and I wanted to know where all those helicopters came from. I also wanted to know where the war came from. To a certain extent, then, this book is an effort to rationalize the profoundly irrational—armed conflict. Upon reflection, I believe it was in part an attempt to exorcize the demon of my war, but I fear that this endeavor will end in failure.

My hope for the book itself is more positive. Yet I realize the difficulty of attaining accuracy when so much of the data are drawn from interviews with persons who received guarantees of confidentiality and anonymity.

Such necessary protection of sources may unintentionally foster embellished recollections and other distortions. The fact that there will be no later challenges directed to interviewees must reduce some of their inhibitions to embroider history. So much of the story of Army aviation is colored by rivalries, ambitions, friendships, and even matters of life and death, that it is exceptionally difficult to discern the truth—if there is such a thing as "truth" unaffected by human perceptions. My own limitations must also be considered here. Both the intensity and the ambivalence of feeling about Army aviation and insurgent bureaucratic politics that were present at the beginning of this project were also present, albeit partly cushioned by knowledge, at the end.

Limitations of time, money, and availability of materials forced me to select data, allowing further room for my judgment to intervene. Ironically, the government keeps certain information from the researcher through the system of national security classification, but inundates the same student with masses of other materials, much of it highly technical. I have tried to be fair and to present a balanced account of the events that are depicted herein. More importantly, I believe I have shown that a social movement can exist in a bureaucracy and thereby I have offered an additional perspective on the politics of complex organizations.

There is an urge, possibly universal, to publicly acknowledge the help of others in a long-term project. This occurs at the time of the Bar Mitzvah speech, reception of an Oscar, or completion of a book (which, for me, now seems like the former two combined). Perhaps the basis of the need to share the spotlight has something to do with the fact that public acknowledgment betokens a rite of passage—an awesome experience. In such circumstances one freely acknowledges one's debts and hence one's imperfections. One dare not suggest competencies that would call attention to one's good fortune and attract "the evil eye." It is good that this is the case, for, whatever the reason, recognition of human interdependence is a useful precursor in the effort to reduce man's estrangement from his fellows. I sincerely wish to thank everyone who has helped me, though by no means will each be mentioned.

To the more than twenty persons who sat for interviews ranging from about one-half hour to seven hours in length, I express appreciation for their patience and, in most cases, forthrightness. I came away from most interviews with a sense of respect for the individuals with whom I had just spoken—soldiers and civilians, officers and enlisted men, and men of the Army and Air Force. Interviews were conducted in six states and in Washington, D.C., and related conversations were held in these and other places including the (former) Republic of Vietnam.

I wish to thank those who helped me at the Air University Library, Montgomery, Alabama; the U.S. Air Force Office of Post Historian, Langley Air

Force Base, Virginia; the U.S. Army Artillery Center Library, Fort Sill, Oklahoma; the U.S. Army Aviation Center Library, Fort Rucker, Alabama; the U.S. Army's Office of Military History, the Library of Congress, and the U.S. Archives, all of Washington, D.C.; the Univerity of California at Los Angeles Library; the Vanderbilt University (Joint University) Library; and the Whittier College Library. Those who care for, order, and provide information do vital work for democracy and for scholarship.

I want to thank my students, some of whom typed and filed, and all of whom shared ideas and listened to tales of armed helicopters until they might have found themselves dreaming about such craft as I did. Though not exhaustive, the list must include Chris Croysdill, Becky Hancock, Jim Hickey, Winn McDougal, Katy Murphy, Marilyn Neece, Charle Wallace, Jim Walton, and Mary Weaver.

Many of my friends at Whittier College helped me in numerous ways, most of all the late Ben G. Burnett, who read all of the first five chapters and whose encouragement was vital in the completion of this work. Others who helped were Mike McBride, Cliff Morris, John Neu, Mike Praetorius, Timm Thorsen, Jan Turner, and Warren Hanson, who permitted me to use his air-conditioned office. In addition I want to thank the John Randolph Haynes and Dora Haynes Foundation for a small summer grant that partially supported this project.

Help also came from Al Labriola, Ken McNeil, Elsa Pendleton, and Ed Portis, each of whom assisted in shaping my views of the world of scholarship and my place in it, and Kim Glassco, who constructed my diagrams.

I would like to thank current and former faculty members of Vanderbilt University, including Professors Bernard Gordon and Gary Wamsley, for their interest in my project, and in particular those who read the entire manuscript and offered helpful suggestions—Professors Robert Birkby, Avery Leiserson, Harry Howe Ransom, and Mayer Zald. Especially, my thanks go to Professor John T. Dorsey, Jr., who provided a lifeline across 2,100 miles.

Most important are the family acknowledgements. My mother, Mrs. Harry Fine, and my late father, Harry S. Bergerson, must be recognized for starting me on the path to learning. And to my patient children, Heather and Philip, who would ask plaintively, "When will Daddy be finished so we can go on vacation?" the answer is "Soon!" The final acknowledgment is for the person to whom the book is dedicated, the person who helped me get on with it by combining patience and gentle prodding in a mix that in retrospect seems almost perfect—Irene Rae Bergerson, my wife.

While recognizing how deep the author's debt is to those who have helped him, the reader must place any blame for shortcomings in the book on the author, who accepts full responsibility for its content.

The Army Gets an Air Force

Chapter 1 | **INTRODUCTION**

In the early 1970s the United States Army possessed the third-largest aviation fleet of any military organization in the world. The largest single grouping belonged to the United States Air Force and the second-largest to the Air Force of the Soviet Union.[1] Even before American participation in the Vietnam War reached its high water mark, the American Army had approximately 3,500 more aircraft on the scene in Vietnam than did its sister service, the Air Force.[2]

In fact, there was a general ignorance of the place of the United States Army's air forces in profoundly affecting the conduct and outcome of the Vietnam War. Even the famed *New York Times* columnist James Reston, for instance, appeared to believe that all those men providing close air support and air lift capability for the 1971 incursion into Laos were pilots of the United States Air Force.[3] This opinion followed by three weeks an article in Reston's own *New York Times* dealing specifically with the problem of the Army's concern over a high rate of loss of helicopters.[4]

All of this would be of little more than passing interest if it were not for the intricate process by which the "land army" acquired its own rotary-wing air corps. This study endeavors to search the complexities of that process—in essence by analyzing a case of bureaucratic politics—and to come up with some suggestions about how civilian and military organizations operate. With awareness of the limitations of a case study, a model will be presented that interrelates psychological and structural patterns manifested in bureaucratic political behavior.

Conflict and Combat

One should know something of the intellectual terrain before taking his azimuth of inquiry. It seems that, much as foot soldiers of each generation slog over old battlefields, platoons of thinkers plod through the mire of man's fundamental relations with his fellow beings. One might begin the trek at a high point of generality by asking, Who can imagine a human society without division and opposition? The omnipresence of conflict, rivalry, and competition has been observed and commented upon as much as the ubiquity of cooperation, compromise, and sharing. Who can imagine a polity or an organization without opposition? Yet in this world of disharmony, most differences do not lead to altercations, and most altercations do not lead to violence.

Soldiers exist to settle violent conflicts—foreign and domestic. Despite this basic reason for existence, sometimes the behavior or mere presence of soldiers seems to bring on the furious destruction of warfare. While they are ideally in a state of constant preparation for conflict resolution through armed combat, military forces are called upon to perform this function only intermittently. In fact, just as their existence occasionally foments conflict, in other sets of conditions their presence seems to prevent or deter war.

Both the possibility and the actuality of combat have great bearing on opposition and cooperation within the military itself. For example, as the possibility of combat is believed to grow remote, the role of coercion as well as of monetary inducements in controlling the performance of men in the ranks becomes more pronounced.[5] Further, there seems to be a tendency for governments to allocate less of the available financial resources to their military services, thereby reinforcing the dynamics of scarcity and, at least in the case of the United States after World War II, increasing certain kinds of rivalry among the branches of the armed forces.[6] Contrariwise, as the chance for armed conflict appears to grow, coercive incentives seem to be replaced by normative imperatives,[7] and, at least in recent American experience, the government seems to find resources so that its armies can have the "best that money can buy."[8]

As we have just seen, problematic auguries of war affect the relations between the government and its soldiers. Fluctuating budgets may be only the outward sign of increasing influence in the counsels of government by military leaders. Changes in influence may also be outwardly adumbrated by foreign-policy alterations.

It is not only in the realm of foreign affairs that the elusive probabilities of war have an affect. In relations between citizens and the military establishment, the imminence and popularity of a coming armed struggle affect the future lives of citizens. Military manpower procurement, for instance, has ramifications in all sectors of society. As Kipling has suggested, fluctuations of attitude are reflected among the citizenry:

> For it's Tommy this, and Tommy that, an' "Chuck him out, the brute."
> But it's "Savior of 'is Country" when the guns begin to shoot.[9]

Soldiers as Public Officials

In modern nations, the uniformed warrior-leaders are officers of the military establishment and thus officials of the governmental bureaucracy. As such, their activities provide the stuff of political organizational analysis. Their activities are political in another sense. In the United States, the military is financed, organized, and legitimated by the national legislature. It is supervised, regulated, and maneuvered by the national executive. Its main business—war and the deterrence of war—is at the very heart of the purpose of government. The relationship of the armed forces to other elements of the government and society are objects of popular concern and scrutiny.

Soldiers are also more than political bureaucrats. As General Sir John Hackett wrote, "In the contract of the military man there lies unwritten but all important, what can only be described as a clause of unlimited liability."[10] The dangers of violent combat must affect the attitude and behavior of military men. Thus a challenging blend of political, military, and organizational variables confronts those who seek to understand the realities before them.

America's military has been scrutinized in many ways. Concern about the impact of military institutions on society is expressed in scholarly tomes and in daily press commentaries about the military-industrial complex (also known more benignly in other times as "those brave G.I.'s and their supporters on the home front"). Others have looked at the organization of the armed forces, the conduct of military operations, strategy and tactics, conflict resolution, weapons economics, and a variety of other non-mutually exclusive topics. In fact, there have been studies in several nations of the place of the military in politics and, conversely, of politics in the military. Such studies are clearly appropriate enterprises for those students of the public weal, the political scientists, as well as for others.

I intend that what follows should add to the present body of knowledge about bureaucratic politics by showing how certain factors that are here associated with the military operate, and how they may be relevant in other organizational settings. I further hope that this work will lead to a more complete understanding of certain aspects of America's soldiery.

Roles and Missions

Military policy making in the United States cannot be understood without an examination of questions relating to roles and missions,[11] for the controversy over roles and missions—"a complex matrix of rivalry between service and service, service and function, and function and function"[12] over "proprietary issues and strategic questions"[13]—is a prime characteristic of the post-World War II defense establishment.[14] Roles and missions issues alert us to the fact that there can be far more to the making and implementation of any arms policy than the formal decision making at the top level of government.

In the case being considered, one service's mission is a crucial variable for animating the policy process. This case is the United States Army's acquisition of a major air support responsibility and the weaponry with which to accomplish it. Although scholars have addressed themselves to similar questions of interservice rivalry and weapons acquisition,[15] their work does not seem to explain adequately the Army's acquisition of the armed helicopter, the ultimate instrument for Army control of close air support and airmobile maneuver capability. Moreover, this particular issue is fascinating because the process involved repeated evasions of formal authority (noncompliance) over an extended period of time.

The models that are most commonly used to explicate weapons allocation politics lead observers to overemphasize the rivalry for hardware and domain among the various service elites supporting new weapons systems. Professor Michael Armacost describes his model of the Thor-Jupiter ballistic missile controversy as one of pressure-group activity within a somewhat decentralized policy-making structure.[16] His book is partly a classical "plural-elite" attack on Sir Charles Percy Snow's view of military policy making. Sir Charles seems to suggest an elitist approach when he elaborates his notion of "closed politics."[17]

Both the pressure-group model and the elitist model may have great heuristic value as devices for explaining many weapons allocations decisions. The pressure-group approach is especially relevant when the men at the top agree to disagree and to accept decisions as to which way the resource pie is to be sliced. Perhaps the elitist model is useful in cases where there is a small ruling group sharing executive and legislative leadership. Neither, however, goes far enough in explaining the case of the armed helicopter.

An approach which allows for examination of factors easily overlooked by those using other methods emphasizes the concept of mission. "Mission," according to Joint Chiefs of Staff lexicographers, means "the task together with the purpose, which clearly indicates the action to be taken and the reason therefore," or "a duty assigned to an individual; a task."[18] This definition, while useful in its juxtaposing of task and purpose, is too confining in its insistence on clarity—an insistence which seems to allude to formal and legitimized statements. Further, it seems rather mechanical, the perspective of an obedient subordinate (perhaps the perspective of writers of military

5 / Introduction

dictionaries). These constraints simply do not capture the connotative richness of the concept of mission, especially its purposive aspects. The very ambiguity of "mission" calls forth philosophical, religious, political, and symbolic problems that beckon the investigator. To the soldier, mission may be what he does and why he does it, but the answers to the question Why?, particularly for a decision maker, may be potentially contradictory and unsettling. On the general level, it involves his life's work and the authority to which he is responsive. Furthermore, mission involving vocation and justification for behavior and attitudes can have tremendously powerful emotional and ideological connotations that call to mind the realm of meanings conjured up by religious missions and their missionaries. These issues will be dealt with at greater length later.

From World War II, through Korea, and on into the 1960s, the Air Force[19] leadership considered itself exclusively responsible for the air support of Army troops. In fact, Air Force domain in the control and operation of all weapons so used was authorized by high-level civilian policy makers and accepted by much of the Army leadership as well. The authorization required frequent reiteration as the changing environment brought forth alterations in role and mission assignments. Certainly the classic conception of an Army exclusively responsible for land warfare, a Navy confined to the seas and littorals with its Marines, and an Air Force soaring alone, patrolling the skies, could not be counted on as a rational policy guide for a demarcation of functions. Costs incurred by such an apparently simple solution could well have included exacerbation of political conflict, absurd inefficiencies, ineffective close air support, poor integration of forces, and an inflexible order of battle in the face of rapidly advancing technology. This did not mean, however, that the traditional conception of the services did not affect the self-image of the servicemen in terms of the mission for which they saw themselves responsible. It has always been the Army officer's task to dominate the ground; the advent of aviation provided another dimension to the soldier's notion of what constitutes the battlefield.

Victors in clashes over roles and missions are not necessarily those who operate at the highest levels of government. Rather, victory may go to those in the lower levels who clearly see their cause, who pursue it with vigor, and who can operate in a changing environment without the top administrators being able to exert control over their "subversive" behavior.

This study will be a useful tool for predicting winners in organizational struggles, but it will also examine the components of bureaucratic politics that emerge under certain conditions and the attempt by a complex organization to adapt itself to a changing situation in defiance of its own leadership and formal hierarchical arrangements.

Compliance and Noncompliance

"Civilian control of the military" is the cliche' of American civil-military relations. In the "objective" model of civilian control, the chief executive passes on through his subordinates the orders that mandate the actions to be taken.[20] These orders are likewise passed down the hierarchy of the chain-of-command structure with the task being made more specific at each lower level. This vertical arrangement stops at the lowliest trooper, who swiftly does his duty, as have his superiors before him, and thus completes the chain of compliance.

It has become a commonplace of organizational theory to question formal models of organization and to demonstrate their inconsistency with reality by looking at the behavior of subordinates. Observing the behavior of the middle- and lower-level participants gives one a somewhat different perception of the faces of power and authority. It is here that we must begin to inquire further into matters of compliance and noncompliance.

Amitai Etzioni has sought to promote our understanding of compliance by using it as an organizing concept in an effort to compare complex organizations: "It is a major element of the relationship between those who have power and those over whom it is exercised. . . . Compliance refers both to a relation in which an actor behaves in accordance with a directive supported by another actor's power and to the orientation of the subordinated to the power applied."[21] He further contends that, empirically, certain kinds of sanctions or power correspond to certain types of involvement.[22]

The significance of such a formulation for this study is that it reminds us that issues of compliance may be best understood by analytical observers who perform the difficult task of bearing in mind both psychological and structural factors. Thus, in looking at the other side of the coin, failure to comply (noncompliance), one must be alert to both the type of relationship that exists between those in formal authority and their subordinates and to the orientations of the subordinates. For example, noncompliance can range from direct disobedience of a precise order to partial fulfillment of a long-standing anticipation of a superior. These behaviors likewise may mean different things to the lower participants; and these meanings may range from passive indifference to a fiery commitment that can lead to unauthorized courses of action.

Since the question of compliance arises in so many settings, analysis of this concept is of necessity multifaceted. One seeks to know not only who complies (or does not comply) with whom (or what), but also to what extent, in what manner, and why in fact there is or is not compliance. One must ask if patterns of compliance and noncompliance reflect some other realities that are of a different order than what the apparent issues of compliance would suggest. Merely looking at compliance in its own right would deprive one of more meaningful insights into human behavior.

Historical Examples of Noncompliance

Noncompliance by military men with authoritative direction is neither a new nor a newly observed phenomenon.[23] As far back as *The Republic*, Plato sought devices for insuring that the people, living in a political unit, including soldiers, were in a state of harmony, this state being reached by everyone doing that for which he was best suited.[24] In case there was any question as to what was correct behavior, compliance with the wishes of the philosopher-ruler elite would provide proper direction. Machiavelli advised the "Prince" as to which type of soldier could best be expected to comply with the sovereign's wishes under various circumstances. Examples made plain the fate of those who could not be assured of compliance—for example, the Roman emperors Commodus (killed by his soliders), Pertinax (slain by the Praetorian guard), and Julianus (put to death by soldiers avenging Pertinax).[25] Though the Founding Fathers of the United States may have failed in their intention to provide for simple civilian control of military activities, the "speeches and writings of the Framers of the Constitution abound with statements that the military should be subordinated to civil power."[26] Yet, oddly enough, it was the very Constitution that they authored which, by dividing civilian responsibility, produced many of the traditional difficulties in gaining compliance to a single source of authority.[27]

Before continuing with American civil-military relations, it might be useful to mention a few notable examples of military noncompliance in foreign settings. These examples may serve to illustrate further the age-old problem (from the perspective of the superiors) of evasion of formal authority. One should be cautioned that extraordinary individual action will be stressed.

Admiral Horatio Nelson clearly disobeyed the order to withdraw at the Battle of Copenhagen. He believed disaster would be the outcome of disengagement. When his commander hoisted the signal to withdraw, it is reported that Admiral Nelson put the glass to his blind eye and said, "I really do not see the signal."[28]

Orde Wingate was a British Captain in Palestine in the late 1930s. Wingate organized and supported Jewish fighting men, laying the foundation for what would become the Israeli Army. His reasoning was that such a policy would be beneficial both to the British Empire and to the Zionist settlers. Several of his superiors felt that his behavior, which included leading night patrols against Arab irregulars, openly contradicted the policy of His Majesty's Government.[29]

On June 30, 1940, the French Embassy in London notified forty-nine-year-old Brigadier General Charles de Gaulle of the order to surrender himself at the Saint-Michel prison in Toulouse, there to be tried by the *Conseil de Guerre*. On June 18, de Gaulle had spoken on the B.B.C. of his plan to continue to resist the Germans in the name of France, in spite of orders flowing from the Armistice signed by the Pétain government. He chose to be faithful to his conception of France rather than to obey the new formal authorities.[30]

Generalleutnant (Major General) Dietrich von Cholitz was specifically named by Adolph Hitler a *Befehlshaber* in August 1944 and thus became the fortress commander of Paris and bearer of the *Führer's* personal orders. His reputation as a man willing to carry out the harshest orders was the crucial reason for his selection. Hitler was determined that Paris not fall into Allied hands or, if it did, that nothing be left for the conquerors but ruins. Von Cholitz chose to save the city and thus the lives of many of his troops. Disobeying the orders of his superiors, he surrendered Paris after offering only token opposition to th Allied forces.[31]

These examples are intended to demonstrate the historical importance of noncompliance and to illustrate its occurrence in varied contexts. In this regard, they serve as a suggestive backdrop to the main thrust of this investigation, the role of noncompliance in American bureaucratic politics.

NONCOMPLIANCE AND THE AMERICAN SOLDIER

General of the Army Douglas MacArthur was rightly famous for his extraordinary performance at West Point, for his daring in operations against the Mexican bandits, and for his leadership in World War I. He gained national recognition as Chief of Staff of the United States Army during the bonus marches, and as commander of Philippine and American troops in the Philippine Islands. He attained international stature through his "I-shall-return" leadership of American forces in the Southwest Pacific and through his benevolent despotism as ruler of Japan after World War II. Yet, it is for his actions as commander of United States and United Nations forces in Korea that he is probably best remembered by political scientists.[32] Even before the brilliantly engineered Inchon landings, it seems that MacArthur was at odds with the wishes of his superiors in the American chain of command. Partly because of the post-Inchon optimism about the outcome of the Korean conflict, and partly because of MacArthur's stature, President Truman ignored his advisers and MacArthur's superiors, who found the General to be insubordinate, and who wanted him restrained or relieved. After the Chinese Communists' intervention and repeated instances of failure by MacArthur to comply with directives against certain public pronouncements by senior officers, Truman

9 / Introduction

relieved the old soldier of his command. The uproar that followed indicated that compliance, with all its ramifications, is the great issue of civil-military relations in modern nations. In the United States, the nature of the relationship of soldiers to civilian authority is a crucial symptom in diagnosing the health of our democracy.

Consider recent examples from the Vietnam struggle. In one instance officers of a division continued to use the dangerous defoliant "Orange" for almost a year after they were ordered to stop.[33] In another case, an order to avoid unnecessary destruction was violated by a unit which plowed up large amounts of land to carve out its identifying patch on the Vietnamese countryside.[34] In the most prominent case, that of General John D. Lavelle, it seems that North Vietnam was bombed in direct violation of the rules of engagement laid down by President Richard Nixon. Further, the deed was covered up over an extended period of time, in high places, and possibly damaged peace negotiations that were in progress and certainly misled the President of the United States.[35]

NONCOMPLIANCE AND CIVILIAN CONTROL

Civilian control of the military is a shorthand phrase for the complex interrelationships between the various legislative and executive power centers in American government and the officer corps and enlisted ranks of the branches of military service. Elaborating these interrelationships leads to one of the most pressing questions of the postmodern American polity: Can American democracy survive in the nuclear era? Defense of American democracy rests on the defense of America from her enemies and even from a "victorious" general war. Moreover, the measures taken to defend the nation, and the manner in which they are taken, can impinge upon the conduct of political life as we know it today. Further, the question of how America will defend herself from overeager friends and too zealous "patriots" adds an additional element of complexity.

It seems clear that no treaty, no strategy, no hopeful scheme for arms limitation or any other device to reduce tension, can be successful if those persons with direct access to the weapons of war do not comply with the provisions of such an agreement. To come face to face with the terrible implications of the problem of noncompliance, one need only reflect for a moment upon the hypothetical possibility that those assigned to be weapons confiscators could become instead weapons concealers.

WHY COMPLY?

Why do soldiers comply with the wishes of their superior officers? The problem of understanding motivation has hounded social scientists and philosophers concerned with human action. There is no graduate seminar in mind reading. Some have tried to describe motivation in terms of physiological drives, while others have avoided entirely the treacherous terrain of the human mind—by claiming that one cannot know its contents empirically or by stating that there is no such thing as a mind. Some have posited a rather simple social psychology which might be described as a rewards-sanctions (or costs-benefits) paradigm. Such dichotomies are inadequate for a number of reasons. So many factors would not clearly fall into either category, and thus would not add to our understanding. In addition, the probabilities for accurate measurement would be minuscule. Further, an exterior exchange may reflect a variety of mental processes. On the other hand, one might limit his taxonomy to rather obvious, easily measurable gains or deprivations. Such an approach would miss the possible component processes and differing levels of salience that enter into compliance behavior.

For soldiers, one might list endlessly the costs and benefits associated with life in the American armed services. The notion of instant obedience found in military dogma—that of subordinates to superior officers and of superior officers to civilian chiefs—will do nicely in stressing the kinds of questions I am posing. If an officer complies with the wants of his superiors, one might assume that he is fulfilling his sense of duty, adhering to a professional norm, and improving his chances for being rewarded. By using extreme examples, however, we can see the difficulties involved in utilizing this approach. Does a soldier fulfill his sense of duty when he fires upon noncombatant civilians because he is so ordered; does he adhere to a professional norm when he has his men torture prisoners to obtain information; and does he improve his chances of being rewarded in this world when he charges out of a relatively safe trench into withering enemy machinegun fire?

All of this is to suggest that one cannot be certain in matters of motivation for complex human action. One must be quite careful of unarticulated psychological assumptions in one's explanations. This not intended to be an attack on the so-called psychological reductionism of the social sciences. Rather, it is an admission that much of what will follow will be based on implicit assumptions about human beings in general, and about contemporary American officials in particular. Assumptions about what actions mean to people should be made as explicit as is reasonably possible, even in studies (such as this) that emphasize structural variables. As Dennis Wrong wrote:

But isn't this psychology, and haven't sociologists been taught to forswear psychology, to look with suspicion on what are called "psychological variables" in contradistinction to the institutional and historical forces with which they are properly concerned? There is, indeed, as recent critics have complained, too much "psychologism" in contemporary sociology, largely, I think, because of the bias inherent in our favored research techniques. But

11 / Introduction

I do not see how, at the level of theory, sociologists can fail to make assumptions about human nature. If our assumptions are left implicit, we will inevitably presuppose a view of man that is tailor-made to our special needs; when our sociological theory overstresses the stability and integration of society we will end up imagining that man is the disembodied, conscience-driven, status-seeking phantom of current theory. We must do better if we really wish to win credit outside of our ranks for special understanding of man, that plausible creature whose wagging tongue so often hides the despair and darkness in his heart.[36]

Likewise, political scientists must be wary lest they end up espousing a view of political man as an interest-aggregating, group-defending elitist—a calculating bargainer—or a cog in an overpoweringly deterministic complex system.

ASSUMPTIONS

Though the contents of men's minds are elusive shadows for social science observers, there are "best guesses" that we can make about what certain things and symbols mean to particular collections of individuals. We derive these guesses partly from empathy, logic, personal experience, the utterances of some of the persons involved in the activities to be related, and other data, and additionally from the context of the situation and the perspectives of the persons involved. Understanding the context is itself a particularly difficult challenge. With this caution expressed, and in the knowledge that wish does not necessarily equal realization, let the assumptions of this study be made explicit:

Officers who share similar recruitment, socialization, and career patterns share certain value patterns as well. Not all soldiers share all values, nor need every soldier have the same world view, but it is possible and legitimate to construct an analytical model of what may be called the American military officer's outlook. According to Edward Shils, an outlook is "one variant form of those comprehensive patterns of cognitive and moral beliefs about man, society, and the universe in relation to man and society, which flourish in human societies."[37] Shils later states that "*outlooks* tend to lack one authoritative and explicit promulgation. They are pluralistic in their internal structure and are not systematically integrated."[38] Outlooks thus do not require consensus on all issues.

American military professionals share an outlook which includes a number of values, norms, and goals and implies a professional identity. This outlook intentionally resembles Samuel Huntington's definition of the professional military ethic as an ideal type to which no individual or group will consistently adhere.[39] Huntington stresses tradition, corporate values, the primacy of the nation-state, and the tendency to view with alarm the capabilities of potential enemy states.[40] Examples of norms that are included in the soldier's outlook are obedience to orders, use of saluting and symbolic gestures and actions, frequent repetition of certain words and phrases, and various social obligations. Goals are more specific and flexible than values and can logically be derived from or justified by outlook, which also serves to justify certain norms and to delineate elements of one's professional identify. Rue Bucher has suggested that a professional identity involves the following components:

1. A definition of the field with which the professional ... is identified—its boundaries, what it encompasses, its major body of knowledge and associated methods;
2. A mission which the field serves—its place in a scheme of values;
3. The activities which are proper to the field; and
4. The relationships that should obtain both between members of the field, and with persons in other fields.[41]

MISSION

Bucher's second point, which relates mission to values, is most important for this study. Mission is thus distinguished from its component element, task, which does not call forth the purposive connotations clearly required by the military dictionary definition referred to above. This purposive element suggests the resonances that can accompany the use of the term "mission" in certain contexts, and these reverberations bring to mind persons who are willing to take great risks in order to go forth and accomplish those things required by higher values.

Along with passion and dedication, mission implies rationality. The concept of rationality is important in the linkages that it provides with two notions about authority: Friedrich's and Willer's. Carl J. Friedrich has defined "authority" as a communication which has the potential capacity for reasoned elaboration.[42] Thus, authority derives from the experience, wisdom, even rightness, of the authoritative source. Moreover, the value-oriented rational behavior that might be observed leads us to Weber's hidden concept of ideological authority as elaborated upon by David Willer.[43]

Willer sought to strengthen Max Weber's famous authority typology by identifying an additional category. Weber originally proposed three grounds—tradition, charisma, and reason—on which to base the belief in legitimate authority.[44] Traditional authority rests on the premise that what was done in the past was right and continues to be correct in the present. Charismatic authority is a mighty force for change brought by an extraordinary individual in turbulent times. Rational-legal authority is exemplified by the subordinate obeying a superior because of laws and rules that establish the rights of office without regard to the identity of the incumbent. Willer's addition to Weber's classification scheme is derived from the latter's political writings. Willer states: "The conception of value-rational behavior determined by 'the conscious faith in the absolute worth of the conduct as such' leads to the ideas of legitimacy 'by virtue of value-rational faith' and in combination with the ideas of domination and organization results in *ideological authority* which rests upon *a faith in the absolute value of a rationalized set of norms.*"[45]

Therefore, values—as well as tradition, charisma, and legal-rationality—can legitimize certain types of domination. In the world of the soldier there is no clear single basis of authority, or legitimate domination. Whether authority refers to motives for obeying, represents different power structures, or is an essentially normative justification for obeying the commands of the power holder, in terms of an explicit psychological metaphor, one might think about the "pulls" of different types of authority on a military officer.[46]

Thus, within one bureaucratic structure, an officer might be open to traditional, charismatic, and rational-legal injunctions. Accordingly, he might respond to the almost sacral formulations of tradition expressed in manners, custom, dress, and so forth. In terms of charisma, combat requires authority that will supersede the normal human fear of death and killing, which persists even after efforts to eradicate it through such intense socialization as basic training.[47] As for rational-legal requirements, surely obedience imposed by chain of command through hierarchy constitutes a readily recognizable form.

Beyond this mix of Weber's authority patterns, something resembling the analytically pure form of ideological authority also can have its effects. However, ideology implies too orderly and comprehensive a world view for it to be the most useful concept with which to describe the officers' points of view. While forgoing some of the coherence and strength of the concept of ideology, the term "outlook" provides greater accuracy in describing the perspectives of military men. Within the military outlook exist notions of what is the mission of each branch of service. This sense of mission, which includes ideas about the overall military mission, suggests a prototypical ideal authority that justifies the power for those who serve to implement the values and tasks understood to be required in pursuit of the mission. Above all, this ideal authority resides in the military's paramount mission: the protection of the state.[48] It is the hallmark of the professional soldier's expressed views on the nature of his obligation to duty, honor, country. Furthermore, mission serves as a secular "theodicy," providing an explanation and justification of why men are maimed or die in battle and legitimating the organizational structure that requires soliders to face hardship and death.[49]

Each service has its classic mission. For the United States Army, it is to control the battlefield. Subsections of the services also have their particular missions. For instance, one might describe the Signal Corps' mission as providing the communication required for control of the battlefield.

The picture is further complicated because the means of achieving goals tend to become values themselves—maintenance of a hierarchy with an instant-obedience behavior model, gaining professional expertise, acquisition of the best in weapons and equipment, and so forth. The values are part of the intellectual and emotional baggage carried about by the soldier. Compliance with orders for some becomes the highest values. Such an attitude might be promoted by the exigencies of combat and by the efficiency norms of bureaucracy. Certainly obedience is stressed by the values of civilian control of the military, which is often depicted in simple terms as a purely vertical pattern of relationships.

Additional complexity is introduced when one considers that a military officer pursues other important goals. Examples include completion of the assignment of the moment (task), promotion and maintenance of the welfare of his troops, promotion and maintenance of the particular service of which the officer is a member, and promotion of the officer himself. It is logical and natural that so many values, norms, and goals will come into conflict over time. In such situations the simple and often most popular answer is to deny that such conflict exists. This can be done by asserting the good judgment and authority of superiors and then following their orders. But what about those occasions when such a route seems unsatisfactory? What about men who through psychology or circumstance operate under a different priority of values or interpretation of mission-imposed obligations? How is this "deviance" to be explained? Although there is no all-encompassing explanation, the case presented below offers a fairly comprehensive interpretation of just such a situation.

Plans and operations for carrying out the task portion of the mission become the manifestations of the value-laden, purposive aspects of mission. It follows, then, that mission has consequences for the role, or daily activities, of the soldier, in that it at least sets parameters for that role. Within the parameters set by the mission, the role is likely to affect the priorities associated with the outlook or service mission. Subsequent carrying out of the mission may affect the outlook or the values implied by the service mission.

When the tensions caused by the different ordering of priorities within the shared outlook become so great that they cannot be accommodated, one might anticipate certain consequences. For instance, one might predict rivalry between coequal units. This rivalry might take various forms, such as those associated with the interservice struggles that developed immediately after World War II. Within one service, where the interpretation of the mission generates tensions over program or weapons, one might expect deviant behavior from certain subordinates. Thus, when the Army's high officers accommodated their differences in outlook with their Air Force counterparts, in certain quarters of the Army a sense that these officials were not doing enough to carry out the Army's mission was generated.

Mission can thus deny a particular kind of legitimacy to formally constituted authority, and can justify an interpretation of doctrine which appears to require noncompliance in matters relating to implementation of program. In a sense, then, mission establishes a rival, nonpersonal "authority" which is distinct from the formally constituted authorities. It limits the legitimacy of the latter while legitimating unusual behavior and a rather different type of organization based on a "cognitive minority" of middle-level officials.[50] This organizational phenomenon will be termed a bureaucratic movement.[51] The foremost political outcome of such a movement will be designated insurgent bureaucratic politics.

Bureaucratic Politics

I hope to show that mission can act as a unifying force among those groups and individuals who desire to alter the official policy enunciated by their superiors. It unites various people—perhaps technicians, tacticians, old ground soldiers, future pilots, and men of bitter memories—with an innovative idea that is coupled with a charismatic doctrine. This can create the formidable characteristics of all insurgencies: secret supporters, the same disobedience appearing in a number of places remote from the source of authoritative power, men willing to risk their careers, fellow travelers willing to shield them, and individuals or cabals not in communication with each other operating independently from centralized control.[52] Insurgents need not seek the overthrow of the established authorities. Rather, in such cases, mission serves the purpose of providing direction for insurgent activities. And in such bureaucracies as the armed forces, these activities take on a political character. Those who undertake them are, in a very real sense, politicians.

As Weber pointed out, "One can say that three preeminent qualities are necessary for the politician: passion, a feeling of responsibility, and a sense of proportion."[53] Let me briefly discuss these qualities as they apply to mission-related insurgency and more specifically to the case of the Army's acquisition of close air support.

16 / The Army Gets an Air Force

In a state of heightened emotions, the belief that one's comrades must risk their lives because of an organizational misarrangement—arbitrary distinctions made among the functions of the armed services—can be a compelling motivation for political action. The recollection of a soldier of the 506th Parachute Regiment in Normandy shortly after D-Day as he prepared to attack Carentan brings home the sense of powerlessness faced by those in such situations: "We watched a few scattered German troops wandering across the bridges heading into Carentan, but the longer we watched the greater their number became. Finally we stood there powerless to do anything but pray for the Air Corps to show up. They never did."[54]

It was the political struggle for power to control future battlefields and prevent a repetition of Carentan that resulted in the Army's acquisition of the armed helicopter. Interestingly and importantly, it was not primarily the weapon itself or even who would fly it that was at stake. What the insurgent Army soldiers to be studied here wanted was *control* of a close air support weapon as an answer to their powerlessness. They wanted to be sure that accountability, responsibility, power, and authority would dovetail in the pursuit of their mission.

There is very little question that military men generally tend to feel an unusually strong sense of responsibility to their organization and their nation. Ward Just captures this spirit in his evaluation of a ceremonial initiation of 1,000 recruits: "The ranks were seated after shouting their unit designation. That is part of what the Army is about, identification: with your buddy, your unit, your battalion, brigade, division, the Army, the country."[55]

A "sense of proportion" among military men refers to the balances that must be maintained between several conflicting pressures on a soldier as he pursues his long-range goals. Let us remember that the professional military officer tends to see war as inevitable. He knows that, over the twenty to thirty-five years of his career, he will most likely experience combat or serve in a combat zone. He also knows that his opportunities for exit from and later reentry into the service career hierarchy are limited.[56] Thus, an insurgent officer must conform to such a degree that he occupies positions of trust and responsibility—and protects his career—while at the same time disregarding the legalities in order to introduce devious innovation. Such a person will generally conform to most of the orders and customs of his superiors, yet, over time, he will press for the adoption of a technique that will enhance the future survival probabilities of his nation, his service, his friends, and perhaps himself as well.

The fact that the struggle in the Army for close air support is at least thirty-nine years old is an example of the politics of endurance practiced by the insurgents. Ironically, in the 1930s, some of the men who later helped create the United States Air Force were themselves a mission-oriented group whose policy preferences were not implemented at the top level of the Army hierarchy. The future General LeMay and others stressed the need for strategic bombing.[57] But the military and civilian chiefs at that time were uncertain about the role of air power; several of the military leaders, in fact, played down that role. As the views of those who favored strategic air power and centralized air forces became more widely accepted, there gradually developed within the Army a small group who were not concerned about massive air power organized on a multifunctional basis, but were interested in having aircraft integrated with Army combat operations.

The successful establishment of the Army Air Force prior to the United States' entry into World War II divided the Army on a functional basis, and since all flying was to be done by those whose concern was with strategic bombardment and direct aerial combat (the predecessors to the present Air Force officers), the Air Force "left the battlefield"[58] because of the way its leaders interpreted its mission. The Army group that wanted air power integrated with Army operations thus became the new insurgents, seeking for the Army an Air Force to replace the one it had lost.

Thematic Approach and Method of Analysis

To peer into the operations of a vast bureaucracy and to come away with any sense of enlightenment is itself a challenging task. The confused patterns of legitimacy, authority, power, accountability, and responsibility give the impression of a huge maze with its own "inexorable operational laws,"[59] if indeed its operations have any regularity at all. Jacques Ellul, a pessimist who makes woeful order out of such chaos, paints the following picture:

From the very moment that a general policy decision has been made by the minister, it escapes his control; the matter takes on independent life and circulates in the various services, and all depends eventually on what the bureaus decide to do with it. Possibly, orders will eventually emerge corresponding to the original decision. More frequently nothing will emerge. The decision will evaporate in the numerous administrative channels and never really see the light of day.[60]

Irresistably, though, one must wonder what happens in this labyrinth. The present study seeks to analyze the Army insurgents in the bureaucratic maze as they secured the right to develop their own air support. In considering this it is hoped that light can be shed on similar political phenomena in other settings. The main thesis of this study is that when controversy occurs over basic issues of role, mission, and domain, in large-scale organizations under certain conditions a movement can develop which might be called a bureaucratic insurgency. The case of Army aviation highlights several of these conditions: (1) a strong commitment to incompatible conceptions of role, mission, and domain; (2) a landmark decision or policy outcome taken to be a defeat for one of those conceptions; (3) determination of at least a nucleus of those committed to the "losing" conception to remain within the system (although others might exit) and continue over an indefinite period to try or to modify the outcome; and (4) willingness on the part of this remant to, when possible and necessary, engage in a strategy (not necessarily preconceived in any full-blown sense) of various forms of noncompliance, missionary work, and recruitment of strategic individuals into what beocmes the "insurgent movement."

When such a strategy does succeed, the insurgents can eventually become sufficiently established to be accepted into the bureaucratic policy-making elite as bargainers for their share of resources for carrying out the now-legitimate mission in a now-legitimate domain. Conditions of such success are primarily: (1) political skill in getting and using opportunities, exploiting available bureaucratic processes and structures to protect, spread, advance, and legitimize the cause, and in developing sometimes innovative tactics and technology suited to a changing environment; and (2) of greater importance, tenacity and persistence, tempered by flexibility rather than rigidity in form and manifestation over a sometimes lengthy period.

Methodologically, my approach resembles analytic induction.[61] That is to say, it is a case study, and the hypotheses it generates will be open to modification or refutation by other efforts. I am well aware that, by choosing a diffuse phenomenon that took place over a long period of time, I have been forced to pick and choose data and to rely heavily on the memories of some of the participants and on secondary sources. I further realize that my findings are limited by my need to use my own experiences in order to better comprehend the meaning of events described by the participants. I believe, however, that these problems are compensated for by an understanding that can nevertheless be gained about the peculiar nature of mission in bureaucratic politics. Furthermore, I think it is necessary to study diffuse longitudinal phenomena if we are not to be stuck with an elitist bias, a single-decision bias, or a bias toward survey methodology—all of which are appropriate in their own places, but which seem inadequate for the tasks selected here.[62]

Thus, the outcome of this study is a model that may help explain bureaucratic politics generally. It stresses the importance of mission and the role of noncompliance in the process. Clarification of the nature of insurgent bureaucratic politics is important to our understanding of (1) the place of intra-

19 / Introduction

organizational conflict in interorganizational rivalry; (2) the factors that legitimate bureaucratic adaptation to changing situations in defiance of leadership and formal position; (3) the role of politics in the process of technological innovation; and (4) the workings of the defense establishment, which have implications for civil-military relations as well as for foreign policy.

At this point, it is fitting that we move on to an in-depth examination of the mission of the United States Army. I will discuss the historical development of aviation and the impact of this development on military organization and values. The Army, striving to absorb aviation into its sphere, failed to adjust to ongoing events and thus lost its control over the bulk of aviation to a separatist elite that emerged from within its own ranks. The implications of this emergence will be considered from the perspectives of higher- and lower-ranking officers, and it will become apparent that for some in the latter group the very fact of their positions in the Army's hierarchy proved advantageous in the Army's quest to regain control of its own aviation.

Chapter 2 | **AVIATION AND THE DEVELOPMENT OF THE ARMY'S MISSION: THE ARMY ACQUIRES, THEN VIRTUALLY LOSES, AN AIR ARM**

Having considered the general concept of mission in Chapter 1, it is now appropriate to analyze the more specific question of how the advent and growth of aviation influenced the United States Army's conception and implementation of its mission. Such an analysis requires a critical summary of the main sequential events and forces that bear on that view as well as a review of the development of intraservice and interservice disagreement over what the Army's proper mission should be and how it should be effectuated.

Mission can have many sources. It can be derived partly from doctrine, from law, from formal role assignments, from weaponry, from expertise—from almost any conceivable combination of sources that have an impact over time on the content of an organization's constitution.[1] To understand the place of mission in the atomic-age United States Army, it is useful to consider how this constitution, "a historic and conceptually defined normative order," was established in the swirl of conflicting cross-pressures brought about by changes in international politics, in organizational politics and policies, and in technological innovation.

History is so marked by convolutions that its interpreters often take comfort in the serendipitous dovetailing of apparently crucial events in the same year. Fortuitously, 1903 serves as such a year in that it pulled together different currents that are significant for this case study and for American military politics in general.

21 / Aviation and the Army's Mission

On November 6, 1903, the United States confirmed its interest in the creation of a canal to connect the Atlantic and Pacific oceans when diplomatic recognition was extended to the Republic of Panama three days after its establishment by a bloodless secessionist revolt against Colombia. The construction of a canal in Panama marked the growing interest of the United States in world politics. Such a waterway would allow for the relatively rapid movement of American sea power from ocean to ocean and would become a vital world sea lane for American power to straddle.

American interest in international politics was matched in the field of military organization by the reforms associated with Secretary of War Elihu Root. In 1899, President William McKinley asked Root, an attorney with no military experience, to look into the shortcomings of the American Army and, using the prestige and authority of his cabinet position, to try to do something about them. In 1903, three major results of that work emerged. One part was the Dick Act, which coordinated the relationship of the Army to the National Guard and as such was the first fundamental reform of the Reserve or "militia" system since 1792.[2] A second major accomplishment was the establishment of a Joint Army and Navy Board to promote cooperation and planning coordination between the services.[3] Third and perhaps most significantly, Root brought about a basic reorganization of the Army along the lines suggested by the model of the German General Staff. He endeavored to resolve problems of paralysis of command and inefficiency of operation by creating a Chief of Staff who would plan for war and advise the civilian Secretary of War, in whom some authority over military commanders would reside. (Still greater authority rested with the President.)[4] Moreover, Root's reorganization plan stressed the function of education in the preparation for battle. Thus it was hoped that an Army would be created that could deal effectively with other world powers. It was also to provide the organizational structure about which much internal and external strife over the meaning and use of aviation would converge.

December 17, 1903, was a significant date in the golden era of American inventions. On that day the Wright Brothers first flew their gasoline-powered aircraft at Kitty Hawk, North Carolina. As it was improved and altered for purposes of battle, this heavier-than-air craft was significantly to influence political-military considerations and in turn be influenced by them.[5]

As early as 1907, an Aeronautical Division (one officer and two enlisted men) was created in the Army Signal Corps. In 1908, what was to become the Army's first airplane was delivered from the Wright brothers for extensive testing. By 1914, the Aeronautical Division had grown to more than one hundred officers and men and fifteen aircraft.[6] Already a sense of difference in values and styles between the ground soldiers and sky soldiers was becoming manifest and, in short order, early signs of tensions appeared. Seeking to stake out a domain for themselves, the Signal Corps' aviators sought increased autonomy in which to perform their missions aloft. Congress responded favorably in July 1914, when it elevated the Aeronautical Division to the Aviation Section of the Signal Corps, authorized slightly more men and planes, and permitted the new section somewhat greater latitude in its operations.[7]

Combat experiences increased the momentum for air power. The 1916 Punitive Expedition into Mexico permitted limited field testing of aircraft tactical formations of the Army. A year later, with the entry of the United States into World War I, the military's air arm expanded dramatically. By the war's end American aviators had conducted 20,000 combat flights and had lost close to 300 planes while shooting down 800 enemy aircraft. Moreover, they had dropped a total of 138 tons of explosives on a multiplicity of targets.[8]

But more important than the combat activities of the war itself was the clarification of alternative possibilities for the use of air forces that followed. Ideas about air superiority, close air support, artillery observation, reconnaissance, liaison, long-range bombing, and even the dropping of parachute troops were considered during this period. Still, the evaluation of the ultimate worth of aviation in combat was uncertain, as was the selection of the most appropriate organizational form. Some saw the airplane as the key weapon upon which the outcome of all future wars would turn. Others saw the airplane as a potentially useful instrument of war, but not necessarily the dominant one. Still others felt that it was a weapon of limited capability and potential.

Congress became a battleground for defining the proper place of airpower and made important (though tentative) steps in this direction during America's war years. A new, more powerful Air Service superseded the Aeronautical Division in 1917.[9] One year later the Air Service was separated from the Signal Corps as an immediate result of the sweeping win-the-war reorganization permitted by the War Powers Act.[10]

Nevertheless, these changes did not satisfy those officers who argued that the mission of Army aviation was different from the Army's mission. For example, one of the more vocal dissenters, Major William "Billy" Mitchell, believed that aviation should be divided into two categories. One would be attached to divisions, corps, and armies to support ground operations. The other would be used for strategic operations in the bombardment of enemy men and materiel at a distance from the fighting line, as well as for the pursuit of enemy aircraft. The strategic use of aviation was analogous to the use of independent cavalry (as distinguished from divisional cavalry), which carried

23 / Aviation and the Army's Mission

the war directly into the enemy's homeland.[11] Related views were held by Major Carl Spaatz, who insisted that air power was quite capable of winning future wars on its own—an attitude that hardly endeared him to the officers who felt that teamwork with ground troops was the sole purpose of Army aviation.[12]

The minority status of the Mitchell-Spaatz position was emphasized by a meeting held shortly after the Armistice by a board of officials who came together to discuss questions of aviation organization. Only one officer who had actually commanded an aerial unit in combat and was still on active duty could be found in the entire United States.[13] This officer, Carl Spaatz, was one of the only 234 regular Army aviators on active duty one year after the conclusion of the war.[14] These officers formed a group that was not by any means wholly committed to strategic aviation at the expense of cooperation with the ground forces, yet from whose ranks a hard core of supporters for a separate aviation mission was to be drawn. These autonomy seekers shall be referred to as "separatists."

The separatists faced several obstacles. Among those were their small number, the lack of an accepted coherent doctrine, limited funds, a public unduly preoccupied with peacetime interests, mixed congressional feelings about aviation, and a potentially hostile Navy. But above all there persisted among Army ground officers an overriding concern that the desire for a separate Air Force meant a lack of attention to air-ground cooperation, unity of command, welfare of the ground soldiers, and indifference to accomplishment of the Army mission.

Since they constituted such a small group, the separatists endeavored to enlarge their numerical strength by lobbying Congress to increase their size as well as their autonomy. Between 1919 and 1933 no fewer than fourteen principal boards and committees studied the development of aviation as it related to national defense.[15] Two major laws, the Army Reorganization Act of 1920, which made the Air Service a combat arm of the Army, and the Air Corps Act of 1926, which created the office of Assistant Secretary of War to help promote aeronautics and which authorized increased strength for the new "Air Corps," were landmarks in the interwar development of Army aviation.[16]

About the same time the separatists adapted the military strategy of Giulio Douhet, an Italian and the foremost theorist of offensive air power.[17] From 1926 to 1940, a modified form of Douhet's strategy was taught at the Army Air Corps tactical school. This strategy reinforced the aviators' intense desire for autonomy.[18]

The 1920s and 1930s also saw the general public's expanding fascination with aviation. All over the world, aviation boosters continued developing aviation tactics and techniques. Much of the interest was civilian in nature, but the military implications were present. In the Soviet Union, sports parachuting was especially popular. In Germany, gliders swarmed in the sky. In the United States, Mitchell and others sought to capture the interest of the peace-minded public at the same time that they were trying to influence Congress. By appealing to the civilian sector, however, they only further alienated the already suspicious Navy and Army traditionalists.

The *Ostfriesland* Affair was the visible tip of the interservice and intraservice disputes over the capacities of, and proper place for, military aviation. The test sinking of the "unsinkable" German battleship in 1921 by Air Service pilots before Navy witnesses fueled the flames of bitterness in which the determination of the partisans was tempered.[19] The sinking of the *Ostfriesland* did not convince many Army and Navy skeptics (who lacked the benefit of prescience) of the utility of air power in actual combat situations of the future. But Mitchell and his band, who now had some further empirical verification for their beliefs, knew what they wanted and were not about to permit the opposition to stand in their way as they struggled to establish the mission of the air arm.

After the crash of the Navy dirigible *Shenandoah* in 1925, Mitchell issued an extreme statement assaulting the leaders of the Army and Navy and charging them with the "almost treasonable administration of the National Defense." Press interest remained high as Mitchell was required to face a court martial, which he himself desired, on charges of insubordination. The lengthy trial offered an opportunity to shower the public with tales of air power. After Mitchell was declared guilty and was sentenced to five years' suspension from duty, he resigned his commission in order to continue to publicize his viewpoints.[20]

Although many of the Air Corps officers relished the possibility of autonomy equivalent to that which had existed in the British armed forces since World War I, most separatists continued their struggle by using the temporary strategem of seeking to place control of all combat aviation units under a General Headquarters Air Force (GHQAF) commanded by an Air Corps officer. However, when this was attained in 1935, rivalry persisted between the Commanding General of GHQAF, who favored autonomy for the air arm, and the Chief of the Air Corps, now responsible for logistics and training, who opposed separation.[21] This source of discord was removed three years later when the GHQAF was assigned to the Chief of the Air Corps in a War Department consolidation plan. Nevertheless, such organizational rearrangements did not dispel the fundamental disharmony between those who felt that the basic mission of air power was to support the ground troops and those who saw aviation's function as centralized power that was to be aimed at the vitals of the enemy homeland and bring quick victory.

25 / Aviation and the Army's Mission

As it turned out, when World War II began, all the men at the top of the war-making machinery in the United States were aviation-minded. President Roosevelt proved his committment to air power when, in May 1940, he called for an annual production of 50,000 aircraft. For some time, the importance of aviation was taken for granted, especially in its deterrent role. Secretary of War Henry Stimson agreed with Roosevelt that World War II would be largely an air war and selected the very able Robert Lovett (later appointed Secretary of Defense) as his deputy for air matters. Generals George C. Marshall, Lesley J. McNair, and Henry H. Arnold were believers in the use of air power, and Generals Mark W. Clark and Dwight D. Eisenhower were among the many commanders who were aviation supporters.[22] Admiral Ernest J. King, the Chief of Naval Operations, though often bitterly at odds with the Air Force, stressed aviation in his capacity as chief naval organizer.[23]

As a result of the pro-separatist leanings of the top political and military leadership in World War II, the Army traditionalists were swept aside as the Air Corps acquired increased resources, autonomy, and power. At the same time, though the traditionalists had lost the day, the issues they represented surfaced among Army officers who were remote from the decision-making councils in Washington, D.C., and who were less likely to be perceived as "obstructionists" of air power.

This situation created the conditions that were conducive to bureaucratic insurgency. Analytically, in the remainder of this chapter we will look at World War II from two perspectives. At one level, the men at the top sat in the inner councils of government, where they secured the Air Force's preeminent position; at the other level, certain lower-echelon Army officers who adhered to the concept of ground control of air support gained the assent of those dissatisfied with Air Force performance.

Men at the Top

The course of Army aviation is inextricably interwined with two significant events that occurred on September 1, 1939: the German invasion of Poland, which marked the beginning of the World War II, and the swearing in of George Catlett Marshall as Chief of Staff of the United States Army.[24]

Marshall is a focal point in what we may call the relatively "closed" politics of the men at the top levels of government. For the military leaders within this group, the possibility of a long-range war from air or sea, a war that would threaten the American homeland, spurred them on in their planning labors.

When Marshall became Chief of Staff, the Army Air Corps was expanding toward a recently authorized increase in total aircraft strength of 5,500.

Within the year, President Roosevelt called for production of 50,000 military planes each year. Every bit of bad news from Europe seemed to call forth an altered planning goal for Marshall's staff.

Marshall's acquaintance with military aviation had originated in 1911, when he used courier pilots on maneuvers. Marshall had taught Billy Mitchell at the Army Staff College, and his long-standing friendship with General Henry "Hap" Arnold dated back to the 1914 American Army maneuvers in the Philippines. Marshall had observed the difficulties associated with aviation in World War I and became something of an air enthusiast as his career advanced. It is easy to understand how he became so receptive to some of the ideas of aviation supporters. His own career had been marked by the "battle against military scholasticism." It was to the fight against "school solutions" that Marshall devoted his greatest energies while Assistant Commandant and Head of the Academic Department of the Infantry School.[25] He was also known as a man who would not hesitate to use unorthodox solutions to resolve training-maneuver problems.

Marshall's close friendship with Arnold was characteristic of the importance of personal interrelationships at the top level of military policy making. Arnold graduated from West Point in 1907. Four years later, after service as a ground officer, he was taught to fly by the Wright Brothers. In 1938, he became Chief of the Air Corps at the same time Marshall was becoming Deputy Chief of Staff of the Army. Arnold and his former boss Colonel Frank Andrews took every opportunity to impress upon Marshall the importance of the development of air power. Though Marshall was never to give the Air Corps advocates all they wanted, he did realize that many of the General Staff officers were hostile to the air arm and that, in the absence of recognition and without a great deal of representation on the General Staff, many of the younger air officers were going to Congress, stirring up the situation. Marshall fought against the almost unified opposition of his civilian superiors and military peers in bringing Andrews into the War Department as chief of the G-3 division that dealt with training.[26]

The creation of the Army Air Forces on June 20, 1941, and the increased authority given the Chief of Army Air Forces were major steps forward for those who sought autonomy for the Air Forces.[27] Nevertheless, there was still to be a great deal of conflict between the Army GHQ and the Army Air Forces over their missions.[28]

This difficulty over operational planning and control was presented to still another board for consideration. Marshall was being pressured on several fronts, and he was determined to seek a more effective overall reorganization. He recognized the serious problems inherent in the existing General Staff situation.[29] His primary concern was that Root's masterwork, the General

Staff, was commanding rather than "staffing" ("the knowing, thinking, and planning functions"), which required a tremendous amount of attention to detail.[30] This concentration on small matters clogged up the channels of command because there were forty large commands and 350 small ones reporting to the Chief of Staff. The War Department reorganization of 1942, Marshall's triumph, consolidated many agencies into three major commands and delegated command functions downward to these commands. All combat components were grouped into the Army Air Forces and the Army Ground Forces. The many bureaus and special staffs were brought into the Services of Supply (later to be known as the Army Service Forces). Each of these major components had its own headquarters and staff. The Army Air Forces gained almost exclusive control of the airplane.[31] It organized its own units, trained its own personnel, and established its own system of supply. The man responsible for putting the reorganization into effect was Lieutenant General Joseph T. McNarney, an aviation officer respected by Marshall for his toughness.[32]

Marshall's sensitivity to political realities was clearly demonstrated by the manner in which he chose to bring forth his fundamental reorganization. Since his plan involved downgrading the General Staff divisions, eliminating the Chiefs of Arms, subordinating the Chiefs of Services to a Supply Chief, and abolishing the GHQ, he knew that many powerful individuals with influential friends supported by long-standing traditions could create an outcry that might interfere with the conduct of the war. Timing the matter so that the tours of duty of two of the Chiefs of Arms and the Adjutant-General would expire while two other Chiefs of Arms were promoted was just one of the techniques employed by Marshall to defang his potential opponents. A series of forcefully conducted, swift meetings held in the shadow of Pearl Harbor permitted Marshall to get his way with less disturbance than would otherwise have been the case, especially after he gained the support of President Roosevelt.

Marshall played the politics of crisis, authority, and bold movement to the hilt and won the day. The outcome was major change initiated from the top. Between January 25, 1942, when McNarney first met with Marshall, until February 28, 1942, when Marshall succeeded in convincing Roosevelt to issue an executive order authorizing the changes, Marshall reduced the number of people who had direct access to the Chief of Staff from sixty to about six.[33] On March 9, the War Department circular implementing the changes became effective and the Army Air Force assumed a still stronger position.

It is not surprising that Marshall was able to secure the support of President Roosevelt for such an important matter. Marshall's relations with Roosevelt were generally characterized as close-working, though not personal.[34]

Nevertheless, Marshall did not move totally into Roosevelt's confidence until at least one year after Pearl Harbor.[35] Marshall apparently relied on Harry Hopkins, presidential intimate, as his channel of communication and advocate with Roosevelt. Roosevelt's heavy reliance on Marshall, so great that it seriously downgraded the roles of Secretary of State Cordell Hull and Secretary of War Henry Stimson in the conduct of wartime national security policy, would not have been possible in a peacetime climate.[36]

Roosevelt's prewar caution about United States intervention in European affairs stemmed from congressional and public isolationist sentiment. A 1937 poll showing that nineteen out of twenty Americans wanted to stay out of a European war set narrow limits on Roosevelt's freedom of maneuver.[37] Roosevelt was further restricted by the elections of 1938, which did not "purge" his Democratic opposition and, in fact, added a host of opponents to his domestic policy to go with his already formidable isolationist critics in the foreign policy realm.[38] Hopkins, who headed the Works Progress Administration (WPA), shared the concern of General Marshall and others about an isolationist Congress not wanting to appropriate sufficient funds for national defense. Hopkins saw to it that more relief funds were allocated for military purposes. Several million dollars of WPA funds were secretly transferred to begin the fabrication of machine tools for the manufacture of small-arms ammunition.[39] It seems, then, that the elements which made possible Marshall's success as a war leader given broad freedom of movement by the President included Hopkins's support of Marshall; the exigencies of war, which stressed executive action and minimized congressional intervention; Marshall's personal attributes; and his track record of effectiveness.

When Marshall hand-picked his top Army commanders, he turned to people with whom he had previously worked closely. As Commander of the Army Air Forces he chose Major General Henry H. "Hap" Arnold, and as Commander of the Ground Forces he selected Major General Lesley McNair. McNair had shared a cabin with Marshall as they crossed the Atlantic on their way to World War I. Later, in 1939, Marshall chose McNair to reform the Command and General Staff School at Fort Leavenworth, which Marshall felt had an antiquated policy, particularly in regard to the Air Corps.[40] McNair was called to Washington in 1940 to raise the American Army to combat readiness. He was a strict disciplinarian who, in the course of directing the tremendous training effort, compiled long lists of officers he thought should be removed and those whom he thought could be entrusted with leadership in case of war. Helping McNair was Lieutenant Colonel Mark Wayne Clark, who came to GHQ as Chief of Operations in 1940 and within the year was made deputy to McNair with the rank of Brigadier General. Marshall knew Clark as a planner in the joint Army-Navy exercises

29 / Aviation and the Army's Mission

in Monterey in 1940, and before that Clark had written a favorable evaluation of an unorthodox field maneuver carried out by Marshall. Because of a hearing disability, McNair often sent Clark to represent him in meetings with Marshall. Marshall's opinion of Clark grew steadily higher as the two men worked on the details of raising divisions for the Army.

Grouped around Marshall, these men operated in Washington, D.C., during the dark days of the Allied cause before America's entry into World War II, and they formed an inner circle of leadership wherein the politics of high-level decision making was played out. Such decision making was heavily laced with doses of personality, international relations, and strategic policy making. The group was strengthened by Marshall's reorganization and in turn strengthened the position of those who favored autonomy and strategic bombing. But events far removed from this power center related to different perspectives and involved a rather different kind of politics.

Lower-Level Participants

Many of the old leaders who, to keep control of aviation for the Army Ground Forces, had opposed the development of strategic air power were left out in the cold by the rapid turn of events that unified the civilian and military leadership behind a strongly pro-air power military policy. This did not mean, however, that the idea of close ground-air coordination had evaporated. The Artillery Branch of the United States Army was a particularly fertile field for those who sought land-force control of air power—an authentic *Army* aviation. Among the major objectives of artillerymen was the use of light aircraft for observation of enemy areas that would both improve target selection and promote accurate firing. Knowledge of the locations of hostile concentrations in order to kill before being killed is, of course, imperative to every soldier. From World War I until the beginning of World War II, there was conflict between the Air Corps and the Artillery over both the provision of observation planes and their organization for utilization. Thus, if reconnaissance missions were required, the Air Corps preferred to utilize all their aircraft from a centralized, unified command under Air Corps control—their standard organizational preference regardless of task. Many in the Air Corps felt that simply furnishing a pilot and a plane to carry an artillery observer would serve to reduce the Air Corps' status.

It was in such an environment that 1st Lieutenant James McCord Watson III telephoned Piper Aircraft Corporation in the summer of 1940.[41] Watson informed Piper of Army maneuvers to be held at Camp Beauregard, Louisiana, in August, and asked for light aircraft to observe artillery fire. Satisfaction with the performance of an L-4 Cub flown by Piper civilian pilot Tom Case led to continued communication between Watson, the soldier, and Case, Piper's representative.

Such interest in light aircraft existed in other parts of the Army. For example, Brigadier General Adna R. Chaffee phoned Piper in February 1941 to discuss having light aircraft brought to the Armor School at Fort Knox, Kentucky. He wanted to evaluate the possibility of using light aircraft to control armored columns and direct heavy cannon fire from tanks. No formal or direct communication was required among like-minded soldiers of differing ranks and locations such as Watson and Chaffee. They were able individually to conceive that their own aviation might help them accomplish their mission.

As Piper Aircraft Corporation became aware of the utility of light aircraft in support of ground forces, the company opened new fronts to apply pressure, supply expertise, and provide a source of informal communication and transfer of information for those who were already concerned about Army aviation. One front was opened on February 18, 1941, when William T. Piper, Sr., wrote a letter to Secretary of War Stimson.[42] Other efforts were made at a variety of military posts by several Piper Aircraft officials. One such official, Henry S. Wann, was district sales manager for Piper Aircraft in the western United States. While trying to find the appropriate individual to convince at Fort Lewis, Washington, Wann contacted a lieutenant colonel who was extremely interested in light aircraft. This officer, who had a private pilot's license, was later to continue his discussion with Mr. Wann at the Louisiana maneuvers. The conversation between Wann and Lieutenant Colonel Dwight D. Eisenhower provided an opportunity for both men to exchange ideas about the potential value of light aviation. In addition, a lobbyist, John E. P. Morgan, campaigned in Washington for light aviation on behalf of Piper, Aeronca, and Taylorcraft—firms which produced aircraft that were potentially appropriate for promoting efficient cooperation between the Army and industry. As a consequence, Major Benjamin W. Chidlaw was made an official consultant to industry and became the visible contact point between industry and the Army. During this period, other officers attempted to bring the higher-ranking officials to see tests of light aircraft. The search for sympathizers seemed endless.

Major William W. Ford was interested in having organic aviation—that is, aviation assigned to and part of a military organization—for the Field Artillery.[43] Ford prepared an article outlining his concepts and sent it to a potential ally, Major General Robert M. Danford, the Chief of Field Artillery. The article later appeared in the *Field Artillery Journal*.[44] Danford became an advocate of Army aviation and Ford became a tester of concepts and the first Director of the Department of Air Training at Fort Sill, Oklahoma. Over time, such random contacts established a pattern out of which emerged insurgent bureaucratic politics.

Light planes appeared at several military posts and performed at the Second Army's maneuvers in June 1941 in east Tennessee; at the desert maneuvers at Fort Bliss, Texas, in July 1941; and at the famous Louisiana maneuvers. The exploits of the "Grasshopper Squadron" of civilians who flew the craft were to become part of the saga of Army aviation. The success of the aircraft in these maneuvers was not automatically well received by the highest officials, however. After the desert efforts, the Army was denied permission to purchase twenty light aircraft. This is hardly surprising in light of the skepticism of Major General Lesley McNair, then Chief of Staff of Army General Headquarters and later Commander of the Army Ground Forces.

The attitude of the Army Air Corps toward aviation not controlled by the Air Corps also hindered development. Perhaps the best indicator of the low status of such aviation was the apparently casual addition of these aircraft to the training exercises. In fact, the civilians who participated in the maneuvers paid their own way and provided their own aircraft.[45] As a token of interest, however, Robert Lovett, Special Assistant to the Secretary of War and later Assistant Secretary of War for Air, approved the request of Lieutenant Colonel Eisenhower to have the aviators and planes placed on a *per diem* rental and expense basis. Such apparent nonchalance may have masked the widespread activities of the friends of Army aviation from its potential enemies. Consider the military-industrial implications of such behavior. One must realize that, as in other aspects of insurgent bureaucratic politics, military-industrial relations in certain cases are possibly more significant at the lower levels of the Army hierarchy than at the elite level.

After the Louisiana maneuvers, in which W. T. Piper, Sr., himself took an active part, General Danford and the division and corps commanders unanimously supported a recommendation to the War Department that light aircraft be made organic to division and corps artillery units. General McNair felt that a fair trial had to be given to a centralized support approach and disapproved the recommendation.[46]

But such setbacks did not deter those who believed that, as the Air Force established its relative autonomy as a separate service, steps were necessary to assure that the Army would have airplanes with which to perform Army-oriented missions. In the summer of 1941, a young artillery lieutenant obtained twenty L-4's—the military version of the Piper Cub light aircraft—in a manner that was designed to avoid the scrutiny of Air Force officials. When the request went to the Pentagon, a high-ranking subordinate approved it in the absence of General McNair, who was out of town. As the decision moved up the chain to Marshall for final approval, it was reportedly kept hidden to avoid Air Force complaints. There is even some question as to whether Marshall realized what he was signing. When McNair returned, he is supposed to have stated that he would not have done it, but that he would have given the Air Forces one more chance to provide proper support. It is very possible that this "one more chance" could have seriously damaged the Army's attempt to get such planes, for it is now believed that McNair "never would have permitted it."[47] Though such tactics appear to be an individual action in a unique situation, they do in fact augment insurgent bureaucratic political activities. For, as the generals were making their formal decisions at the highest levels, lower-level officers and their supporters pursued alternative courses of action.

With America's entry into World War II, the need for tests of artillery observation aviation became obvious. William Ford, now a lieutenant colonel, was joined by Second Lieutenant Delbert L. Bristol and First Lieutenant Robert R. Williams in setting up the testing program at Fort Sill. With planes provided by the Army Air Forces, the tests got underway in early 1942. These tests were conducted by pilots who at the same time were being trained as Army aviators. At the end of February, training was completed with the graduation of the "class before one."[48] Testing continued, and on June 6 the War Department formally established organic Army aviation.

As a result of the testing-training at Fort Sill, the War Department directive called for two pilots and one mechanic for each Field Artillery battalion, two pilots in each divisional Field Artillery Headquarters, and two pilots in each Field Artillery brigade or group headquarters. The average infantry division thus required ten aircraft; each armored division, six or eight. Thus, an authoritative decision instituted a minimal structure within which the makings of a future bureaucratic social movement could incubate.

The Army Ground Forces were to provide training of pilots and mechanics while the Army Air Forces procured the aircraft and maintained them. The Department of Air Training, which prepared the pilots, was established under Lieutenant Colonel Ford. This school served as a training ground for most of the pilots, whose exploits later developed into a lore that would be shared by those seeking an expanded role for Army aviation. Furthermore, it prepared many leaders for that movement. While adjusting fire for over 90 percent of observed artillery missions,[49] chauffeuring all manner of individuals, and performing other tasks, these pilots endeared themselves to those ground soldiers who benefitted from their flying.

Armed Combat and Mission Discordances

Most crucial decisions about the use of air power rested on considerations of grand strategy and were quite literally made by the top men of the Allied political-military elite and affected them as well. Decisions to stress strategic bombing—which had obvious consequences for the individual soldier—came from the highest hierarchical level. In 1943, for example, the attack on Germany, for which there was not sufficient fighter support for American bombers, created military and political consequences of the first magnitude.[50] The decision to attack transportation and communication centers in France—the so-called Transportation Plan—was seen as a victory for tactical aviation advocates over the strategic plan to bomb petroleum centers, the so-called Oil Plan.[51] But both plans required aircraft to go beyond the eyesight of the ground soldier and thus did not seem very "tactical" to him. Though air support for the ground troops improved as the war in Europe drew to a close, the effects of the Air Force's lack of coordination with the ground troops (not to mention the Navy) were to persist. This is because the mission of the United States Army required more air support than organic Army aviation could provide for successful completion. Hence, much of what was expected from air forces by ground officers would have been furnished by the Army Air Forces. While most Army Air Force officers agreed with this, some ground officers disagreed with the preoccupation with strategic aviation and were not satisfied by the organization or performance of tactical aviation.

Even the most extreme partisans of strategic bombing of enemy population centers and industries admitted that there was some small role for air forces in coordinating with ground troops. Still, this function would be minimal because the role of ground forces would be minimal—strategic bombing would win the war by bringing the enemy population to its knees. Some of the less extreme partisans of strategic bombing believed that strategic bombing was a kind of support bombing at the combat theater level.[52] Thus, the Army in that theater would ultimately benefit. But for the most part it was understood that tactical aviation was to be the major means of air support of the ground forces.[53]

The main functions of tactical air power as seen through the eyes of ground soldiers were outlined in a memorandum prepared for the Chief of Staff in September 1940. They included: "(1) close, direct support fire missions on the immediate front of ground forces; (2) air defense of friendly ground forces and installations in the combat zones; (3) air attack against targets in hostile rear areas; (4) support of airborne forces; (5) reconnaissance, observation, liaison."[54] But such ground-oriented viewpoints did not reflect the attitudes of most Air Force officers. Their views were expressed after combat experience in North Africa in Field Manual 100-20, *Command and Employment of Air Power.*[55] As the Air Force struggled for autonomy, its officers stressed their equality with the ground forces and their belief that aviation assets should be organized under the control of an Air Force officer.

In 1943, Field Manual 100-20 listed in order of priority the three primary missions of tactical aviation. The first mission, to gain *air superiority*, stressed the destruction of hostile air fields and hostile aircraft, both on the ground and in air action. The second priority, *isolation of the battlefield*, included disruption of communications and destruction of supply dumps and troop concentrations in the rear. Only third priority was given to *combined actions with ground forces*, and the difficulty of such operations and their limited utility was stressed. Strategic aviation was quite clearly beyond the purview of the Army's ground forces. Nowhere were there any affirmative words for true close air support that would require communication and cooperation at the level of the field commander. Nowhere was there stress upon on-call missions in which ground officers at a low level could insist upon support on their immediate front. This does not mean that such close coordination did not occur during the war, but, rather than provide a later sense of appreciation for the air forces, successful examples of close support tended to verify that such missions were possible but were ignored by the "fly boys," who had other fish to fry. Certainly the ground forces thought that the Air Force pilots could gather very little glory from close air support.[56]

Many in the Army seemed to nurture an enmity toward the Air Forces that was to provide a receptive environment for those who felt that the situation was not helping the Army carry out its mission. Complaints varied from failure of air support to appear when needed to too much comfort and glory for Air Forces personnel. Even when the Air Force performed the desired mission, there was often a taste of bitterness. The terrible misdropping of several parachutists on the night before D-Day in Normandy was not to be easily forgotten by men of the "airborne club" who would later have leading positions in the Army.[57] In fact, fouling up air support through misdropped bombs took many lives, including that of General McNair, who was inspecting the front before the breakout at Saint-Lô when he and hundreds of other American soldiers became casualties of carpet-bombing planes that missed their markers. How such errors affected the troops can be seen in the words of Ross Carter, who described his experience as an airborne infantryman in Europe:

One day the men of the "Wild Blue Yonder" got messed up and bombed our shower bath at the foot of the mountain. Olson and the Big Polack had to dash naked out of the shower tent in freezing weather, hell-bent for a

35 / Aviation and the Army's Mission

foxhole. The Air Corps apologized to us, explaining that they'd mistaken us for Krautheads, but the dead men couldn't be present to acknowledge or to receive the apology. The Big Polack never forgave the incident. Every time he got drunk he would seek out the Air Corps boys, tell them their error, and wait for them to apologize. If they sassed him, he'd lower the boom and come back to us contented.[58]

Linking the Lower- and Higher-Level Participants

Characteristically, low-level efforts to obtain air support occasionally emerged in the high levels of the military structure. Because General Patton was able to get satisfactory use of tactical aviation to screen his advance through France, a lot of the low-level disgruntlement probably stayed bottled up.[59] Decisions dealing with "tactical" aviation did not stress the grievances of the lower-level soldiers, and in many ways did not appear to bear on them, for the action was still to be controlled by the Army Air Corps and was to take place well beyond the battle lines.

The decision to divert aircraft for fairly close support right after D-Day until a beachhead could be secured and the decision to carpet bomb at the Saint-Lô breakout do not appear to have been made as a consequence of pressures from below (though they do appear to reflect the desires of the low-level soldiers). This is not true in the case of the battle-by-memoranda between Generals McNair and Arnold.[60] The Air Force was always uncomfortable with control of aviation assets by the Army Ground Forces. Command generally was a very sensitive issue. The Air Force opposed the creation of organic aviation for the Field Artillery. When such aviation was proven successful, the Air Force formed liaison squadrons to perform the observation and liaison missions of organic aviation. These squadrons were used only at the corps and army levels, while the Army "puddle-jumpers" continued to gain in popularity. There was confusion over the aviation squadrons, and it is likely that many in the Army were not anxious to have them succeed. The European Theater of Operations Headquarters recommended that the liaison squadrons be disbanded and the aircraft be used to provide organic support for ground units other than the Artillery. This request was disapproved. It took a relatively low level event to bring in the very high decision makers—a lesson that was to have an impact throughout the struggle over Army aviation. The lesson was to grow out of the Italian campaign.

The fighting in Italy was extremely difficult because of mountainous terrain. Certain Army Artillery pilots feared for the capacity of their aircraft to cope with the required high altitudes and therefore pleaded for more powerful engines. Such requests came to the attention of the Air

Forces. Their vigilance in protecting their domain was well known, and this relatively minor request was one example of a group in the Ground Forces trying to improve its organic aviation to enable it to accomplish its mission more effectively. In this instance, when the significance of this request was recognized, it energized the highest levels of the Air Force. On January 29, 1944, General Arnold himself wrote a memorandum to General Marshall requesting that organic aviation in the Army Ground Forces be discontinued on grounds of economy and flexibility. Arnold's recommended actions would probably have wiped out Army aviation:

11. *Action recommended* . . .
1. All liaison aviation service be provided by the Commanding General, Army Air Forces. In theaters, liaison aviation service will be provided by Theater Air Force Commanders.
2. That organic air observation for Field Artillery be discontinued; Field Artillery T/O's be amended accordingly; that all personnel now holding rank or grade in organic air observation for field artillery be carried on as excess until absorbed into Field Artillery units except as indicated in paragraph 3 below.
3. That all Air Corps property now in organic air observation for Field Artillery be returned to the Army Air Forces and all personnel assigned be transferred to the Army Air Forces except for such personnel as the Commanding General, Army Ground Forces desires to retain in non-flying duties in the Army Ground Forces.
4. That appropraite adjustments in the Army Troop Basis be made to reflect action directed above.[61]

General McNair, it will be recalled, was an advocate of air power and reluctant about Army aviation at first. It was his former subordinate General Mark Clark who personally made great use of Army aviation and supported it. McNair challenged Arnold's writings in a memorandum of his own to General Marshall on February 16, 1944. He tersely offered his analysis before recommending no change in the use of liaison aircraft:

The basic memorandum contains a number of debatable statements. However, the main issue really is satisfactory air observation for field artillery. The present system is outstandingly successful—one of the remarkable developments in connection with the effective artillery support which is being given the infantry in all theaters. On the other hand, field artillery air observation by the Air Forces had been unsatisfactory since the advent of military aviation. There is abundant reason to doubt that the results would be otherwise if this task were returned to the Air Forces now. Especially would it be hazardous to make so radical a change at this particular time. The cost of liaison aviation, regardless of who mans it, is microscopically small as compared with the cost of the air force as a whole, and is hardly a material factor in the discussion.[62]

The issue was resolved when the War Department disapproved Arnold's request, stating, however, that in the event Army aviation promoters tried to extend their program, the Air Force could resubmit its memorandum. Such a threat, by suggesting political costs, may have inhibited the growth of Army aviation. The exchange of correspondence insured the existence of a base of operations for advocates of Army aviation. It also showed the political problems that could arise from the exposure of plans for improving the Army's organic air arm. The low-ranking officers who wanted to deal with formal decisions by the top leadership saw that they could provoke a response by effecting a linkage between the men at the top and themselves. But among those who wanted increased Army aviation capabilities, a few saw that such a link-up was something to be avoided in most cases if they were to more realistically obtain assistance in the completion of the Army's mission.[63] They preferred to avoid having their mission-attainment capacity hindered by formal orders from above.[64]

Mission: The Bomb

Strategic aviation was not tactical support of the ground troops on the theater front. To the men of the Air Force, who were to take its positions of leadership following World War II, strategic bombing was to be the weapon of destruction to use against the homelands of the enemy forces. With the advent of the atomic bomb, such Air Force attitudes, previously quite widely held, became overwhelmingly dominant. All during World War II, Arnold's desire for air autonomy was kept in check. One obstacle stemmed from the requirement that the Air Force provide support for the Army Ground Forces in the completion of land missions. Moreover, Marshall was limited in his ability to act because some of the most significant military decisions of World War II were based on questions of military organization and tactical aviation, and thus involved other powerful officials. Eisenhower typically sought commanders who were interested in both strategic and tactical aviation and who could cooperate with ground commanders.[65] Further, General Arnold could not fulfill his dream of a separate and equal Air Force, because Marshall was reluctant to permit the establishment of a separate service until enough experienced staff officers could be trained.[66] Finally, Arnold faced a persisting doubt about the efficacy of the strategic-bombing doctrine on which separation was to be based.[67]

With the conclusion of the war, in the minds of Air Forces leaders and their supporters, no such necessity for significant ground-support aviation existed. But the technological innovation of an atomic weapon that was to radically affirm the strategic mission of the Air Forces was not to alter fundamentally the Army's view of its mission. Though the Army was required to accommodate its strategy and tactics to the nuclear reality, its mission, in its own eyes, was to remain the same. The upcoming Army-Air Force schism, therefore, would not affect each service equally, for this continuing conflict, so easily dismissed as a struggle for service autonomy and recognition, or for the political spoils of congressional appropriations, drove at the very heart of the *raison d'être* of the United States Army.

In Chapter 3 we will consider the ways in which an organization establishes its domain as part of coping with its environment. We will seek to understand the impact of various factors that produce turbulence in the environment and the ways in which the Army and Air Force sought to clarify their roles and missions in the atomic era.

Chapter 3 | **DOMAIN CONTROVERSY IN A TURBULENT ENVIRONMENT: EXTERNAL PRESSURES ON THE ARMY**

The main focus of this study is Army bureaucratic behavior. However, it would be incorrect to picture the Army as a static organization with an elite pitted against its subordinates. On the contrary, the Army is a constantly changing, large, complex organization. It is influenced by external factors that are often out of its control, and its reactions to these developments affect the setting and hence the conduct of intra-Army politics.

Every organization must come to terms with its environment, often by carving out its place in the scheme of things.[1] In this way an organization establishes its "domain." Domain may be described as the claims an organization stakes out for itself in terms of (1) technology involved, (2) populations served, and (3) services rendered.[2] Because domain refers to claims, it is a dynamic concept that can vary according to who is doing the claiming, how the content or process of the claims varies, and how well or widely accepted these claims are. A high level of acceptance at crucial points is termed domain consensus.[3] These crucial points are located in what is called the "task environment" of the organization being considered (the focal organization).[4] The task environment denotes those parts of the total environment which are "relevant or potentially relevant to goal setting and goal attainment."[5] Since organizations depend on their task environments for necessities such as legitimacy and sites for disposition of goods and services, regularities in the relationship between the focal organization and its environment might be anticipated. One especially important aspect of individual behavior or role-set relations is the network of role-sets of boundary personnel—those whose roles require significant interaction with others beyond the boundaries of the focal organization (the organization under study)—and their role partners in other organizations. The various transactions that occur at organizational boundaries involve the flow of people, cash, and goods and services or perhaps power, influence, and information. Such regularities might be perceived as part of the organization-set of the focal organization. An organization-set consists of the complex interactions that take place between an organization and other organizations in its environment.[6] These interactions are analogous to the complex of roles and role relationships that the occupant of a given status has by virtue of occupying that status.[7] Thus, just as role-set implies social location, organization-set implies a locating of the focal organization within its environment. But this location may become doubtful as changes occur within the environment. In this aggregate of external conditions and influences, one may look for clues concerning organizational disruption—a change in interorganizational relationships, in organizational structure or process, or even the replacement of one organization by another.[8]

One may look to the organization, the environment, and organization-environment relations to better understand human behavior. This suggests what has been called an "open systems" approach to organizations.[9] F. E. Emery and E. I. Trist have outlined just how open and vulnerable organizations are to their environments in their work on the causal texture of environments, which presents four ideal types of causal texture ordered on the basis of the degree of system connectedness that exists among components of the environment.[10] The simplest type of environmental texture is that in which "goods" and "bads" are relatively unchanging in themselves and are randomly distributed. This they call the placid, randomized environment. The second type is a "placid, clustered environment" in which "goods" and "bads" are relatively unchanging in themselves, but are clustered. The third type is dynamic rather than static. It is called the disturbed-reactive environment. It consists of a clustered environment in which more than one system of the same kind exists and competition is present. The fourth type is dynamic in an additional respect, for its dynamic properties arise not simply from the interaction of identifiable component systems but from the field itself. These are termed turbulent fields. The turbulence results from the complexity and variety of causal interconnections.[11] Keeping in mind types three and four may be helpful in an examination of the Army's organization and the question of its domain from the 1940s to the present.

What follows is an attempt to clarify the situation of the United States Army in the post-World War II years in light of the above concepts. The impact of international uncertainty, compounded by extraordinary advances in weapons technology, profoundly affected the crucial elites concerned with foreign and military policy. These contingencies also influenced calls for military reorganization and brought into question the very need for the United States Army only a short time after its greatest triumph. This extraordinary turn of events, along with others, created a turbulent environment that seemed to threaten the very existence of the Army.

International Setting Upset

Unlike the end of World War I, conditions during the years immediately following World War II did not permit the United States to return to a policy of isolationism. International instability and domestic economic and scientific achievement required America to play a new role in the world community.[12] Possession of the world's most productive economy, as well as a monopoly over atomic power, ended whatever possibility there might have been for a reversion to exclusively domestic concerns. An additional problem confronted both America and the world community: the death, shortly before the end of the war, of Franklin D. Roosevelt and his replacement as President by Harry S. Truman, a man of unknown quality and questionable leadership ability.

However, neither concern over presidential leadership nor the novel situation that characterized the end of the war had much effect on public sentiment. A "return to normalcy" was expected, and following the custom of previous wars, demands were made and fulfilled that the troops be brought home and the strength of the armed forces be reduced to a minimum by means of a general demobilization.[13] These moves were later to have serious repercussions in the international arena.

The international scene soon changed the minds of many who thought that America could return to the tradition of isolation. United States officials joined with their British counterparts in the formation of the United Nations, but even before the charter was signed, and increasingly thereafter, questions were raised as to the role the United Nations would have in the postwar world. The uncooperative attitude of the Soviet Union damaged the prestige and status of the fledgling organization and adumbrated its weaknesses.

It was also rapidly becoming apparent that the forces that had managed to ally themselves against a common enemy had little left to hold them together. A division among the Allies split the major powers into two camps, each mistrustful and uncertain of the other, and the actions of the Soviet Union at this time increased the antagonism, in spite of a reservoir of American good will resulting from the Russian war effort.[14] Even during the last years of the war, dealings with Stalin had been increasing difficult. True, Soviet expansion into Eastern Europe and annexation of the countries of the U.S.S.R.'s eastern border as satellites was cause for little action in the United States, but as the Soviet Union made moves to include Turkey, Iran, and finally Greece in its sphere, it became necessary for the United States to adopt a more realistic foreign policy to deal with the situation.

A policy of containment evolved and was manifested in part in the Truman Doctrine. In response to the apparent Soviet expansionist threat, the United States declared its policy to be aid for "free people to work out their own destiny in their own way" whenever such aid was necessary.[15] Thus, when Britain could no longer provide aid to Greece in the Greek effort to oppose Communist guerrilla forces, President Truman asked Congress for both financial and military aid.

Appropriately, the military now attempted to define its place in the new scheme of things. Those who had recently reaped fame and glory for their successful prosecution of a "hot" war diverged profoundly in their opinions on how to deal with the "cold" war.[16] Much like the discordancies that were occurring on an international scale, conflicts within the United States military that had been subordinated during World War II now rose to the surface.

Public-policy and public-opinion elites were very concerned that the United States meet the Soviet challenge with an effective and efficient military machine. Within the winning military team there had been serious differences among the services over strategy, organization, resource allocation, and even style. These conflicts were not fully exposed to public scrutiny during the war itself, but now, as America was buffeted by the alternating winds created by the rush back to civilian pursuits and the rising perception of a Soviet threat, the record was brought more clearly into view. The evidence, however, was hardly decisive.

Air-power supporters contended that strategic bombing had not been given the resources needed to destroy Germany without requiring considerable ground combat.[17] In this regard, many believed that more bombers, more bombs, more freedom in target selection, and more time would have won the war with far less cost in pain and treasure for the land armies. Others pointed out that the Air Corps did get the cream of the recruits, vast sums of money, and many strategic-bombing opportunities, but that these did not slow down German industrial production to any signficant extent.[18] Perhaps air support closer to the front would have allowed swifter movement to take and hold enemy territory by destroying or cutting off his armies in the field.

Generally, though, strategic recrimination was not a major popular pastime. Rather, there was at first a sense of security and hopefulness associated with the rapid return to peaceful pursuits by the people of the nation that was the strongest in the world industrially and economically and that was the sole possessor of atomic power.

Lessons learned during the war opened up possibilities for all kinds of remedies for real or imagined defects in coordination between the military services. These were increasingly verbalized at several levels, and, above all, the push for an autonomous Air Force that had been quieted during the war now emerged full blast. The arguments for this approach became intertwined in the arguments for a general reorganization of the national military establishment. In order to place the struggle for Army aviation in its proper context, it seems useful at this juncture to offer a summary of the reorganizational disagreements that dominated military politics immediately following World War II.

Military Reorganization

Instability in the relationships among the services was heightened by the conflict over proposals for military unification. Despite opposition from the War and Navy departments, there was a considerable history of congressional efforts to consolidate the armed services by one formula or another. When World War II came, General Marshall was able to reorganize the War Department to his own liking through bold political action that enjoyed vital support from President Roosevelt. Perhaps he thought that another bold stroke at a time when the outcome of the war was in doubt could cut the Gordian knot of legislative-interest group-military service politics, or perhaps he simply anticipated the necessity for some concrete reform on which to base postwar military planning. In any case, neither political nor strategic considerations were to serve as significant time restraints on the struggle over military reunification. When on November 3, 1943, Marshall submitted his proposal to the Joint Chiefs of Staff for a unified military establishment, he initiated a power struggle which has yet to be resolved.[19]

Major alterations were anticipated in the call for reorganization, and it was to be expected that the United States Congress would become an important arena for organizational struggles. In the House of Representatives, a Select Committee on Postwar Military Policy was established under the chairmanship of Clifton A. Woodrum.[20] The Woodrum Committee included seven members of the Military Affairs Committee, seven members of the Naval Affairs Committee, and nine representatives drawn from the House at large—a sign of recognition of the great importance attached by congressional tradition to the close links between committees and their constituent agencies.[21] The War Department and its supporters took the offensive in favor of complete unification. The Navy—under the proficient leadership of its civilian chief, Secretary of the Navy James V. Forrestal—did not directly oppose unification, but simply picked holes in the Army's proposals while reminding the congressmen of their own prerogatives.[22]

After World War II, the Army and the Army Air Forces found themselves in coalition against the Navy. The phenomenon tended to be significant largely at the elite level. From Army-Navy football traditions to Joint Chiefs of Staff battles over allocation of airplanes, the Army-Navy rivalry loomed. The Army seems to have accepted as an accomplished fact that the Air Forces, which had been virtually autonomous since World War II, would become autonomous. This resignation on the part of top Army officials may be further explained by two factors. First, the Army leadership felt that top-level unity of command was a traditional organizational imperative now to be realized on a broad basis. Second, having been part of the War Department team, Air Force and Army leaders had left a record of pushing for unification. Thus an informal compromise position was taken by men from both camps—the Air Force would gain autonomy as a separate service, but at the same time would become more closely unified with the other services on the basis of equality within the general reorganization scheme.

The organizational strategy inherent in the Army and Air Force's outlook was that the services should be organized by weapon or by medium, with riflemen controlling the destiny of the Army and all other land combat units (such as the Marine Corps), and airmen controlling all airplanes (including naval aviation). The Navy's view was that organization should be on the basis of mission. That is, the Navy should control all the ships, Marines, and airplanes necessary to accomplish its basic mission—control of the seas and sea coasts. For some in the Army, the Navy's view was to have great appeal.

Aviation questions were naturally central to the discussion. Yet there was great reluctance to endorse specific proposals about allocation of air assets. Thus, close air support could not be clarified when broader questions, such as who would control naval aviation, remained ambiguous. The perplexed Woodrum Committee continued its hearings in a restricted way, but attention shifted to the work of another group, one selected by the Joint Chiefs of Staff and known as the Richardson Committee. The creation of the latter committee testifies to the significance of the matters under consideration. When great questions of policy, personnel, and finance are raised, interested parties often use such devices to seek information and attract publicity.

Admiral James O. Richardson and his colleagues pursued their investigation of military reorganization by speaking with the foremost military authorities available, apparently to insure political support for whatever plan emerged in the final report.²³ They spent the summer and fall of 1944 interviewing high military officials in Washington, and then in the late fall and early winter traveled to the European, Pacific, and Mediterranean theaters. An array of high-ranking officers was collected to testify to the need for military reorganization. Despite dissent from Richardson himself, the Richardson Committee garnered heavy support for merging the armed forces into one Cabinet department from such preeminent commanders as MacArthur, Eisenhower, Nimitz, and Halsey.

The only question that remained was how to bring about consolidation. The search for this answer involved constitutional, political, administrative, and economic issues, as well as practical and ethical questions, and was to consume several more years.

As the war drew to a close, the Navy began to resist the popular appeal of unification. Secretary of the Navy Forrestal chose a moderate strategy of education and gentle prodding that focused on public officials.²⁴ For example, he selected his friend Ferdinand Eberstadt, a respected expert on business and industrial aspects of military matters, to prepare a report that would be the basis for the Navy's bargaining position. Eberstadt was not considered a strong Navy partisan, and his findings suggested a hint of independence that would make them more credible. His report endorsed the notion that there should be more coordination between service departments, and further, between military and foreign-policy machinery. But it differed from the official Navy position by advocating the creation of a separate Air Force from the old Army Air Forces, a position that further elevated Eberstadt's status as an objective observer and hence increased the impact of his report.²⁵

The battle continued in the Senate Military Affairs Committee, where the most famous generals and admirals came to testify. Judging by the Army's case it was predicted that the interservice cooperation that had prevailed during the exigencies of war would deteriorate into squabbling during peacetime. Stressing economy and efficiency, the unification proponents insisted that national defense could not be provided on a "piecemeal" basis.²⁶ In many ways, the struggle became a classic case of rational versus incremental decision making.²⁷ On the one hand, the Army argued for a large-scale, comprehensive unit in which plans would be made at the top of a hierarchy that by its very nature ostensibly encouraged the free upward flow of information on which decisions are based. These decisions would be carried out by subordinate units with efficiency and dispatch. It seems tactically appropriate that those who proposed such a sweeping approach should go on the attack. On the other hand, one sees the worldly-wise Navy fighting a holding action by pointing up the flaws in grand schemes that might work on paper, but that suggest problems of application. In fact, Admiral Nimitz specifically turned against unification on the grounds that, while it looked good in theory, it would be of questionable value in practice.[28]

In the midst of the turmoil over unification, questions of close air support were occasionally raised, ironically often by the Navy. Arguing that separate development of similar weaponry was not wasteful, the Navy pointed to innovations in close air support and dive bombing made by the Navy and originally opposed by the War Department.[29] It seemed, though, that all the Air Force generals and many of their Army comrades were captivated by the big bombers and the big bomb. Close air support just was not that important in a world dominated by atomic bombers.

The generals also seemed to be attracted by the mystique of large-scale organization with its intrinsic notions of economy and efficiency. It was the Navy that stressed questions about the implications for democracy of a huge defense organization under a single military boss. The position of the Army seemed to resemble the formal, apolitical character of "scientific" public administration and governmental reform.[30] Navy officials continued to question the wisdom of the hierarchical view that unity in the field required a unified commander in the Washington bureaucracy.

Clearly, the call for a classifical model of decision making with one individual at the top was deeply embedded in the Army's outlook. Since the Root reforms of 1903, there had been a trend toward bringing the various subunits in the Army under control of a single Chief of Staff. Simply stated, the belief was that one man could make a decision while groups of men haggled over problems; in warfare, any decision, however rashly made, was better than waiting around for judgment. Such an attitude was later to become a tool on both sides of the close air support argument when interwoven with the idea of unity of command. But it was to prove more beneficial to the Army officials, who viewed the joint procurement of air support systems and joint acquisition of combat close air support as intolerably slow and weighted down with too many individuals who could alter or even merely be involved in decision making.

NATIONAL SECURITY ACT OF 1947

Congress finally ended the immediate controversy by enacting the National Security Act of 1947, which legitimized the impetus for the move to centralized military planning and operations by authorizing the creation of a national military establishment to replace the separate Departments of War and Navy.[31] This reorganization also separated the overwhelming bulk of

Air Corps materiel and personnel from the Army, creating a separate United States Air Force. Further reorganizations took place in 1949, 1953, and 1958.³² Each of these major structural realignments served to enhance the power and prerogatives of the Secondary of Defense and the Chairman of the Joint Chiefs of Staff. Thus, the Office of the Secretary of Defense and the Chairman of the Joint Chiefs (with the Joint Staff, which is comprised of a collection of middle- and upper-middle-level officer-bureaucrats) increasingly impeded interactions between each service and its task environment. Disorganization replaced organization-set, thereby creating instability within each service and its environment and altering hierarchical authority patterns that had provided the rationale for instant obedience within the chain of command.

Prior to World War II, service domains were fairly clear-cut. Supporters in Congress, in industry, and in private life contributed to the domain consensus, for there was little overlap between service organization-sets.³³ Even aviation questions were relatively minor and for the most part reflected intraservice matters. After the war, however, due to the new technology, the international situation, and the increasing complexity of government, the organization-sets of the military services became unsettled. The reorganization acts and amendments introduced during this period were, in part, attempts to define the domains of the services with regard to novel technological and environmental factors.

Reorganization of the military was incorporated into the National Security Act of 1947. In turn, this statute was a portion of the move toward reorganization of much of the national government, as evidenced in such other actions as the Atomic Energy Act and various domestic reorganization measures.³⁴ As a subset of this movement, the National Security Act was an attempt by political and military elites in the United States to come to terms with the new world conditions they faced in the period following World War II. Thus, while the individual services at this time were primarily interested in questions of domain, this was not the chief concern of Congress in 1947 or thereafter.

Congressional interest in the maintenance of each service was, however, deep. Congress did inject individual statements on the roles and missions of each service into the 1947 National Security Act. Specifically, the duties required of the Army were:

The Army, within the Department of the Army, includes land combat and service forces and such aviation and water transport as may be organic therein. It shall be organized, trained, and equipped primarily for prompt and sustained combat incident to operations on land. It is responsible for the preparation of land forces necessary for the effective prosecution of war except as otherwise assigned and, in accordance with integrated joint mobilization plans, for the expansion of the peacetime components of the Army to meet the needs of war.[35]

Parenthetically, it was not until 1950 that Congress codified the combined responsibilities of the military services: "(1) preserving the peace and security, and providing for the defense of the United States . . . ; (2) supporting the national policies; (3) implementing the national objectives; and (4) overcoming any nations responsible for aggressive acts that imperil the peace and security of the United States."[36]

The 1947 National Security Act marked the decline of the services from the institutional status they had enjoyed to the position of organizations in service of a new establishment.[37] The Military Establishment (later to become officially the Department of Defense) became an additional layer of authority with which the services had to deal. While the Air Force finally gained official recognition as a separate service, all the services suffered a loss of autonomy to this new superagency. The new authority imposed upon them was repeatedly transformed and became increasingly powerful in the next several years. Most importantly, the changes were made at the highest levels, where the emphasis is on planning, programming, and weapons systems. In such circumstances, made more difficult by the requirement to plan for the prevention of war as well as for combat itself, war tends to become more of an abstraction, more numbers and charts with little of "the tang of concrete and human events."[38] This combination of effects altered the "disturbed-reactive" environment in which the services had operated. The new environment was decidedly turbulent.

The new environment was also dualistic. Wartime brought the tempest of combat, but the single overriding mission tended to reduce turmoil within the organization. Peacetime increased organizational unrest, but because of the peculiar international Cold War atmosphere, the military faced the turbulence of both situations.

Reorganization is a traditional device used in trying to cope with a variety of organizational ills associated with a shifting environment. Efforts to adapt the civilian and military defense bureaucracies to such change included four major restructurings—in 1947, 1949, 1953, and 1958—as well as several lesser alterations. Each of these resulted in many apparent changes, all pointing in the direction of increased centralization, but certain aspects of confederation endured.

ORGANIZATION

As outlined in the 1947 National Security Act, the overall organization of the military was not drastically changed. The most obvious change was the separation of the Air Corps from the Army, and thus the formation of the new Air Force.

In point of fact, the Military Establishment was headed by the Secretary of Defense, who was a Cabinet member, but who was not the head of his own department. Instead, each of the three services constituted a department and was headed by a Secretary who was also a member of the Cabinet and who had a great deal of independence. For example, any service Secretary could see the President or carry a case to Congress or the Bureau of the Budget—the only requirement being that the Secretary of Defense be informed. At the highest level of the military hierarchy of each service was the Chief of Staff (or the Chief of Naval Operations), with the three service leaders together forming the Joint Chiefs of Staff.

In 1949, reorganization took a more drastic form as even anti-centralization Secretary Forrestal found the organization unwieldy.[39] The services remained separate, but the department heads lost their Cabinet status as the new Department of Defense was officially formed. The service Secretaries still had access to Congress, but were required to route all budget and policy matters through the Secretary of the superior department. The military protested such a development,[40] and in 1953 it became necessary to further clarify the powers of the Secretary vis-a-vis the services (now four in number, since the Marine Corps was for the most part established as a service in its own right in 1952, though it retained special ties to the Navy).[41] The services were still autonomous, but they were to be responsible to the Defense Secretary in matters regarding efficient and effective operation. In 1958, the Secretary of Defense received a further grant of power in which the services became subject to the direction of the Secretary in all matters except personnel, supply, weapons research, and doctrine. Thus, from a position of budget supervisor, the Department of Defense became a complete layer of insulation between the military and the policy-making levels of government.

JOINT BOARDS

Joint boards were part of the scheme to provide for interservice cooperation and coordination. The boards were concerned with munitions and research. A war council was included among them, but it fell into disuse soon after its formation.[42] There was an attempt to strengthen the munitions and research boards in 1949 by giving them a higher rank within the military establishment, but this attempt failed and the boards were eliminated under the 1953 reorganization plan.

JOINT CHIEFS OF STAFF

The Joint Chiefs were officially recognized by the National Security Act of 1947, though they had in fact existed during World War II. Once legally authorized, the Chiefs were expected to provide a common military direction for the services and thus were provided with their own secretariat and staff. Their responsibilities also included such duties as developing a structure of common planning and command, acting as advisers to the President, transmitting orders from the President to the services, and preparing strategic plans. These tasks called for close cooperation and a large staff, neither of which existed at the time. Each member was a partisan of his own service, and this fact, combined with the turbulence in the environment, resulted in insufficient coordination during peacetime planning.[43]

In 1949, an effort was made to improve these conditions. Staff size was increased and the position of Chairman of the Joint Chiefs of Staff was instituted. The Chairman was to be senior to all other members. The Chairman could bring to the attention of the Secretary of Defense matters on which the Joint Chiefs were divided, and he had personal access to the President and the Bureau of the Budget. The acquisition of a Chairman for the Joint Chiefs freed the other Chiefs to run their own services, but it reduced their status and effectiveness as a joint planning board.[44]

The power of the individual Chiefs was further reduced in 1953 when the Secretary of Defense was appointed the executive agent for the unified command. The duties of the Chairman were also increased to include control over the personnel and management of the Joint Staff. In 1958, the individual Chiefs regained some of the power and status they had lost due to the alterations in structure already identified.[45] Deputy Chiefs of Staff were appointed and were delegated the responsibility for training and equipping troops. This allowed the Joint Chiefs to concentrate more fully on the comprehensive overview of national security planning. The Chairman's power was again increased, and permission was granted to abolish the Joint Staff committees, where each service was represented by an equal number of officers, in favor of a more truly unified Joint Staff. Indeed, the effect of these reforms was to virtually eliminate the planning and strategic role of the individual services, except as they were represented on the Joint Chiefs, and to further isolate them from the formal policy-making forces within the government.

OTHER INTERNAL AND ENVIRONMENTAL FACTORS

Reorganization, while important, was by no means the only disorienting factor in the interservice relations of the post-World War II era. Other factors at this time also contributed to the organization-set dislocation of the United States Army. These factors, while analytically separable, overlap empirically. Hence, in the following analysis, categories are fairly arbitrary. In an attempt to separate out this tangled skein of relationships, I will present the material under the rubrics of the budget, conventional weaponry, the Korean conflict, roles and missions, strategy, nuclear weapons, public support, Congress, industry, the Office of the Secretary of Defense, and foreign policy.

Budget. After World War II, budgeting practices became especially troublesome. President Truman, in particular, insisted on a rather rigid budget ceiling.[46] The services still interacted with Congress and with external groups, but their bargaining position was essentially changed. Before the war, each service had worked with Congress through a Secretary who was partial to its interests for an absolute gain—that is budget gains by one service were relatively independent of gains by the other services. After the war, the services were given a single budget figure to work with, and this meant a parceling out of what was rapidly becoming a scarce resource. Each service, therefore, logically compared its own situation with that of the others. An additional problem arose in that the magnitude of money contained in this single-figure budget made the military an increasingly likely department in which to exercise economy as a part of the general fight against inflation.[47]

Due to the additional layers of authority imposed upon the military, then, relations in the budgeting process had changed. Officials in each service were dealing with people at a new level, and the Secretary of Defense could not be counted on as a service partisan. The style of requisition also was altered, for no longer were plans formulated and then funded; rather, what planning there was, was done with the purpose of acquiring the largest possible portion of the budget. Thus, such glamour items as missiles became the mainstay of the service budget.[48] The problem was succinctly expressed by one congressman: "The real question is just how much is enough? If there is peace, a $13 billion budget is entirely too much, and if there is war, this is entirely too little."[49]

Conventional Weaponry. Technological innovation resulted in the adoption of a variety of new weapons and artifacts of war besides the atom bomb. In one area, the impact of jet planes, which could fly faster, farther, and higher than other aircraft, increased the insecurity of the Army concerning the ability of their personnel to provide close air support. The Tactical Air Command (TAC) hungered for a piece of the strategic mission.[50] By 1960, certain concerned soldiers believed that no jet fighter was equipped to carry conventional bombs, but rather that TAC had become a miniature Strategic Air Command whose offensive compentencies stressed delivery of the nuclear weapon.[51]

During this time, the Army's weaponry was not updated. In fact, the hardware with which the Army was to meet the challenge in Korea was largely left over from World War II.[52] Because of the preoccupation with atomic devices, some officers foresaw this obsolesence of Army weapons.[53] As early as 1947, attempts were made to gain access to the atomic stockpile, and in 1951 such attempts were partially successful.[54] At first, however, the main interservice weapons battles were between the Air Force and the Navy.[55] The Air Force was involved with the Navy in a major controversy over the flush-deck carrier and the B-36 bomber, a controversy in which the Army played no major role.

The Army, was of course, hungry for fire power and mobility, but the Air Force had its own priorities, which did not include filling the Army's needs. The actualities of combat during the Korean War heightened the anxieties of Army officials.

Korean Conflict. The struggle over helicopters was manifested during the Korean War, and the contention was a life-or-death matter. Questions arose as to who would evacuate the Army wounded from the battlefield, where delay caused by disagreement or uncertainty could be fatal.[56] Such weapons rivalry was part of the general uncertainty associated with the Korean conflict: was it to be an all-out crusade in the manner of the two previous world wars? Or was it to be a limited conflict with carefully circumscribed roles and missions? Factions developed in the Army, with the men who tended to have a background in the European war accepting limitations as they concentrated on the Russian threat, while those with an Asian background favored a more aggressive posture.[57] The insubordination and removal of General MacArthur and the absence of victory heightened the turbulence surrounding the military in general and the Army in particular.

Also during the Korean action there was great concern about close air support. Ground troops desire as much fire support as possible. The Army expected that much of this assistance would come from close air support missions flown by the Air Force. But the average soldier on the ground was unable to bring air-power assistance to his area because of a policy requiring complex radio communications in order to gain access to forward air controllers.[58] For such men, roles and missions questions about air support were no small matter of grand policy.

Roles and Missions. The controversy over roles and missions continually influenced performance during this time. Such questions were not new in Army-Air Force relations. Attempts to resolve roles and missions assignments had been dealt with initially in two post-World War II reorganization conferences, but, in fact, the uncertainty and the controversy continued as intensely as ever.

53 / Domain Controversy

The first of the conferences was held in Key West, Florida, in March 1948.[59] The agreement reached there codified the obvious—that is, that the land medium was the domain of the Army, as the sea and air belonged to the Navy and Air Force respectively. These areas corresponded to the primary functions of the services. The Joint Chiefs further agreed that secondary missions might overlap, but that no service was to develop weapons or capabilities that could serve only its secondary capabilities. The roles and missions problem was further elaborated at the conference held in Newport, Rhode Island, during August of the same year. Here it was determined that each service was to be given exclusive authority for planning in its primary domain, but that the capabilities of the other services in carrying out these plans could not be ignored.[60]

The major outcome of these conferences was the assurance of naval air capability. The primary missions, as they were made explicit, reflected the status quo with respects to the domains of the services. The problems arose with regard to the secondary missions. Each service was to support its primary role with whatever secondary functions were necessary, yet these secondary functions could not conflict with the primary mission of another service. In this respect, the Army and the Air Force had asymmetrical responsibilities,[61] for while many in the Air Force perceived the Army to be functionally of little account because of the future nature of warfare, soldiers not only did not view themselves or their serivce as insignificant, but they were also uncomfortable with the notion that they were perceived to be this way by the Air Force. At the same time that the Army's value to the Air Force was in question, the role of the Air Force vis-à-vis the Army was one of indispensability, for the Army's primary mission (ground warfare) could not be carried out fully without Air Force support. Despite the discomfiture of the Army, support by armed aircraft was assigned exclusively to the Air Force in every roles and missions assignment or agreement until 1966.

Thus, major reorganization did not prove to be a cure-all for the problems that plagued the military following World War II, but rather signaled an increase in complexity for the services. On May 20, 1949, Joint Army-Air Force Adjustment Regulations 5-10-1 appeared under the title "Combat Joint Operations, Etc.: Employment of Aircraft for Performance of Certain Missions."[62] This order set weight limitations and outlined certain specific functions for the use of Army aircraft in ground combat operations. The Army was to pay for its requirements, but the Air Force was to be responsible for procurement, maintenance, and research and development of all Army aircraft.

During the entire Korean conflict, there was disagreement as to the effectiveness of Air Force support for the Army. The Army accused the Air

Force of lack of support,[63] but the Air Force countered with the charge that the Army was encroaching on the structure of integrated air power.[64] The Air Force wanted specific limitations on Army air power; the Army, in turn, wanted promises of support, a more difficult task since support flows from the combat situation.

In all another attempt to resolve air support disagreements, Secretary of the Army Frank Pace, Jr., and Secretary of the Air Force Thomas K. Finletter met periodically from May through October of 1951. They agreed to by-pass weight limitations and attempted to phrase an agreement based upon function. The concept developed that the Army was to use its aircraft strictly within the combat zone (not expected to exceed sixty to seventy-five miles) for improvement of logistics, communications, and other combat-related functons.[65]

Within a month after the signing of this agreement, however, dissension concerning the helicopter arose again, largely regarding evacuation of Army troops. On October 13, 1952, the Secretaries of the Army and Air Force met with their respective Chiefs of Staff and the Assistant Secretary of Defense. With apparent pressure from Secretary of Defense Robert Lovett (seemingly originating from the White House), an agreement was reached on November 7, 1952.[66] This agreement reinstated weight limitations on Army aircraft, but made them subject to review by the Secretary of Defense. On the other hand, the Army gained when Army transportation of Army supplies, equipment, and personnel within the (slightly enlarged) combat zone become a primary rather than a limited or emergency function. In addition, observation, control of Army forces, command liaison, and courier missions became primary Army functions, and two new functions were added—artillery and topographic survey, and, most importantly, limited air-medical evacuation, including battlefield pickup of casualties.[67]

Despite these efforts, significant Army-Air Force rivalry persisted, for the agreements touched only the surface of the dissension and did not deal with the underlying questions. With the exception of the first Pace-Finletter accord, these agreements were little more than bargained compromises at the service Secretary level, designed to be as inoffensive as possible, while the Pace-Finletter agreement was too general to be of much use.[68]

The year 1953 saw the coming to power of a new national administration headed by one of America's great soldier-heroes, Dwight D. Eisenhower. With his presidency came an end to the Korean War and implementation of the "New Look" in defense policy by Secretary of Defense Charles Wilson. The turbulent environment continued, however. The Army had been buoyed up by its limited success in Korea under General Matthew Ridgway following its earlier defeats at the hands of the North Koreans and then the Chinese.

55 / Domain Controversy

Nevertheless, it was still unsettled in its organizational environment. In 1953, Secretary of Defense Charles Wilson attempted to update the Key West Agreement, but brought forth no real change.[69] When the Army later borrowed the T-37 jet fighter for maneuvers, it exacerbated the existing tensions by alerting the Air Force to this new infringement on its domain.[70] Eventually, Wilson was forced to deal with the situation. Continued bickering led him to try once again to resolve roles and missions issues.

Thus, in November 1956 Wilson circulated a memorandum which supposedly reaffirmed previous roles and missions agreements while providing additional clarification. Its major thrust was to restrict Army missile and aviation activities (supposedly, in part, to produce more interservice harmony).[71] Utilizing a static model (of questionable relevance in an atomic era), it limited the Army to use of its own avaition within 100 miles of the forward edge of the battle area (FEBA). The memorandum also decreed that airlift and tactical air support were Air Force missions. The weight limitation for Army aircraft was to be 5,000 pounds for fixed-wing craft and 20,000 pounds for rotary-wing craft.

Certain pro-aviation elements in the Army reacted to this memorandum as though it were a bitter pill,[72] but at the same time steps were taken to circumvent the meaning of the agreement. The lack of success of this memorandum is seen in the fact that by 1966, the time of the next major agreement, the Army had well over 400 aircraft (predominately helicopters) in combat as part of the equipment of one "airmobile" division alone.[73] Even such aircraft as the Caribou fixed-wing transport were in use by the Army, also an exception to the 1957 memorandum. The Caribou was later given up by the Army in return for certain concessions from the Air Force. The circumstances surrounding their relinquishment as well as the 1966 agreement will be discussed in Chapter 5. The war in Vietnam seemed to require such items as an airmobile division and the Green Berets, and in this situation the Army managed to come to terms more effectively with its narrowly conceived environment.

Strategy. Samuel Huntington suggests that, in the post-World War II decade, four major stategic missions were considered as priorities for those concerned with national security: Continental defense, defense of Europe, limited war, and strategic deterrence.[74] These priorities did not present themselves in any self-evident order. In the struggle to rank these priorities, the Air Force tended to favor those programs which corresponded to strategies that assured them primacy and that, by their own interpretation, virtually assured them almost exclusive control of United States air power. The Army, on the other hand, promoted policies in which its role was not so clear, and which, given even the most favorable interpretation, involved shared powers.

In years immediately following World War II, the Army pushed for a universal military training (UMT) program that was intended to provide a large pool of not-quite-combat-ready forces held largely in reserve status.[75] With hindsight, this seems incongruous with the need for compact, highly trained, combat-ready forces. The Army lost this fight, for not only was it out of step with strategic necessities but it was also asking for more than Congress was willing to provide. UMT was interpreted as a means to assure organizational survival,[76] but more importantly it provided the Army the wherewithal to renew one interpretation of its mission, the ability to mobilize a large number of men to accomplish great feats. At that time, given the uncertainty as to who the enemy would be, the question of the effectiveness of atomic power, and the type of war the future promised, the concept of UMT seemed less unreasonable than it may now appear.

Providing air defense for the protection of the United States became a focus of interservice rivalry associated with strategy, weaponry, and roles and missions. Should the major defense be provided by long-range interceptors flown by Air Force pilots as one of their classic functions? Or should defense be provided by anti-aircraft artillery, a classic Army task? As weapons technology moved in the direction of missile development, the question became abstracted. The Army, for instance, could contend that the Nike-Hercules missile was an extension of the anti-aircraft concept, while the Air Force might insist that the BOMARC missile was a pilotless interceptor.

Nuclear Weapons. It is in the area of offensive weapons with atomic capabilities that the Air Force-Army rivalry appeared most intense. No one understood the possibilities raised by atomic power, yet everyone understood the immensity of the possibilities only too well. How were the services to cope with the possibility that there might be no more war and no need for military services, or every need for at least one service? Did the bomb mean that thermonuclear war was inevitable, or did it mean there would be only limited wars, without atomic weapons? There were no sure answers, but in trying to assure itself of a place in the sun, each of the services sought a piece of the atomic action.

Several officials in the Army tried to adapt military doctrine to the nuclear reality. The Army reorganized itself in the mid 1950s so that it could fight with well-dispersed battle groups in a "pentomic" division structure in Western Europe.[77] Ideally, the Army would have its own intermediate-range missiles, and its own aviation assets would provide dispersion for forces under attack and concentration for troops about to launch an offensive. Some of the helicopters that would be used in these operations were, in fact, described as "air cavalry" and were to perform the same functions of reconnaissance, screening the flanks, and shock that had historically been performed by mounted troops.[78]

Public Support. The romantic view of a swashbuckling air cavalry gamboling across an atomic battlefield was probably presented for public consumption partly as a device to win public support. The struggle for public support occupied much of the time and attention of Army planners; and even though atomic weapons would not have fit in well with the traditions of a land army composed of individual fighting soldiers, it was clearly recognized that popular support and money lay in the direction of the glamorous, antiseptic big bomb.

Efforts were made to enlist the aid of professional associations, industry, and Congress in procuring for the Army more of the stuff of future wars. In these efforts lay the beginnings of many changes in civil-military relations. Until then, the military had been insulated from much of the day-to-day political wrangling because of its professional status. The new environment forced the services to become part of a political and public relations scene they did not know, but they learned quickly. The Air Force was most skilled at public relations, but all the services found themselves involved in such activities as speechmaking, offering expert advice and assistance to the film and television industries, writing articles and books, making public service announcements for recruiting, conducting tours for industrial and civic leaders, testifying at public hearings, and being called upon to offer support regarding political-military decisions.[79] An example of the last situation is the public backing given by many high-ranking officers to Truman's dismissal of MacArthur.[80] In addition, there was the development of various "backstop" organizations, which aided the services in their bids for favorable publicity.[81] Composed of retired service personnel and other civilian supporters, these organizations had freedom of movement in areas in which military participation would have raised questions.

Congress. The military attempted not only to establish its status in the community but also to reorient its relationship with Congress. Congressmen had become less the partisans of a single service and more attuned to overall issues of national security and defense.[82] At the same time, military budgets (which had become the essential method of congressional military policy making) were presented in the Defense budget, in which individual service claims had already been considered. The Armed Services Committees in the House and Senate now had less influence on military policy than did the Appropriations Committees, in spite of section 412 of the 1959 Military Construction Authorization Act, which states that appropriations may be made only for programs that are authorized.[83] Moreover, the double focus of oversight stipulated by section 412 had paved the way for less-effective overall congressional control of the military establishment.[84]

Relations with Congress involved more than budgetary processes, however. The military was able to repay congressional favors in two ways. One was by handling constituent problems referred to a particular service by an individual congressman. The other involved the establishment of bases or the alloting of contracts, especially arms-related contracts, within a congressional district. In these cases, the military's influence with congressmen came from helping their constituents and was therefore more effective than simply relying on service preference or ideological similarity in obtaining favors.

Industry. One major environmental development insofar as armaments were concerned was the birth of the first significant peacetime munitions industry. This industry, with its involvement in the tremendous financial resources available, became a force with which each service had to deal as best it could. Again, the Air Force was particularly successful in this regard, largely because much of its research and development was handled by a relatively homogeneous and consistent group of corporations, those associated with aircraft production. While this pattern repeated itself for the Navy and its shipbuilding supporters, the Army faced a different set of circumstances. Because the Army required such a broad variety of products and because it did so much of its own research by means of the so-called arsenal system, no single industrial bloc emerged to stabilize the Army's environment.[85] The Air Force gathered great political support through the ability of the aircraft industry to advertise effectively and lobby in Congress; in contrast, the Army's support was diffuse. An additional problem for the Army was that the agreements regarding roles and missions placed aircraft development under the auspices of the Air Force. Thus, the Army was faced with a situation in which its rival stood between it and the technical elements important to its domain.

With the move of the Army into missile development in the mid-1950s, some changes took place. The Army tried to catch up in the propaganda race by encouraging Western Electric to place advertisements for its Nike-Hercules missiles, which were then competitive with the Boeing BOMARC.[86] The Army found some support in corporations belonging to its backstop organizations and began to reap benefits similar to those of the Air Force-industrial relationships. Yet such developments did not ensure certainty within the environment, even though these activities were partially efforts by the services to establish organization-set. General Gavin, for example, stated that "what appears to be intense interservice rivalry . . . in most cases . . . is fundamentally industrial rivalry."[87] If accurate, his statement suggests that the Army was not in control of its destiny, and his words in fact suggest perception of a turbulent environment. This interindustry turbulence may have partially justified claims by some officers that the services were not responsible for the rivalry, since the services were swept along by the impact of relationships among the industrial giants.

Office of the Secretary of Defense. Given the vast sums of money involved in weapons research, development, and procurement, and the complexity of management problems also involved, there was an increasing policy focus on the Office of the Secretary of Defense. Budgetary matters became increasingly important, and the Secretary of Defense, who always had primacy in such questions, likewise grew in power. To the soldiers, huge amounts of money might have created an atmosphere of unreality, but the need for management of organizations required to deal with such sums was producing civilian economic technocrats. When Robert S. McNamara became the Secretary of Defense in the Kennedy administration, there was a pronounced stress on achieving, through the most modern cost-effectiveness techniques, economies of expenditure.[88] The requirements for cost effectiveness meant that each service faced a comparison with the other services concerning how well each program contributed to some general defense goal. Such comparisons further weakened the ties between the services and their traditional duties, thereby somewhat affecting the military ethos associated with these traditional military missions. The insistence upon cost-effectiveness techniques, later formalized as PPBS,[89] also damaged the military's sense of professionalism because it promoted the opinions of young, computer-wise technocrats at the apparent expense of the military judgment of experienced officers.[90] Interservice rivalry increased, thereby promoting unsettling domain relationships, but there also existed a sense of kinship among high-ranking officers in their battle with the youthful civilian managers. In any event, greater sums of money were expended. The defense establishment appeared to increase in power and efficiency, and as the Department of Defense was strengthened, so was its role in the making of foreign policy.

Foreign Policy. Although international developments set in motion a variety of activities that in turn promoted turbulence in the environment of the United States Army, the Army, as part of the military, paradoxically began to move in the direction of reestablishing an organization-set within the matrix of foreign policy. For a certain segment of military officers, the militarization of foreign policy by both civilian and military officials provided an opportunity to develop new relations with elites interested in foreign policy. These relations suggested a civilianization of some military offices in a manner that was incongruent with classic professionalism.[91] At one point, military advisers abroad outnumbered State Department officials by more than two to one.[92] Much of national security decision making was based on information gathered by the military, even if its relevance to military matters was dubious. As a result, a large number of military advisers performed quasi-diplomatic chores and militarized America's relations with many nations. By supporting containment, military men increased their opportunity to become actively involved in the global struggle against Communism. In this struggle, the whole world provided a potential arena for international conflict.

As the Joint Chiefs of Staff grew in power, dependence on their advice in military matters grew as well, though in specific cases, such as their advocacy of the Safeguard Anti-Ballistic Missile System, their recommendation was partially rejected.[93] The top military planners' perspective tended to stress the possibility of the "worst case" occurring, but it did not diverge greatly from the views of civilians with parallel interests.[94] In joint planning sessions, it was quite natural for military men to stress the military aspects of diplomatic or economic international relations. Soldiers pressed for more weapons in order to provide a broader range of options for civilian policy makers to choose from in the application of force.

Among the options provided by the Army were the AR-15 (M-16) lightweight rifle intended for use in jungle combat, Special Forces A-team units trained to combat Communist-supported insurgencies in developing nations, and airmobile, large-scale Army units sustained by troop-carrying and arms-bearing helicopters. Such options opened up the possibility—or perhaps created the probability—of intervention in "wars of national liberation" on the side of the non-Communist forces.[95]

Thus, the Army's domain came to include nonatomic limited wars on the periphery of a supposed Communist monolith. Faced by the inability of the national government to deal with such challenges, economically or diplomatically, the interest of the Armed Forces hierarchy in general, and that of the Army in particular, moved from peacetime turbulence to the surface regularity of wartime demands. For soldiers performing their mission in Vietnam, the turbulence of peacetime was replaced by the chaos of battle, which, paradoxically, brought with it a stability provided by the need to accomplish their mission. However, while the Army was engaged in combat, the environment in which it operated continued to fluctuate. The declining popularity of the war and the dimming possibility of victory affected popular

61 / Domain Controversy

support for the Army itself. Distaste for the draft, for the policies on which the war was based, and for the manner in which the war was conducted provoked passionate attacks on the Army as well as on the war itself.

With an irony that for some soldiers was almost as cruel as war itself, the Army found itself actively engaged in pursuing its mission with weapons that appeared to fit into traditional modes of operation, while at the same time turbulence in the environment and internal dissent threatened the Army's existence as an institution. The youth culture of the 1960s, American policy regarding Vietnam, and the Army's role in the war spurred the dissent, which, coupled with the continued turbulence, made the future of the Army uncertain. Technology that provided the needed weapons may have prolonged the "helicopter war"[96] and threatened the existence of the Army, but the Army still looked for salvation through such devices as the electronic battlefield in a search for technological solutions to organizational dilemmas.[97] It is precisely this question of technology in the struggle for Army aviation that requires more detailed elaboration.

We will consider the attitudes and orientations of important subgroups within the Army and Air Force in order to suggest how Air Force officers' orientations inhibited their ability to meet the needs of the Army and how the Army's outlook tended to free it to select from any available technology that seemed to meet its needs. The place of doctrine in the development of aviation will be stressed, and attitudes toward procurement and budget will be considered. A brief history of the helicopter will be presented, followed by a tracing of the development of the armed helicopter, in order to show the mix of technology and politics within which bureaucratic insurgency can take place. Techniques of innovation will be highlighted in order to clarify the politics of putting inventions to practical use.

Chapter 4 | **HELICOPTER TECHNOLOGY: POLITICAL IMPERATIVE OR OPPORTUNITY?**

"Science is the quest for more or less abstract knowledge, whereas technology is the application of organized knowledge to help solve problems in our society. . . . There are many important, creative, innovative activities which, if they draw on science, draw on it only incidentally."[1] Technology, then, may be thought of as the application of scientific knowledge, methods, or research for practical purposes.[2] Understanding the development of aviation equipment can provide a clearer comprehension of the interrelationships of technology and politics in general and of helicopter technology and insurgent bureaucratic politics in particular. It is the very human touch of application that brings to technology the possibility of alternate modes of decision making and administration. These modes may be repeated over time to form discernable patterns or styles. These patterns may further suggest, though by no means determine, an underlying state of mind which can be called a "psychology of technology."

Psychology of Technology

Simply looking at the manifestations of this psychology of technology has suggested to certain concerned military men distinctions in style between the approaches of relevant personnel in the United States Air Force and those in the United States Army. Some of these distinctions have been collected in an effort to suggest ideal types that would be useful in promoting understanding of a far more complex reality.

After gaining its autonomy, the Air Force had continually stressed bigger, higher-flying, longer-range, faster aircraft.[3] This passion for high speed was significant in that it focused the attention of the Air Force away from helicopters and other low and slow aircraft in favor of big bombers and quick-air-superiority fighters, and beyond them to towering, fast ballistic missiles. The Air Force, for the most part, simply preferred the faster, fixed-wing configuration to the rotary-wing helicopters. Even when involved with helicopters in Korea, it held to its tradition by choosing the larger, more complex RH-12 over the Army's smaller, simplified H-13.[4]

Furthermore, the Air Force had been oriented toward atomic weaponry since the beginning of its use. Its great clashes with the Navy centered on control of the air-delivered atomic weapon, initially in the form of the B-36 delivery system.[5] The Air Force's reluctance to share this particular type of weaponry is congruent with its own notions of mission, which require that the Air Force control the air and have the strategic capability of destroying the enemy through air power.

While many officials in the Army were concerned to obtain atomic weapons for themselves, especially tactical nuclear weapons, such actions seemed as much an effort to assure organizational survival (getting the Army's share of the atomic action) as a reflection of a real sense that the Army's mission *required* such weaponry. Furthermore, while the atomic delivery system was an end in itself for Air Force officials, tactical atomic weapons actually spurred additional innovations in the Army (the pentomic division and the Sky Cavalry).[6]

In short, the Air Force was very much aware of its glamorous position and sought to fortify it.[7] Such glamour was enhanced by the incredibly expensive and complex hardware associated with the atomic mission. The Air Force was literally "above it all" and, in the minds of the Army, had departed the battlefield.[8] The Army, in contrast, was not so wedded to complexity. In fact, in many aspects of Army life the motto is KISS ("Keep it simple, stupid!"). Being close to the earth, many soldiers had the experience of fighting against dirt and moisture in such simple mechanical processes as keeping their rifles and machine guns clean.

As the Air Force soared high to the sky, stressing its lofty image, it further insisted on extremely high standards of safety so that nothing would mar that elevated image.[9] Soldiers, on the other hand, used their aircraft for flying close to the nap of the earth and accepted their casualties from the accidents that resulted.[10] The Air Force was accustomed to thinking in terms of loss rates per mission from its combat experience in World War II, and would adjust tactics if a rate rose above a certain point.[11] The Army, in contrast, could not change its tactics as readily to reduce casualties below some magical number in the midst of fierce, enemy-initiated combat.

The Air Force's approach was essentially linear. If it was faster, traveled farther, was more complex (and more expensive), it was, by this logic, bound to be better. Being charged with the mission of deterrence through the destruction of the enemy homeland and immediate retaliation, it is not surprising that the Air Force resembled a swift greyhound pursuing the rabbit of its mission with blinders on to keep it from distractions. In contrast, the Army appeared to be a bloodhound whose desultory rambling from post to post masked a deliberateness of purpose. Air Force linearity has conditioned that service to insist upon newness in its technical tools, and innovations have had a particularly futuristic cast.[12] The Army, on the other hand, perhaps from necessity, has had to make do in large part with apparently obsolescent, discarded materials and has by-passed many new developments suggested by newer products.[13] Thus, there exists a viewpoint that in various matters of technological innovation, the Air Force is usually first, followed by the Navy, and followed after a rather long time by the Army. This pattern has been termed "technological lag."[14]

There is now some evidence that Army psychology is no longer immovably on the side of improvisation. Rather, there is evidence that a research and development strategy stressing large sums of money and complex systems with long lead times has become increasingly attractive to Army aviation planners, who are themselves becoming increasingly established and visible as part of the defense establishment.[15] In particular, the development of the Lockheed AH56-A (Cheyenne assault helicopter) resembles other large-scale weapons development projects.[16] However, the Army aviators may still have been too new at the game of large-scale development to be able to tolerate contractors' misdeeds. This is suggested by the cancellation of production of the Cheyenne due to default of contract, a step which forfeits the Army's opportunity to obtain its "dream" helicopter.[17] In any event, prior to the Cheyenne venture, the Army's style appears to have been a mixture of the venerable and the novel which produced an approach that stressed makeshift invention and doctrinal flexibility.

Technology and Doctrine

For the Air Force, technology was inextricably linked with mission. This was so because, in order to go aloft, a technological presupposition is required. Further, great advances in capacity are associated with technological advances. This has been less true of the Army, though the situation may be changing.[18] For the Army, mission was closely linked with human beings—that is, it was labor-intensive in contrast to the technology-intensive mode of the Air Force.

Doctrine, being principles expounded upon by a body of believers in the mission, was logically derived from the mission for both the Army and the Air Force. The mission of the Air Force, as stated, was highly dependent upon technology. As such, the insistence on the part of students of doctrine that armed services adopt doctrines concerning tactical and strategic applications of new weapons prior to the actual application of those weapons reflects a failure to differentiate between the place of technology in the Army and its place in the Air Force.[19] Winning weapons with the doctrine to guide their use was appropriate for the service of technology. Winning soldiers with weapons used as tools was appropriate to the service of manpower.

For the Army, doctrine told how to organize, lead, and maneuver troops.[20] Weapons were neither the basic necessity of such doctrine nor mere accretions on the body of the Army. Rather, weapons were tools to be applied in furtherance of basic military principles. Therefore, any doctrinal alterations stemming from technological changes still fell within parameters set by the mission.

The Air Force particularly had been limited by its doctrine that requires a stress on the offensive capabilities of its weaponry.[21] Such problems were far less important for the Army, whose timeless (if internally inconsistent) principles of war seemed applicable to all situations facing ground troops.[22] The Air Force did endeavor to protect what Thompson calls its core technology.[23] This core technology was, in fact, a technology associated with particular types of hardware. The Army also sought to protect its core technology, but in this case its technology stressed "proper" use of the organization and leadership of men. Such technology was suited to the Army's role as defender of the terrain. The soldiers were literally "down to earth," and their style reflected the vicissitudes of natural forces—cautious, slow, close to the ground. The Air Force had "slipped the surly bonds of Earth"[24] and, as such, found itself defending air. In such an ethereal atmosphere, it is not surprising that these men clung tenaciously to the tangible air vehicles which took them and their identity aloft.

Air Force doctrine accentuated the impact of technology on warfare. As such, it was a part of an intellectual tradition of which General F. C. Fuller was an exponent. Fuller has stated, for instance, that "tools, or weapons, if only the right ones can be discovered, form ninety-nine per cent of victory. . . . Strategy, command, leadership, courage, discipline, supply, organization, and all the moral and physical paraphernalia of war are as nothing to a high superiority of weapons—at most they go to form the one per cent which makes the whole possible."[25]

Some might wonder at the notion of inanimate invention as a creator of social change. While it is true that humans mediate between technology and society, they themselves are nevertheless affected by the things they choose to manipulate. However, these inanimate objects can vary in their impact on the minds of men.[26] In particular, ideas about these objects can become an unshakable part of an outlook on life. Thus, each new aircraft or missile flying higher, faster, and farther could symbolically imply the correctness of the idea that progress in weapons must increase at an accelerating rate and that such progress is virtually inevitable.

Such a perspective, while perfectly understandable, was by no means the only view of the appropriate role of technology in military matters. For those men whose view of their mission was not tied to any particular technology, a greater detachment seemed possible. Some developed an attachment to increasingly complex tools, but others looked for a variety of ways to complete a task.[27] For many, though not all, men of Army aviation, the armed helicopter became a substitute invention which expediently replaced much of the air support that might have been provided by the Air Force.[28] Thus, had the Air Force taken up serious research and development in fighter helicopters, or even permitted control of some portion of their current inventory of attack planes and transports to be maintained by ground commanders, it is likely that Army aviation would not have developed as it did. The helicopter provided aviation support in a "regime" or realm of flight that was neglected by the Air Force. However, there is no need to deem inevitable the development of helicopters, as opposed to other kinds of obstacle-crossing, armed vehicles. That Army aviation developed in the manner in which it did is largely related to interorganizational relationships, Air Force doctrine, and Army political activities rather than to technological determinism.

Technology and Procurement

Army and Air Force differences existed in the realm of the service-industrial aspect of technological politics. The Army had traditionally made use of Army-controlled capabilities through the device of its own proving grounds and arsenals. The Army chose to continue those relationships developed during the war which stressed intramural research and development.[29] It took part, for instance, in battles to improve the civil service status and pay of government scientists.[30] The relative absence of Air Force tradition was manifested in its acquisition of weapons. The newly established Air Force preferred a policy of close relationships with contractual sources to the extent that a Second Hoover Commission subcommittee commended it for relying on private contractors.[31]

The Army continued to operate laboratories along the lines of arsenal systems in conventional weaponry. This promoted the possibility of appraisal of new weapons by persons not necessarily committed to a particular private corporation. It was contended that to obtain the complex technical resources needed for Air Force systems, outside rather than intramural arsenal expertise was needed, though in-house capabilities would be maintained.[32]

The politics of this distinction produced a variety of allies for each side. Relationships of trust between contractors and the Army were less in evidence than those warm relationships which existed between the Air Force and its industrial supporters.[33] The Commission on Organization of the Executive Branch of the Government, also known as the Second Hoover Commission, tended to support the Air Force's approach, while the General Accounting Office (GAO), the efficiency-oriented arm of Congress, issued reports critical of the operations of service contracts (attacking in particular the Air Force's controversial contract with the Ramo-Wooldridge Corporation). Congress was reluctant to accept the recommendations of the GAO, its own investigatory arm.[34]

Technology and Budgeting

The complexity of the equipment desired by the Air Force required expenditures of vast sums of money for its acquisition, and since the federal government's budgeting approach was to provide a huge lump sum and then distribute it among the services, the Air Force tended to get the largest slice of the defense pie.[35] After all, its long-range jet bombers and sleek missiles clearly fitted into policies of deterring the Soviet Union and were evidence of the power of the United States military as well as of the strength of the United States economy, especially in the eyes of Congress. Because the Secretary of Defense permitted each service to operate largely independently, many projects were started by each service that could not be completed at existing budget levels.[36] While this meant a great many "stretch outs" and cancellations of programs that would not have been started if costs had been anticipated accurately, the very ability to start so many small programs tended to benefit the service that could keep such programs small. In the case of the Army, some of these programs were associated with the airmobile Army.

In the face of changing management technologies, criticisms of former budget systems brought forth new techniques associated primarily with Secretary of Defense Robert McNamara. The Air Force, in fact, went on record as endorsing a new budget management technology stressing systems on the grounds that the "complexity of its weapons, the long lead time and extensive resources involved, and the urgency of achieving and maintaining maximum operational capability" made systems management necessary.[37]

Technology was not the determinant for Army aviation supporters. They were able to use the new management technology, much as they were able to use the new hardware technology, and make it work for them. Technology, in short, provided obstacle and opportunity. It was up to the men of mission of Army aviation to make the most of this opportunity (as we shall see in Chapter 5), and the helicopter itself provided the primary opportunity for them.

Technology and Invention

The story of the airmobile Army appears to revolve around that product of technology known as the helicopter. Without laying too much stress on the hardware aspects of Army aviation, it will prove valuable to trace briefly some of the historical milestones in the creation of this machine, varieties of which were to become the workhorses of the airmobile Army.

THE HELICOPTER

A helicopter, generally speaking, is a type of aircraft whose support in the air is derived solely from the reaction of a stream of air driven downward by propellers revolving around a vertical axis. Leonardo da Vinci, in fact, perceived that the spiraling motion of the Archimedian screw could potentially lift itself into the air.[38] But it was not until the French inventor Louis Breguet rose five feet for two minutes in August 1907 that the principles became potentially practicable. Ironically, while others worked on various craft, it was Breguet who demonstrated the first genuine helicopter performance (as opposed to simple flight) in July 1935.[39]

During World War I there was an increasing impetus to study the helicopter as a device that would hover over the enemy for intelligence and reconnaissance purposes. In 1915, an Austrian lieutenant, Stefan Petroczy, assisted by a young professor of aerodynamics, Theodore Van Karman, produced a captive helicopter (held by cables due to lack of maneuverability) which boosted a pilot, observer, and machine gun for one hour. Lack of the ability to stabilize these craft disappointed developers in many countries, however, and most then turned to fixed-wing craft.

One exception was George de Bothezat, who worked in Russia until he was forced to flee in 1917. Exiled in the United States, he convinced the

American Army that his machine possessed inherent stability and maneuverability and, as a consequence, he received $20,000 with which to produce it. Though the de Bothezat helicopter rose six feet and stayed aloft for a minute and a half, additional expenditures of more than $200,000 still could not fully satisfy the Army, and the plan was abandoned in 1924.

The Spanish inventor Juan de la Sierva y Cordorina provided impetus to helicopter development with his invention of the first rotating air foils. He saw that by designing the rotor properly, he could make use of air flow across the blades as if they were so many wings. The autogiro, Sierva's creation, which was a rotor without an engine attached (the engine turned a normally positioned propeller), provided many ideas essential for the development of the helicopter, but was not itself to be a prototype for the creation of most future models. Eventually, the United States Army Air Corps tested two autogiros in 1936. While the tests proved unsatisfactory, they did suggest what an effective helicopter might someday do.

In 1939, Igor Sikorsky put on a masterful helicopter demonstration before representatives of the United States Army and other governmental agencies. By making the most of the ability to hover, his VS-300 captured the interest and imagination of the observers. Sikorsky's XR-4, a later mock-up, was subsequently demonstrated for General H. H. Arnold, head of the Air Corps. The Navy, as well as the Army Air Corps, placed orders for this model, and orders were later placed by the Coast Guard, the Air Corps, and British units for the XR-6, a newer model. The major use of the helicopter by the military services was for air rescue, a function performed at the very end of World War II. It was in the years after World War II that the helicopter became a major tool in the struggle for Army aviation.

ORIGINS OF ARMY AVIATION

No one individual can claim to be the founder of Army aviation. During World War II, there developed a tradition of using field expedients to make available equipment more effective. Thus, airplanes came to carry arms to provide suppressive fire capability. One source credits Colonel Frank Forrest with the original gunship design,[40] but claims are also staked for Tommy Haynes and Bryce Wilson, who are said to have designed the first aerial armament system.[41] Credit is also given to a Major Carpenter, who is said to have put bazookas on L-14's in the Fourth Armored Division in World War II and destroyed several tanks.[42] In all these cases, the armed aircraft were fixed-wing, but the precedent was established for the armed helicopter. Also established was the practice of superiors issuing countermanding orders to remove the armament. Needless to say, since such modifications were not authorized, these orders failed to deter the persistence of the "garage mechanics in their own shops" in the combat zone, where there were other priorities.⁴³

Immediately following World War II, Army aviation existed in a state of uncertainty. General Arnold had perceived the threat of Army aviation to the all-inclusiveness of air assets that he desired for his anticipated autonomous Air Force.⁴⁴ From 1945 to 1947, the number of organic Army aircraft declined from approximately 1,600 to an estimated 200 craft.⁴⁵ During this period the future of Army aviation was unclear. It was uncertain whether there would continue to be an organic Army aviation program, or whether those army pilots who chose to remain in the service would move into the newly created Air Force. It is perhaps paradoxical that the very National Security Act of 1947 that brought into existence the United States Air Force also recognized the possession of organic aircraft by the United States Army. This act was to be the legitimizing basis on which Army aviation would be built.

While Army aviation did have an excellent charter for its existence, it did not have control over its own research and development or the procurement of items required for the maintenance of its aircraft. On March 23, 1950, the Army and the Air Force jointly prescribed procedures related to the development, procurement, supply, and maintenance of Army aircraft.⁴⁶ These regulations indicated that the Air Force would still control procurement of aircraft and aircraft equipment; the conducting of research and development when requested by the Army; the classifying of types in coordination with the Army; and the handling of the actual purchase, inspection, and acceptance of Army aircraft. The Air Force agreed to coordinate with the Army in conducting engineering, user, and troop tests. The Air Force was to evaluate recommended modifications of Army aircraft, handle storage, take care of issuance and shipment at the depot level, and perform depot maintenance at its own expense.

Still, the Army maintained some appearance of discretion since it could determine military characteristics for Army aircraft and aircraft equipment, approve specifications thereof, and make final decisions regarding proposed modifications. The Army would, of course, provide the Air Force with funds for research and development, purchase, and any other expenses associated with the modification and testing of aircraft. The Army also retained responsibility for receipt, storage, and distribution of its aviation equipment below depot level, as well as for organizational and field maintenance. It was on this last, quite unremarkable provision that the politics of invention was to be based for some time.

THE ARMED HELICOPTER

Though Army aviation was restricted by reliance on the Air Force for a variety of technical and materiel needs, forces were at work that would provide recurring impetus to the drive for an airmobile Army. In the development of Army aviation, both increased mobility and improved fire power were significant factors.[47] In order to increase the fire power of a helicopter, fixed armament was required. Efforts to arm helicopters were more significant manifestations of the effort to improve close air support than were other developments. Thus, while improvements in speed and range were important, stress will be laid upon that which caused most consternation within the Air Force and provided the greatest test of strength of Army aviation—the arming of helicopters.

Although General Carl I. Hutton is often called "the father of the armed helicopter," it is not known who actually first armed a helicopter. Interest in the idea began as early as 1940, with Sikorsky's development of the R-5. The French lay claim to use of armed helicopters in Algeria in the mid-1950s, but, due to the Korean conflict, experimentation and use of helicopters, armed and otherwise, had already taken place.[48]

The Korean War marked an acceleration in the growth of Army aviation. The field-expedient style demonstrated earlier was further manifested by the shooting of weapons by individuals on helicopters, by the airmobile landing of troops by the United States Marine Corps, and by the early use of helicopters in the evacuation of wounded troops.[49] It is in this last area, medical evacuation, that the Army made the greatest use of its aviation opportunity. Between 1951 and 1953 alone, more than 21,000 casualties were air-lifted by formal Army medical evacuation units, a figure which does not include thousands of other evacuations.[50]

In addition to medical evacuation, commanders learned the value of other functions suggested by activities of the helicopter. General Maxwell Taylor learned to appreciate the saving of an important battle flank through the use of helicopters for resupply. Lieutenant General Reuben Jenkins observed an important battle from a helicopter and recognized the potential for battlefield command and control from above. In addition, new aviation equipment was introduced during the war and was tested in action for efficacy.[51] The fixed-wing L-19 became the favorite aircraft for reconnaissance, while the H-19 helicopter, which served the Sixth Transportation Company, was part of the first unit of its kind to support American soldiers in combat.[52]

The cessation of the Korean War did not halt interest in the potential of Army aviation. In 1953, the 24th Infantry Division, stationed in Japan, began experiments with a grenade launcher mounted on an OH-13.[53] In the United States proper, the ballistics research laboratory of the Aberdeen Proving Grounds armed a YH-32A helicopter with launcher tubes for two-inch rockets.[54] These efforts, known as Project Sally Rand, appeared barren, for this particular helicopter was never adopted by the Army. Nevertheless, they form part of a pattern of experimentation which was eventually to come to fruition.

Army war games provided additional arenas for helicopter experimentation, Exercise Sagebrush, conducted in 1955, included sky cavalry experiments.[55] Equally as important as the exercise itself was the formal analysis made by official evaluators, for the non-aviators who authored the less-than-favorable report unknowingly set in motion unauthorized tests at Fort Rucker, Alabama. Two other Army exercises—Able Buster and Baker Buster, which were designed in part to test armed light aircraft in the anti-tank role—also were negatively estimated.[56] Still, these too contributed remnants to the stockpile of odds and ends later used in the decisive arming of helicopters.

Sky Cav, Fort Rucker. The experimentation that is generally credited with initiating the developments that would lead to the armed helicopter began in June 1956, when Brigadier General Carl I. Hutton, Commandant of the Army Aviation School at Fort Rucker, determined that, for the helicopter to be an effective means of transportation for the ground soldier, fire-suppression capability was required to inhibit hostile ground fire.[57] The transport helicopters had to be armed for use during air assaults.

Hutton, a rated aviator, asked Colonel J. D. Vanderpool, a non-aviator assigned to the Combat Developments Office at Fort Rucker, if he would devise and test weapons systems for use on Army helicopters.[58] Hutton was well aware that it was unlikely he would receive the approval of his superiors for his activities.[59] The unfavorable attitude of higher officers toward Army aviation was based on a combination of several factors. Many of these higher officers were simply skeptical about the effectiveness of a low-flying, slow-moving aircraft in armed combat. Others had their own pet projects and did not care to share their limited resources. Still others found Hutton recklessly outspoken in the manner of Billy Mitchell. Some saw other resemblances to Mitchell that made them feel as if Hutton were embarking on a self-serving crusade. Still others were reluctant to embark on any course that would tend to create a new Army Air Force that would seek autonomy at the price of another painful schism and thereby reflect on the unpleasant residues of the orginial break between the United States Army and the Air Force that were manifested daily in bitter rivalry. Others felt that roles and missions accords forbade such experimentation and, like all other directives from higher authority, were to be obeyed in letter and in spirit. Added to these reasons was the inevitable desire to avoid "making waves" that might bring on unanticipated consequences by upsetting existing conditions.

Such obstacles did not deter Hutton. Tests were to be conducted on a volunteer basis in the evenings and on weekends.[60] At first glance, it appeared that use of volunteer personnel not on duty would somehow be more acceptable since the Army would be spared providing men who had to be diverted from their assigned tasks. In fact, the development of an unauthorized project by use of a moonlighting military task force compounded the exceptional nature of the situation.

Whatever the case, Vanderpool, who was later to be Director of the Combat Development Office and a member of the 1970 Blue Ribbon Defense Panel studying defense policy and organization,[61] was enthusiastic about the possibilities suggested by Hutton. Activity got under way immediately.

Hutton himself received United States Continental Army Command (CONARC) Training Memorandum 13, dated June 4, 1956, which emphasized the need for new concepts in mobility. On June 27, 1956, more than three weeks later, Hutton, in a display of bureaucratic wisdom, wrote a letter to General W. G. Wyman, Commanding General, United States CONARC, explaining that his answer to the mobility question was to send ground soldiers aloft. He further suggested that industry develop a fighting aerial vehicle and that he (Hutton) be permitted to experiment with existing helicopters organized into tactical formations in accordance with Training Memorandum 13.[62] In a letter dated July 13, 1956, General Wyman approved the request and expressed his desire that a general plan be coordinated with the United States Army Infantry School at Fort Benning, Georgia, and then be submitted to him.[63]

Vanderpool and his volunteers (later to be known with proud irony as Vanderpool's Fools) did not wait idly for Wyman's response.[64] The weapons discarded from the Able Buster and Baker Buster exercises were sifted for parts, ammunition, and equipment that could serve to arm a helicopter. Various scrounging trips were made to Air Force depots, Navy supply dumps, and other such locations. At this time, Vanderpool initiated contacts with industrial arms manufacturers. Each of these activities highlights the lack of funds for the program.

Vanderpool toured the country asking air-frame manufacturers how much punishment the helicopter air frame could take.[65] Thus, he not only obtained an idea of helicopter toughness but also alerted industrial suppliers to potential future development. Vanderpool also visited ordnance plants looking for weapons systems, but these visits were unsuccessful.[66] Finally, at a General Electric branch office in Vermont, accompanied by Lieutenant Colonel F. C. Goodwin, he met Farell T. Mayhood, G. E.'s chief engineer at the branch. Armed with only a drawing on a paper napkin and no money, Vanderpool asked General Electric to build a rocket kit for a helicopter. Mayhood, in concurrence with his associate Jack Hardy, agreed to fabricate a kit and deliver it within three months.[67]

Also during this early period, close relationships were formed between the Army aviators at Fort Rucker and the personnel at various weapons-related military offices (in particular the Rock Island Arsenal, the Aberdeen Proving Grounds, the Springfield Arsenal, and the Ordnance Weapons Command [OWC] Headquarters). In April 1958, the OWC Headquarters outlined and recommended a series of potential projects that would assist Army aviation and sought appropriation of funds with which to finance the Army aviation weapons war.[68] The OWC was familiar with projects under way at Fort Rucker, inasmuch as it had maintained liaison officers there since the previous year.

The team at Fort Rucker was racing to create a *fait accompli* by showing that weapons could, in fact, be fired from a helicopter. Officers and enlisted men assumed unusual roles as they invented the first kit suitable for live-fire tests. Working as machinists, designers, and laborers, they created an armed helicopter with a .30-caliber machine gun secured to a roof platform.[69] Almost simultaneously, a homemade weapons kit consisting of two .50-caliber machine guns and four Oerlikon rockets was mounted on an H-13 helicopter.[70]

As would be expected, the early tests were conducted with a mixture of daring and caution, since no one knew what might happed when rockets and machine guns were fired from helicopters. First, Captain James Montgomery, the group's test pilot, fired machine guns from a helicopter on the ground; then the guns were fired from the craft at a hover and later still when the helicopter was in forward flight.[71] Since there were only minor ill effects—for example, structural cracks—from such firing, further tests of the rockets were undertaken.

Later, as different combinations of weapons were tried, various mechanical difficulties were encountered. At one point, the plastic bubble of the helicopter burst into fragments during a machine gun firing.[72] But Vanderpool purposely overtaxed the air frame to see what kind of punishment it could take.[73] The willingness to accept negative results and hence the appearance of failure is a particular asset to experimenters. It can be imagined how failure on a multimillion-dollar project could have damaging repercussions for the further development of a particular weapons system. Despite numerous mechanical failures and the ever-present possibility of personal injury, Vanderpool's men maintained their momentum.

Fabricating successful inventions for arming the helicopter was only a secondary objective of Vanderpool's work, however. The real objective was to study "armed airmobile tactical organizations or formations," and the outcome of this study was an invention as well—a doctrinal creation including old elements and new ideas in combination with old ideas and new elements.⁷⁴ The original organizational ideas were borrowed from the Duke of Wellington, whose cavalry fought from their horses, whose dragoons were horse-mounted infantry who dismounted to fight, and whose forces were supported by horsemobile artillery.⁷⁵ Tactical ideas were codified as a training test by combining lessons learned from Sky Cavalry operations with horse cavalry doctrine taken chapter by chapter from the last field manual written for horse cavalrymen in 1936.⁷⁶

Sky Cav, Fort Benning, and Other Developments. Invention efforts were not restricted to the confines of Fort Rucker. General Hutton, for instance, had prepared a helicopter armaments kit at the United States Army Ordnance Plant in Mainz, Germany, sometime after he joined the Seventh Army in Europe in 1959.⁷⁷ Private companies, such as Emerson Electronics, conducted experiments on their own.⁷⁸ One especially interesting parallel effort was conducted with the encouragement of General Herbert B. Powell, Commander of Fort Benning, home of the Army Infantry School.⁷⁹ General Powell was a graduate of a special course for high-ranking officers at the Army aviation school and had received his aviator's wings. To forward the state of the art in helicopterborne infantry warfare, Powell requested Major William A. Howell to undertake experiments in arming the helicopter. Howell, the executive officer of the Lawson Army Air Field Command adjacent to Fort Benning, appointed Chief Warrant Officer James P. Ervin, Jr., as project officer.⁸⁰ Fort Benning, like Fort Rucker, became the home of a Sky Cav experimental unit, and frequent trips were made between Benning and Rucker to share knowledge and swap equipment.

Much of the activity at Fort Benning paralleled that at Fort Rucker. Weekend and night operations became part of the Benning group's new way of life as it learned about gunsights, weapons, and electrosystems. Items were obtained in quantities that ranged in amount from one unconverted intervolometer (a device for timing the firing of rockets) to thousands of rounds of ammunition.⁸¹ Equipment was scrounged from Fort Rucker, the Birmingham Naval Air Station, an Alabama Air National Guard unit, Robbins Air Force Base, an Atlanta naval unit, the Pensacola Naval Air Station, and Tyndale Air Force Base, as well as from Fort Benning itself. Cooperation was not always forthcoming, however, even from Fort Benning: A Colonel Linton, the G-3 (operations and training officer) on General Powell's staff, was frequently notified of the unit's progress and problems.

Howell's men also contacted industrial representatives. It appears that some of the experiments were performed for the Hiller and Bell helicopter companies by the Sky Cav unit at Fort Benning. Especially close relations existed between the Sikorsky Company, represented by a Mr. Albert and a

Mr. Carney, both engineers, and by Harry Generous, who played a liaison role regarding the arming of the Sikorsky H-34 helicopter. Mr. Generous was in frequent contact by telephone with the Sky Cav unit, and the project officer, Ervin, and others visited Sikorsky on more than one occasion.

The Benning experiments eventually were terminated in early 1958—supposedly due to a lack of command support and sufficient weapons.[82] Such a view suggests that the work was incomplete, that further goals remained out of reach, and that the project's mission was unfulfilled. Considered from a different perspective, however, the functions and contributions of the Powell-Howell-Ervin efforts can be more clearly discerned. First, it is helpful to think of the Benning endeavors as a back-up system for the primary efforts at Fort Rucker, which, being the home of the Army Aviation Center, might have been subject to special scrutiny by the Air Force or the Secretary of Defense. Second, the experiments revealed new talents in aviation techniques among the men employed on the projects. Third, new patterns of friendly relations were established among various groups, especially between those in the helicopter industry and the concerned soldiers. Fourth, new techniques in procurement were developed. Fifth, the improvisations of Powell's group stood as evidence of the decentralized nature of Army aviation. Indeed, it was to be quite common for Army aviation supporters to undertake projects—much as General Powell had—that were designed to improve the use of helicopters in conjunction with their own special areas of expertise.

While the work of Sky Cav had vast significance for the development of Army aviation, it also had an impact on the promotion of a specific air cavalry concept. Army planners initiated the development of the Aerial Reconnaissance and Security Troop (ARST) in 1960.[83] The ARST was formed to further test the ideas of using armed helicopters for classic cavalry mission—reconnaissance, flank security, and shock. After much testing and training, it was determined that armed helicopters were capable of performing traditional cavalry missions, and in 1962 an air cavalry troop became a part of the divisional armored cavalry squadron. But the supporters of Army aviation were in no sense content to lower their sights by limiting themselves to one company-size unit for each division.

Growth and Accomplishments of Sky Cav. While the Sky Cav at Fort Benning was short-lived, a Sky Cavalry Platoon, Provisional—organized to make use of Vanderpool's inventions—was more accurately to mirror the mutable course of Army aviation. On July 11, 1957, this unit of eleven officers, sixteen enlisted men, and ten helicopters was placed under the operational control of the Director of Tactics, United States Army Aviation

School. In mid-1957, there were, then, two sky cavalry units, one at Fort Rucker and one at Fort Benning. Ostensibly to avoid the confusion that existed over the different types of sky cavalry, the Rucker unit was renamed the Air Combat Reconnaissace (ACR) Platoon, Provisional (Experimental), in November 1957, but the brief history to be presented now of the redesignation of this unit suggests that there may have been other reasons, either organizational or political, behind the repetitive name changes. Thus, on March 24, 1958, the unit was reoganized as the 7292nd Air Combat Reconnaissance Company (Experimental). It was designed for school and not tactical use, was placed under the Second Battle Group, 31st Infantry Regiment, and was made part of the school troops at Fort Rucker.

On March 25, 1959, the unit was redesignated the 8305th Aerial Combat Reconnaissance Company. On September 24, 1962, it became Troop D (Air), 17th Cavalry, after which it moved to Fort Benning, becoming part of the 3rd Squadron, 17th Cavalry Regiment, 11th Air Assault Division (T). Later, Troop D's designation was changed to A troop. (The 3rd/17th Cavalry was later to be renamed the 1st/9th Cavalry and sent to Vietnam in 1965.)[84]

The early Sky Cav formed a very close fellowship and called itself the "Royal Order of the Fighting Hoverbugs."[85] Its personnel had nicknames such as Chief Piddler, Chief Scrounger, Chief Operator, and Chief Inventor. Later, in Vietnam, where the 1st/9th was part of the 1st Cavalry Division (Airmobile), this unit became the "Cav of the Cav," the "First of the First Team," the elite fighting arm of the elite division. It was still a closely knit unit and nicknames reflecting the unit's role remained important, the unit's essential role being to score the highest body count.

The early work involved in producing the armed helicopters at Fort Rucker signified consequences for later developments. Experimentation with the 2.75 folding-fin aerial rocket (FFAR) allowed later developers to determine that it was the best available rocketry for helicopter armament.[86] Likewise, the mounting arms for the rocket pods later used on the UH-1 were originally developed by the ACR Company.[87] Even the XM-2 helicopter armament kit, which underwent development tests at Springfield Armory in 1962, had been effectively experimented with at Fort Rucker.[88]

In a related development, some of the earliest small research and development contracts were provided to companies interested in Army aviation. It has been suggested that one intent of such programs was to keep together teams of competent technicians who would then be available during the expansion of Army aviation.[89] Vertol, which armed the H-25 helicopters with rockets from the Rocketdyne Division of North American Aviation; Bell Helicopter Company, which installed the SS-10 wire-guided missiles on the OH-13, thus giving the helicopter anti-armor capability, and which later began to develop the Huey Cobra on its own initiative; Lycoming, which provided the turbine-powered equipment that became the mainstay of a new generation of Army helicopters; as well as General Electric, Sikorsky, and others previously discussed, are examples of companies that provided great support for Army aviation.[90]

A particiularly interesting case of development and acquisition that required technology produced by a sophisticated team was the UH-1 (Huey).[91] Orginially, the Huey was designed as a battlefield ambulance. It has been described as being designed so that litters could be inserted crosswise. Since it was understood that some medical evacuation was an Army responsibility, funds were available for the development of such a helicopter. No longer did the Army have to shop exclusively for "off the shelf" or cast-off equipment.

Research in power plants had been progressing throughout the 1950s.[92] Shortly after a small turbine engine was created that would increase the capacity of the UH-1 helicopter (originally the XH-40), further developments were made on this new craft. In particular, an aircraft designed solely for medical evacuation would not need hardpoints (used in mounting weapons). While the first model of the Huey had no hardpoints, they were included in the specifications for subsequent models. Once something remotely suitable for their purposes was obtained, the men of Army Aviation were on their way to building a force appropriate for their needs.

Further testing of the Huey took place in various areas, including the Republic of Vietnam, as the Medical Corps made do initially with H-19's.[93] The first unit in Vietnam to be equipped with helicopters was the Utility Tactical Transport (UTT) Helicopter Company (in October 1962).[94] This unit was given the mission of providing armed escort for troop-carrying helicopters. Additional efforts to invent more effective armament systems were undertaken in Okinawa and in Vietnam itself.[95] In Okinawa, Chief Warrant Officer Clarence J. Carter was summoned by Major General Norman A. Costello, G-3 of the United States Army, Pacific, to arm some helicopters for a demonstration of armed helicopter capability in an attempt to increase support for the use of armed helicopters. Throughout 1963, as new weapons concepts were created and tested, the entire UTT Company came to be viewed by the Army as a testing ground for determining the feasibility of armed helicopters. Building a bridge between invention and innovation by its performance, it became one comprehensive experimental demonstration.

Innovation and Invention

At this point, it is appropriate to distinguish between the concepts of invention and innovation. Invention is the outcome of a fabrication of the imagination. That is, when one invents something, one makes, through the use of one's mind, many parts into a whole. Innovation implies implementation of conceptions. These conceptions need not be technical inventions. The politics of invention can therefore be distinguished from the politics of putting plans into practical use—the politics of innovation.

The politics of invention deal with those aspects of social life that are concerned with how individuals are constrained to fabricate new technical configurations. For the purposes of this study, I have stressed the inventions associated with creating an airmobile Army, especially the arming of helicopters. These inventions ranged from the most simple, unobtrusive, and inexpensive constructions (for example, the welding of a machine gun on a helicopter) to the most intricate, ostentatious, and costly weapons systems (for example, the Cheyenne).

The politics of innovation involve the promotion, dissemination, and putting into operation of notions which may or may not be based upon technical invention. As such, innovation ranges from the effort to convince the public and Congress of the efficacy of Sky Cavalry by means of articles in the public press, through politically oriented war-gaming, to the attack by armed transport helicopters on suspected Viet Cong in the Republic of Vietnam in the early 1960s (illustrated in the discussion above concerning the UTT Company). The aspects of innovation to be dealt with here are the visible manifestations of the politics of innovation. The more covert aspects, which are part of the realm of insurgent bureaucratic politics, will be discussed in Chapter 5.

The major methods of overt diffusion of innovation are publication, public speaking, and exhibitions. Some publications are particularly aimed at disseminating information among sympathizers. The *Army Aviation Digest* fills this role and will be discussed in Chapter 5. Publication itself can be divided into three categories. First, there are popular or scholarly articles authored by Army aviation proponents such as Generals Gavin and Howze.[96] In addition, public relations efforts induce journalistic coverage of favorable events. These two kinds of articles are designed to build support while disseminating new ideas. A third type of publication is advertisement. The Association of the United States Army, a backstop organization, advertised the need for an airmobile army and the desirability that "the Army be immediately free of the existing limitations on Army aircraft."[97]

Speechmaking offers another opportunity for advocates of a particular program to make their point before what is often a rather homogeneous audience. Supporters of Army aviation, in particular, have often taken advantage of such opportunities.[98]

Demonstrations are the most elaborate manifestations of efforts to promote innovation by public or semipublic display. These demonstrations can vary from the famous *Ostfriesland* sinking, which was referred to in chapter

2, to the lavish fire-power display known as the "Mad Minute," during which an audience is subjected to the stunning spectacle of the mass firing of weapons that represent a full complement of infantry support ordnance. Supporters of Army aviation likewise attempted to use favorable combat simulation to impress selected groups and individuals and hence to enhance their cause.

Early in 1957, the Fort Rucker Sky Cav went on the road to present demonstrations at Fort Knox, Kentucky, and Fort Benning, Georgia. At Fort Knox the target group was the United States Armor Association, a potentially favorable backstop organization,[99] while at Fort Benning those to be impressed were members of an industrial symposium and a delegation of congressmen.[100] In the latter case, the "scope of the show was somewhat limited by representatives from CONARC."[101]

An army aviation-industry symposium sponsored by the Association of the United States Army was held at Fort Rucker on June 6, 1957. The demonstration was witnessed by Generals Taylor and Wyman and other interested military and industrial leaders. Because the transportation function was being emphasized, however, the full implications of the armed helicopter were not revealed at this point.[102] In 1957, additional demonstrations were held at the Redstone Arsenal, Huntsville, Alabama; at Fort Bragg, North Carolina; and at Fort Benning.

In July 1957, there was a change of command at the Army Aviation School. It was at this time, and before an audience whose composition revealed much concerning the tactics of Army aviation enthusiasts, that the decision was made to reveal to the public the capabilities of Sky Cavalry. General Bogardus S. Cairnes, the new Commandant, took the wraps off the helicopter's capacity for fire power before approximately 500 cadets from the United States Military Academy at West Point.[103] Cairnes told the cadets that he wanted to see them as pilots as his aviators presented what was described as a "deadly jack-in-the-box performance."[104] The helicopters were portrayed as "leaping up into sight, firing a burst and then dropping down behind hills or trees, taking cover, and moving on to new positions."[105]

The decision to go public combined press exposure with political recruitment and socialization, but it was not sufficiently all-out to directly challenge the Air Force. Intriguingly, while the implications of such tests suggested violations of the various roles and missions agreements, apparently the attention of the Air Force in general and of certain top Army officials specifically was sufficiently engaged elsewhere to prevent bringing the development of Army aviation to a halt.

The Army aviation supporters then became even bolder. In July 1958, 400 of the nation's top military and industrial leaders, including many high-

81 / Helicopter Technology

ranking Army and Air Force officers and Secretary of the Army Wilbur Brucker, saw Army aviation in action as three H-37 Sikorsky helicopter deposited tons of equipment and crews that prepared and launched on "Honest John" surface-to-surface missile in an exercise termed "Operation Ammo.[106] Before this group, they took a calculated risk by interrupting a missile-oriented exercise to show the potential of the armed helicopter in order to engage command interest.[107]

Other demonstrations were held during this period at Fort Rucker for such VIP's as Lieutenant General Gavin, the G-3 of the Army; General Edward Snedeker, Commanding General of the Marine Corps School of Quantico, Virginia; and Secretary Brucker.[108] Such displays also received appropriate media coverage.

Having discussed the overt efforts to innovate within the Army in helicopter technology, we now need to explore those aspects of the growth of Army aviation which were less open to public scrutiny. It is only by observing both the overt and covert dimensions of innovation that we can begin to piece together a fuller picture of how the Army got an air force.

An effort will be made to pinpoint those persons who might participate in a bureaucratic social movement. The tactics appropriate for members of the social movement and the function of mission will be discussed. The behavior of officers engaged in insurgent bureaucratic politics will be analyzed, and highlights of the Army aviation social movement will be presented.

Chapter 5 | **THE DYNAMICS OF INSURGENCY**

One of the major difficulties in dealing with organizational innovation is the almost irresistible temptation to direct one's thoughts toward readily identifiable organization. But the device of focusing on easily measured individual behavior does not necessarily open up all remaining intraorganizational phenomena to the curious student. What may be required is an understanding of organizational behavior which is neither organizational nor behavioral, according to some traditional uses of these terms.

It would be impossible to understand the development of Army aviation by centering one's attention on the Army aviation branch, since no such branch existed. Accumulating data and revealing percentage figures concerning attitudes of aviators as opposed to, say, non-aviators also would not lead to a deep understanding of the acquisition of more than 12,000 aircraft for the United States Army. It is hoped that an alternative method, a case-study approach that imperfectly blends analysis with empirics, will prove satisfactory in revealing the development of Army aviation.[1]

Let us begin with a limited endeavor to place the innovation of Army aviation in its appropriate context. What follows is merely a conjectural conceptual framework and is therefore open to improvement. Parenthetically, it should be noted that the mutal exclusiveness suggested by the quadrants of the tables used to exemplify aspects of this conceptual framework should not mask the actual overlapping of behavioral patterns which exists in real life.

Governments may be perceived by their employees to be essentially legitimate or nonlegitimate. Those who perceive the government to be legitimate and who agree with its policies are likely to support the government and its

Table 1. Perception of Organizational Legitimacy and Attitudes toward Organizational Goals

Perception of Organizational Legitimacy	Attitudes toward Organizational Goals	
	Agreement	Disagreement
Legitimate	Supporters	Insurgents
Nonlegitimate or irrelevant	Acquiescers	Outlaws

activities and are therefore known as *supporters* (Table 1). Those persons in government service who perceive the government as essentially nonlegitimate, but agree with or accept its policies, may be thought of as *acquiescers* (Table 1).[2] Those who accept the government as legitimate, but who strongly disagree with important policies, can be thought of as *insurgents* (Table 1)—that is, those "who rise in revolt not so much in an attempt to destroy the organization or institution or its laws or conventions as in the hope of effecting changes or reforms believed to be necessary."[3] Such people are, by their very nature, involved with innovation in opposition to the status quo. Those who find the government nonlegitimate or, again, who are not concerned with the legitimacy of the government and also do not accept the policies of the government can be called *outlaws*. In this essay, the insurgents are the crucial actors.

In turn, the insurgents may be further categorized. Those who oppose governmental policy because it will cause them important personal harm and who are inclined to take action suffer a variety of cognitive dissonances. Eventually, they must try to save themselves from harm by becoming active against the government or the policies, or by leaving. For such people, *self-defenders* (Table 2), it is likely that the government will eventually be perceived as nonlegitimate, and they will become *outlaws* or so threatening that they will become expatriate. Those who feel that the government is legitimate and who cannot act against it to prevent personal harm become *submissives*. For some who feel that government is legitimate, but who perceive institutional harm from governmental policies, it appears necessary to remain on the scene to do battle. Those who remain behind, the *persisters*, may stay on the scene for a variety of reasons, including the possibility of personal gain, difficulty of exit, or because of the authority of higher values. The obligations imposed by the need to accomplish a mission constitute a particularly important pressure for standing one's ground in the name of higher values.

There are also those for whom the mistaken policies of government constitute a basic challenge to higher values. For such people who are not fighters, the higher values are often a fundamental part of the institution to which they belong. As in the case of those who do not choose to fight when personal well-being is the chief issue, when institutional problems arise, such men also suffer cognitive dissonance. Such people become *acquiescers, sub-*

Table 2. Categorization of Insurgents

Reaction	Perception of Goal Disagreement	
	Personal harm	Institutional harm
Action	Self-defenders (unstable)	Persisters
Nonaction	Submissives	Abandoners

missives (if the cognitive dissonance becomes such that it constitutes personal harm), or, most likely, they quit the scene and become *abandoners*, possibly avoiding personal harm, but probably harming the institution (Table 2).

One of our central concerns, the capacity for persistence, is variable, as is the type of action to be taken. Among the insurgent persisters, one can find individuals who select a course of overt defiance over a relatively short period of time. A classic example of such conduct is General Billy Mitchell, whose defiance and fate were discussed in Chapter 2 (see Table 3). Some who adopt the public-oriented strategy are enabled, by dint of personality or circumstance, to remain in their official capacities. An example of this type is Admiral Hyman Rickover, whose insistence on an atomic-powered American submarine fleet brought him several times to the verge of separation from his service by disgruntled superiors.[4]

Other persisters feeling dissatisfaction over a particular policy might take the short-run route of forming something resembling a *cabal* (Table 3). Such a cabal seeks through action to "restructure situations and values in the interests of its members."[5] Since cabals are largely hidden from view, it may be assumed that many have existed which have avoided our notice. Nevertheless, it might be suggested that those persons who assisted General John D. Lavelle in the unauthorized bombing of North Vietnam constituted a group that might be categorized under the rubric cabal, wherein status distinctions exist and leadership is important.

While each of these ideal types constitutes a significant, if episodic, example of insurgent bureaucratic politics, it is the next category, that of bureaucratic *social movement*, upon which we will focus, for here the elements of innovation, persistence, resistance, and association come together in a manner that sheds great light on the acquisition of thousands of aircraft for the United States Army. At this point it is appropriate to discuss ideas about social movements in general to indicate something of the genesis of the notion of a specifically bureaucratic social movement. This brief presentation will alert the reader to aspects of the struggle for Army aviation.

Social Movements and Army Aviation

Mayer Zald and Roberta Ash describe a social movement as "the purposive and collective attempt of a number of people to change individuals or societal

Table 3. Categorization of Insurgent Persisters

Duration	Number of Actors	
	Single	Multiple
Short	"Mitchell-type"	Cabal
Long	"Rickover-type"	Social movement

structures."[6] They call attention to the fact that a successful social movement has no further reason for existing and that the goals of the movement can incur hostility or repressive action. They further point out that such movements are characterized by incentive structures in which purposive incentives predominate, solidary incentives are secondary, and material incentives are significant primarily in the short run. The mixture of these motives naturally varies.[7]

The long-term characteristics of social movements are stressed by Preston Valian, who writes: "The term *social movement* denotes a concerted and continued effort by a social group aimed at reaching a goal (or goals) common to its members."[8] Rudolph Heberle has reminded us that all movements have political implications, even if the members do not strive for political power.[9] He also stresses the importance of ideology, especially the element of volition, when he observes that "the belief in a set of constitutive ideas binds the members of a movement together and gives them the *élan* needed for the persistent pursuit of the movement's aim."[10]

Heberle has also attempted to distinguish sociopsychological types of movements according to the prevailing motivation of their members: "(1) the value-rational, 'spiritual community' or 'fellowship of believers in the truth of the constitutive ideas and in the practical aims of the movement'; (2) the emotional-affectual following of a charismatic leader; and (3) the purposive-rational or utilitarian association for the pursuit of individual interest."[11] While Heberle indicates that combinations of these types are frequent, it is worth comparing the value-rational spiritual community (type 1) with David Willer's value-rational authority, which was discussed in Chapter 1.

Thus we arrive at the following ideas about social movements: They are characterized by a particular outlook. They stress purposiveness and solidarity. And they are characterized by efforts and attempts—that is, by a disposition to activity. Further, each of these aspects has a political dimension. Extrapolating from what is understood about social movements in general, we can begin to conceive of such a movement contained within a bureaucracy— a bureaucratic social movement. While it is possible to imagine something resembling a bureaucratic grouping aimed at inhibiting innovation, according to the preceding train of logic some different designation is required here, for *innovation* was the goal of the bureaucratic social movement assigned the task of securing combat ascendency via effective airmobile techniques (CAVEAT).[12]

Perseverance was surely the hallmark of CAVEAT. As noted in Chapter 2, the idea of ground-controlled air power is at least as old as World War I. More significantly, the realization that, in the face of autonomy for the Air Force, the Army Ground Forces would require organic aviation to enable them to perform their mission was acted upon in the early 1940s by some of those who were to be come the pioneers and, in a few cases, the victors in the battle for Army aviation. We have observed how many of the efforts to improve Army aviation were rebuffed and how these setbacks were met with new efforts at later times.

There was so much of this kind of activity that a pattern of dogged efforts at innovation can be discerned. The pattern includes many random instances as well as some deviations, but it might generally be characterized as one of apparent obedience accompanied by less-than-compliant behavior in a relatively narrow realm. Most of the soldiers involved in CAVEAT did not become manifestly disobedient in most of their activities. For by far the largest amount of time, these men were soldierly in their conduct, and thus relatively indistinguishable from their peers. Callous flippancy and outright rebellion were foreign to their nature.

Some of the proponents of Army aviation became very frustrated by the difficulties they encountered. Of these, a number overstepped their authority, a risky situation, for a forward individual could be considered a *personna non grata*.[13] In general, however, the important figures in CAVEAT used what has been described as "the leaning approach."[14] In this football analogy, the ball carrier runs laterally behind his offensive line and tries to "lean" into holes in the defense to make some kind of gain. When the holes appear blocked, the leaning back does not try to plunge through his defensive opponent; rather, he backs off, continues running down the line looking for other possible holes. If he finds all of them closed, he runs around the end. If that fails, he waits for the next play.

Similarly, the strategy of the insurgents was largely one of doing whatever one could, but as soon as it became apparent that one would be rebuffed (especially if there was little that might be done), the individual should not get upset. Rather, he should "back off, and just keep on doing your chores," thereby remaining invisible so that he could make the best of later opportunities.[15] If enough people did this for a long enough time, it was thought that they were bound to be successful in achieving their goal for the Army. Another officer put it somewhat differently when he indicated that one must stay within the system to subvert it. "We subverted the organization, we freed the thinking of others from within, not from without."[16] Continuing, he expressed his affection for perseverance: "I like persistence. A million drops of water on your head will hurt you worse mentally and physically than a ball peen hammer. If you are aggressive and lack tact you will lose. The kindest comment I have received is 'Man, you have been selling this so long,' because that means he realized your persistence."[17] This officer went on to say that if you convince a disbeliever over time, he will note your idea and soon begin to think that it is his idea. Then the subordinate can say, "Hell, he's working for me," and can "put his feet up on the desk."[18] Persistence, in the case of the members of CAVEAT, was not merely hard-headed obstinance that developing technology should be utilized. Their sense of the Army's mission was distinct from that of their fellows and was the driving force behind much of their effort.

Mission: Who Decides?

If *mission* means "the task together with the purpose," it does not follow that there will be general agreement on all subtasks and subpurposes among those who feel they intuitively or empirically know what the mission is. Each area or organization seems to have its own "mission" while sharing in the overall tasks and purposes of the others. Thus, an exchange of views with different officers concerning the mission of the Army might yield varying results. As in the party game where an originator whispers a few sentences to a player who in turn passes it along to the next speaker and so forth until the statements return to the originator, often in distorted form, some of what has happened reflects simple misunderstanding on the part of some listeners, but much of the confusion can be accounted for by the gamesters' (usually unwitting) interpretations of the statements made.

Likewise, disparate perceptions exist within the Army due to the divergent perspectives of those who are charged with the interpretation and development of appropriate strategy for reaching the goals the mission specifies. A simple statement of the Army's mission is that it is "responsible for the preparation of land forces necessary for the effective prosecution of war."[19] Follow this process one step further, however, and you will observe the instant fragmentation of certainty that plagues those who seek comprehensive, rational, organizational purpose. For instance, what does this statement mean? Is the Army to fight on land? Against other land forces? To control the land? And by what means is it to arrive at its goal? By what means is it anticipated that it will be able to accomplish its goal when such diverse tasks as movement of forces, discharging firearms, and communication are involved? (This may be recognized as the soldier's classic guide: move, shoot, and communiate.) In the case of moving forces, for example, is it anticipated that mobility will be achieved by means of foot, horse, truck tank, helicopter, fixed-wing cargo airplane, or deposit by parachute? How are these decisions reached? Are they based upon strategic considerations, tactical requirements, technical imperatives, economic allocations, political bargains, doctrinal specifications, or on the basis of some sort of value notions about correctness or appropriateness? The answer is probably some combination of most of the above over time and in various situations, but each factor does not weigh the same each time or among every group.

Mission and Missionaries

The notion of mission is also helpful because it suggests attitudes and behavior associated with missionaries. Such attitudes and behavior on the part of those who were trying to establish Army aviation did in many ways resemble those of people in missionary service. And this was not merely a chance happening, for in trying to produce actions that confirmed the validity of a general conception of the basic correctness of Army control over its own support aviation, those involved were often required to proselytize much in the manner of missionaries, both among the heathen, and, more importantly, among the lapsed or deviant believers.

Many of these soldiers were conscious of their missionary role. A graduate of one of the first Army aviation classes referred to his early colleagues as "poor missionaries who had done the early work to pioneer."[20] The early aviators also had the "Cub spirit," which, it was claimed, kept them going in the face of adversity.[21]

Missionary interest depends largely on conviction. The soldier inspired by mission is not merely waiting, like a public relations man, for any client, but rather requires that certain conditions be operative before he goes into action. Such an officer will engage in certain kinds of behavior for mission-related aspects of his job that he might deem inappropriate for other aspects. He is restrained from some activities because they tend to conflict with his mission.

Additionally, missionaries do not require a geographical center. Thus, when they are thwarted in one place, there is no requirement that the mission fold up and die. The dispersion produced by the absence of a geographical center not only serves to protect the movement as a whole from attacks on its parts but also allows for flexibility in organization and approach at the several points.[22] On the other hand, dispersion may create communication difficulties which not only hamper the enemies of the movement but affect the movement as well. This dispersion thus requires a heavy dose of the conviction referred to above. Further, centrifugal forces at work upon the various diverse individuals and groups may be somewhat contained by the sharing of mission as a unifying factor.

Many missionaries have sought to establish a sense of unity through symbolic devices such as adopting the clothing and language of the people they seek to reach. When James Hudson Taylor went to China, he chose the identification devices of learning the Chinese language and accepting Chinese dress.[23] One might compare this to the great pressure to get Army aviator wings accepted as part of the uniform and to the development of Army aviation jargon, both of which could promote a sense of comfort and solidarity. Further, such symbolic devices allow potential brothers-in-mission to identify each other in strange terrain. Even for those who do not wear the wings, the "thumbs-up" gesture or casual references to "slicks," "hooks," "autorotation," or any other such terms could signify the presence of a potential friend or ally.[24]

People who have a sense of mission appear to have a certain self-respect of many of those about them through their perserverance and commitment. The inner self-respect can, of course, be carried to the extreme of egotism or even egomania, and the respect of outsiders can be turned into fear and loathing through fanatical zealotry. But as Elton Trueblood says, "Mission has about it an innate nobility because it provides the only known pattern in which the inner life of devotion can be combined with social action."[25] Thus, mission depends upon both belief and action. The absence of either strand fundamentally impairs the viability of mission.

Roles and Missions in a Bureaucratic Setting

Because mission is so dynamic, even the "good faith" efforts to assign roles and missions arbitrarily are unlikely to be successful. Roles and missions assignments by high military and civilian officials are based on their view of service activities as items that are to be distributed as the result of some rational plan based on an elevated perspective or some bargained compromise. But while roles and missions simply denote the visible service activities to the top leadership, to the subordinate men of mission such allocations mean much more.

Robert Linton's definition of "role" as "the dynamic aspect of status"[26] helps us to understand what role meant to the supporters of Army aviation. The constituents of status are rights and duties, and such rights and duties, for these men, were based largely on their view of the Army's mission.

This difference in interpretation is even more profound when the term "mission" is considered, for mission, which encompasses the highest values of the soldier, can hardly be arbitrarily assigned without consequences, and these consequences, in terms of noncompliance, were constantly reaffirmed. As one officer said:

> Army aviation's history is benchmarked by skirting the regulations, or avoiding them, or getting them changed. The Air Force has a history of trying to delineate and build a fence around Army aviation beyond which it cannot step. And this was first done with the first memorandum of understanding which laid down specific weight limitations of Army aircraft. . . . In those memoranda of understanding it was important to realize that Army aviation was in a box both in where it could operate, the kind of missions it could fly, and weights—specific weights it could build things to—which inhibited . . . its development of aviation and inhibited the manufacturers to give any interest to this, what I would call bastard child, in our need, because they could see no real future in this. Only the light plane manufacturers were interested in trying to do anything for Army aviation.
>
> On the other side of this fence that had been built, this arbitrary fence which was supposed to delineate, the Army found itself with a wide gap in which the Air Force was doing nothing. . . . So, we felt that it was arbitrary and inhibiting, and we fought very strongly to get around it. And those two exceptions by the Secretary of Defense at that time—[Charles] Wilson— were immediately made because we had been pushing very hard for both the Caribou program which grossed out, I've forgotten now, somewhere close to 20,000 pounds, and the Mohawk, which grossed out around 7,000 pounds.[27]

Some examples of evading the strictures of roles and missions decisions were presented in Chapter 4, especially in regard to helicopter armament experimentation. The men of CAVEAT also sought loopholes in various restrictions. Flexible interpretations of certain phrases or the omission of specific wording became cues for action. When Secretary Wilson said exceptions might be granted to his statement on roles and missions, he opened a route for Pentagon-based insurgents. Two important exceptions to the 1956 Wilson Memorandum were achieved through pressure and persuasion on the part of the soldiers. Secretary Wilson allowed the Army to "buy" the fixed-wing, twin-engine Mohawk, which was supposed to be used as a reconnaissance aircraft. In this case, Army aviation leaders could point to the great interest of the Marines in the aircraft. This interest, manifested by the Marine money invested in it, proved compelling, and Wilson approved the exception. Shortly thereafter, the Marines withdraw their interest, but the Army was by then well involved with the Grumman aircraft. Serendipitously, Grumman had developed a number of schemes to put the necessary weapons stations on the wings of the Mohawk and to stretch its wings to enhance its weapons capability. This capability was later to be exploited in Army testing.[28]

The other major exception was the Caribou fixed-wing cargo transport, which also was sold to the Secretary on the grounds of economy. In this case, the Canadian armed forces had expended a large amount of money in development, and the economy argument proved irresistible.[29] It seems that each additional restriction on CAVEAT promoted the very outcomes that such inhibitions were designed to prevent.

When people are dealing with an ongoing technology and are motivated by mission in the face of stiff opposition from above, it can rationalized that they "kind of sneaked it" in order to have successful innovation.[30] Had the higher leadership endeavored realistically to control the efforts of CAVEAT, they could perhaps have developed a strategy of subordination through co-optation—that is, keeping the lower elite under restraint while more actively supporting and therefore observing their efforts. Efforts to choke off innovation led to secret experimentation and other deviance. One individual went too far when he stated that "innovation by its very nature is disobedience," but certainly innovation is subversive of the status quo.[31]

Bureaucrats engaged in trying to alter the staus quo can be involved in different kinds of behavior. One type not associated with innovation is bureaucratic sabotage. Arnold Brecht has described a progression of bureaucratic sabotage culminating in large-scale noncompliance among the lower-level groups (representing a lower socioeconomic class) within a bureaucracy.[32] Yet a more appropriate depiction of noncompliant bureaucratic behavior is that provided by Daniel Moynihan in his description of bureaucratic "guerillas":

For a period, the committee [President's Committee on Juvenile Delinquency and Youth Crime], or rather its irrepressible staff, was a force of great influence within the government, waging war on the bureaucracy, attracting ideas and men from the outside and colonizing them within the government. They sometimes referred to themselves as the "guerillas"....

The *élan* and patronage of the President's Committee on Juvenile Delinquency and Youth Crime ought not to lead to the assumption that the program was necessarily successful. Indeed, on balance it would appear it was not. The match was unequal. The concept of the "guerillas"—living off the administrative countryside, invisible to the bureaucratic enemy but known to one another, hitting and running and making off with the riches of the established departments—was attractive, but also romantic. Simply as a matter of firepower, God was on the side of the big battalions. The smaller ones, such as the Children's Bureau could bide their time. (Within three or four years of the height of their activities, it would appear that not a single member of the guerillas was still in government. Certainly, the group had ceased to operate by 1965.) But just as important, it might well be judged that the group had only a weak understanding of the problems with which it sought to deal. At once condescending and naive, it was ahead of its time perhaps, but not nearly abreast of its subject.[33]

92 / The Army Gets an Air Force

The military metaphor is adapted by a military man himself when offering an explanation of why a particular kind of courage is needed in the strife of mission-related bureaucratic politics:

There are some people who fit into the combat environment and feel comfortable in it. And there are people who fit in the bureaucracy environment of Washington and are naturals for it and feel comfortable in it, and they are not necessarily interchangeable. So it's a different kind of a battle and it's just as nasty. And a career is just as likely to be at stake. But there are those people who despise the Washington bureaucracy environment and do anything in the world to avoid assignment there, consider it a real hardship tour. There are others who are naturals in this, and thrive on this sort of thing. There are certain unwritten rules of the game, what you can do and what you cannot do in Washington; and the people who have been burned on these things feel very bitter about it, but this is nevertheless a fact of life. And it's not necessarily just the military, it's all of it.[34]

That some people see bureaucracy as a nightmare of red tape has led Victor A. Thompson to describe those with the most extreme attitudes of this type as "bureautics."[35] Such people believe bureaucracy to be intolerable and find every organizational situation they encounter frustrating. It is quite unlikely that innovation can be spearheaded within a bureaucracy by those who find its procedures and requirements onerous.

There is, on the other hand, a great likelihood that those persons who provide much of the leadership for a bureaucratic social movement will be able to make the most of a hierarchical administrative setting. Persons arrayed throughout the bureaucracy do have opportunities to promote themselves and their cause. Even those in relatively low-level positions can exercise power. David Mechanic has explored various factors that account for the power of secretaries, prison inmates, hospital attendants, and other "lower participants."[36] It is his view that power results from access to and control over persons, information, and instrumentalities. Variables affecting power include normative definitions, perception of legitimacy, exchange, and coalitions. Personal attributes associated with power include commitment, effort, interest, willingness to use power, skills, and attractiveness. He also discusses various attributes of social structure, including time spent in the organization, centrality of position, duality of power structures, and replaceability of persons. The importance of Mechanic's analysis for this study is that, while it has become commonplace in organizational theory to show that bureaucracies can be impeded by the action of subordinates, his study makes it clear that even the lowest-ranking participants are capable of exercising power affirmatively and suggests ways in which this can be accomplished.

In the present study, we are not dealing with the very lowest level of participants; rather, we are concerned with men who tended to range in rank from lieutenant to lieutenant general. Further, the grades of these men changed by means of promotion, and personal career advancement became a factor affecting their social movement. Opportunities are associated with the positions of these "higher" participants who form the "lower" elites in the organizational structure. For these "middle-men," some of the opportunities resemble those of the lower participants and others are similar to those of the elites. The place of colonels, for example, in various political movements is well established. Not only do they have opportunities similar to those above and below them, but additional advantages are provided by their strategic position amidst the flow of information and power.[37]

In our attempt to come to grips with the bureaucratic social movement, we will focus on middle-ranking officers. While enlisted and warrant officer pilots and combat troops were relevant to the drive for Army aviation, as were high-ranking military and civilian defense elites, they were auxiliary to the core of the social movement. In an effort to examine the significance of persistence for a bureaucratic social movement, I have divided the time to be discussed into five-year periods and will attempt to capture the dynamics associated with each period. It is important to remember that the concept of social movement is, by its very definition, concerned with "movement" or change. Thus, each static snapshot that follows is an artificial attempt to stop the action so as to provide a tangible picture for analysis.

PERIOD I: WORLD WAR II, 1941-1945

As we saw in Chapter 2, the provision of autonomy for the Army Air Forces crystallized the concern of those who felt that ground support was the crucial job of Army aviation. It is not surprising that Army aviation was formally created in 1942 after informal tests and promotion by those men who especially perceived the value of light aviation. These aviators found themselves in a battle for their very existence as liaison pilots under the control of ground artillery commanders. Other branches wanted the officers for their services as ground leaders, and the Army Air Forces followed an alternating strategy of trying to absorb Army aviation and trying to resist its expansion.[38]

Army aviation had important supporters in high places, but many important considerations occupied these officers' time.[39] Most close air support was provided by the Army Air Forces, but it was often found wanting. There were airmen who were concerned about the support of ground troops, but the central supporters during this period were the Cub pilots overseas and in the United States, especially at the home of the Field Artillery, Fort Sill, Oklahoma. This is a worthwhile reminder that a social movement does not require a geographic center to be successful.

94 / The Army Gets an Air Force

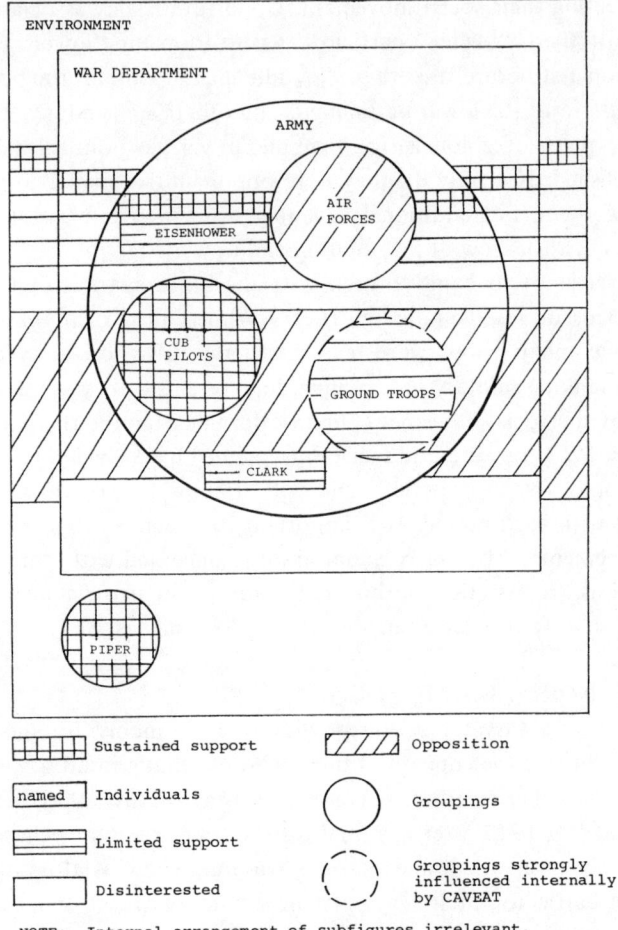

Figure 1. Selected Postures Regarding Army Control of Army Air Support: World War II, 1941-1945

NOTE: Internal arrangement of subfigures irrelevant.

It was the Cub pilots, with their "Cub spirit," who pushed their own views in order to keep alive Army aviation controlled by ground commanders at a relatively low level in the hierarchy of command. Some soldiers, having experienced shelling by their own artillery, associated such mishaps with faulty spotting and thus did not like Army aviation, but these men, plus those who associated Army aviation with the "pampered" Army Air Forces, formed a minority. In general, the Cubs, whose pilots lived near the front with the troops, were well-appreciated or tolerated, while the Air Forces' pilots were envied and resented.[40]

The Army Air Forces, whose primary mission was long-range bombing, were often condemned for failing to provide support. Among those whose distaste for the Air Forces' support was to have a lasting effect were those paratroopers of the XVIII Airborne Corps who were misdropped by the Air Forces' pilots, especially at Normandy.

The utility of the Cub pilots for branches of the Army other than the artillery was formally accepted in August 1945, when the War Department agreed to allow organic aviation for armor, cavalry, engineers, infantry, and tank destroyers.[41] Such a move, which could have broadened the base of the social movement, was rendered relatively insignificant, however, by the demobilization that followed World War II. Thus, the period terminated with the social movement centered on the successful Cub pilots (Figure 1).

PERIOD II: FRAGMENTATION AND REORGANIZATION, 1946-1950

The reduction in forces following World War II threw the Army into disarray (as indicated in Chapter 3).[42] During this period, the Army faced the challenge of adapting to the impact of the air-delivered atomic bomb, the unification movement, and the fluctuating international scene. The position of Army aviation looked particularly tenuous because it was not known whether all of Army aviation would become a part of the new United States Air Force. At this time, pilots were faced with the choice of pursuing their careers in the Air Force or in the Army. Those who selected the Army were often warned they would never rise above the rank of captain or major. Three main obstacles faced them. First, being specialists in aviation, they would not have time to serve in the ground slots in their branch that could lead to their promotion. Second, Army leaders would be fearful of creating an aviation element large enough to open a second Army-Air Force schism. Third, the resentment that remained within the Army toward the Air Force could carry over into relationships with Army aviation.

Many of the pilots were reservists and chose to leave military service at this time because of declining opportunities and professional uncertainties (or the desire to be civilians again). But those who comprised the Army aviation movement continued to pursue their objectives. In fact, it might be argued that those who remained in the service during this time of adversity strengthened their bonds with one another and manifested the special kind of commitment associated with hard-core adherents. This close-knittedness was to continue to large measure even during the later expansions of Army aviation.

In some ways, the aviators' association resembled a favored fraternity. Practical jokes were often attempted, —for example, a fireplug kept "popping up at different places, once at the quarters of a general."[43] One observer has noted that the attitude common to the pilots was like that found among winning ball clubs and winners in general. There was, of course, disagreement among the leaders, but the disagreements tended to be over matters of emphasis, and the disputants displayed less resentment and hostility than might otherwise be expected.[44]

On December 7, 1945, the Army Ground Forces Air Training School (formerly designated the Department of Air Training) was estabished to provide tactical training in the use of other ground arms that were to incorporate organic aviation. The school encountered great difficulties, but after it was redesignated the Department of Air Training in 1946 as part of an academic reorganization, it expanded its facilities.[45] At this time, some middle-ranking officers not previously involved in the program became aviators.

In the reorganization of 1947, Army aviation was provided an essential legitimacy by the National Security Act, which stated that the Army could maintain its own organic aviation.[46] The struggle to establish legitimacy did not end with receipt of a formal charter, however. Even the search for names was to occupy the time of some of the insurgents. As one official stated: "We were changed to the title Air Op to Light Aviation and then to Army Aviation. Most of this was an evolution that we had to tenderly go by, not to get the wrath of our own people because they had a constant fear of the Air Force coming back to take over this mission."[47]

Likewise, in an effort to show their authenticity as pilots, the Army aviators battled to win their own rating system—those aeronautical titles of aviator, senior aviator, and master aviator—but this was not accomplished until 1950.[48] In a related symbolic contest, the Army moved slowly toward getting a design for its own wingbadge. The Air Force would not permit the use of its silhouette for the wings, so the badge became a conglomeration of elements, including the wing size used by the Navy.[49]

Late in World War II, organization of the Army aviation movement in Washington was minimal. Captain Robert Leich became a staff officer in what was known as the Service of Supply.[50] A Major Anderson was the first staff officer to "go up to Department of the Army" from the Army Ground Forces. The only other significant organizational gains consisted of the addition of one staff officer at the grade of lieutenant colonel to each field army and the transfer of some Department of Air Training personnel to Fort Sill's Field Artillery School.[51]

During this period, the aviation insurgents endeavored to solidify an organizational foothold in the Pentagon and elsewhere (Figure 2). Some of their records had been kept quite informally in green loose-leaf notebooks, and the insurgents, with their grasp of bureaucracy, knew that such paperwork would not suffice in their battle for legitimacy.[52] They improved the paperwork, but then faced an acrimonious dispute over the slotting of aviation officers in the Army structure. The insurgents succeeded in getting an aviation officer

Figure 2. Selected Postures Regarding Army Control of Army Air Support: Fragmentation and Reorganization, 1946-1950

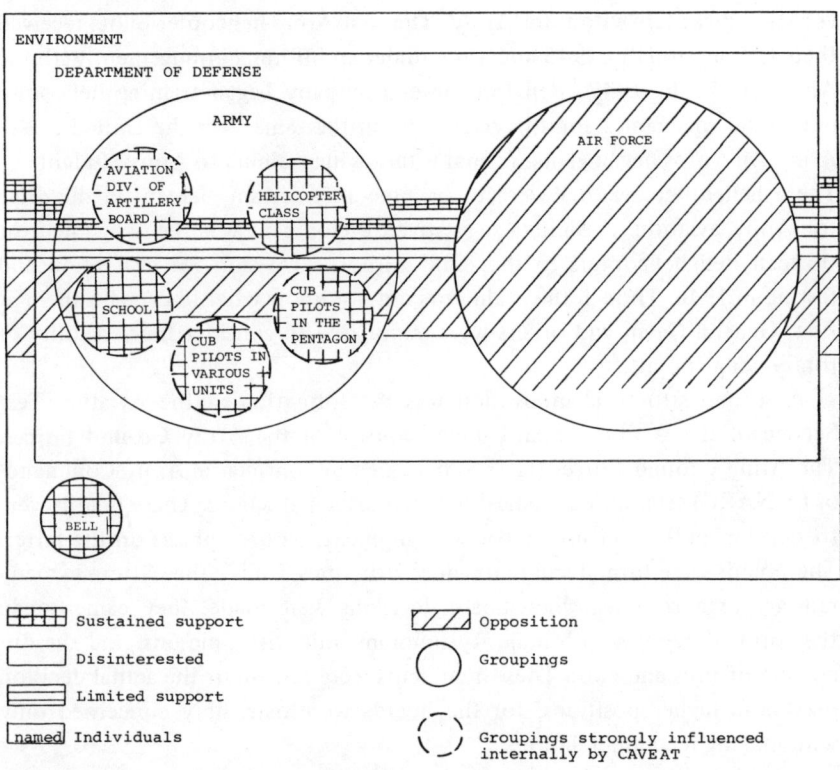

into the Army G-3 (operations and training section)—Colonel Robert Neeley. According to one report, however, Neeley was told by his boss that since he was an Army aviator he was prejudiced and would therefore not be permitted to handle action that had anything to do with Army aviation.[53]

Rather than await selection from above, the insurgents "sent up" an officer who was a member of the first graduating class of Cub pilots, the "class before one." He received the same briefing given to Neeley by his superiors. This officer had been at the Pentagon for only a short time when, according to one report, "they found him with an aviation paper in his pocket going down the hall, he was intercepted, and fighting ensued."[54] Though "fired" by his immediate superior, he was able to discuss his situation at a higher echelon. The superior with whom he spoke supported the aviator, and certain aviation policies were altered.[55] This story should not be considered an isolated incident; the first part of the story is typical in the sense that others fought for recognition and were squelched.

Two other developments external to Washington which were to have long-range consequences occurred during this period. The first concerned the advent of helicopters within the Army. The first Army helicopter pilots received their training in later 1945 and 1946 under an informal arrangement with the Air Corps.[56] In 1947, Bell Helicopter Company began training helicopter pilots and mechanics for the Army and in the same year the United States Army Air Corps began giving formal rotary-wing training to Army students.[57] These helicopter aviators were to become a significant element in the drive for Army aviation. A similar suggestive development was the assignment of thirteen Bell helicopters to the 82nd Airborne Division for evaluation and testing in 1946. Though the evaluators did not know what to do with them at first, General Gavin and others were stimulated to consider the versatility of rotary-wing aircraft.[58]

A second structural innovation was the formation of the Aviation Test Service of the Artillery Board under control of the Army Ground Forces. The Army Ground Forces (later to become the Continental Army Command, or CONARC) established a board for each principal school. These boards were to develop both doctrine and new equipment, with emphasis on the latter. The boards were formal and permanent structures. Unlike the pattern in many military organizations, when board decisions were made, they came out in the form of reports with majority opinions, minority opinions, and the discussion of pros and cons. These arguments were to benefit the actual decision makers in higher positions, for the boards were ostensibly concerned only with making recommendations.

Such boards were the outgrowth of the discovery that procurement decisions have long-range implications. For instance, if one chose a different caliber of ammunition, a logistical nightmare might be created. The decision makers did not want those who made the *de facto* decisions to be the Ordnance Corps; they wanted them to be the users. The boards were designed to represent the ultimate users—the artillery battery, the infantry company, the cavalry troop—as contrasted with the technicians of the Ordnance Corps, Transportation Corps, or similar branches.

As might be expected, the boards were generated as a result of user pressure by the Army's combat arms in opposition to the wishes of certain technicians.[59] Though they were co-located with each school, they did not have to report through a tortuous chain of command; rather, their work went directly to the commanding general of CONARC.[60] Generally speaking, in the 1940s and 1950s the boards were comprised of a full colonel, who was president of the board, and approximately forty officers. Being a board member was a sought-after assignment, especially for those in the research and development field who desired basic experience in testing.

In keeping with their origins, the boards designed their tests to determine how items would function in a simulated combat environment. For example, ordnance might test fire thousands of rounds of ammunition through a tube to see if an artillery piece would wear out. The artillery board, on the other hand, sought to determine whether the field piece could be camouflaged, whether it shot accurately when handled by ordinary troops—the kinds of questions that were unlikely to be given primary consideration by the technical services. The Army aviation field, which started out as a small division of the Artillery Board, became so important that it eventually broke away to become co-located with the newly formed Army aviation school at Fort Rucker during the mid-1950s.

PERIOD III: PREAMBLE, 1951-1955

The Korean War provided a crucial stimulus to Army aviation. In the first place, Korea demonstrated the effectiveness of Army aviation (and especially helicopters) in combat. Second, because of early defeats, weaknesses in the Army were revealed which called attention to the need to improve America's military ground forces. Third, the Army's effective performance under General Ridgway inculcated greater pride and confidence. This, mixed with uncertainty about the Army's ultimate existence and discontent over air assistance, further stimulated Army-Air Force rivalry over aviation support.

In 1951, a group was set up in the G-3 section to provide staff assistance to the Chief of Staff and the Secretary of the Army on aviation matters. It was headed by Colonel Robert R. Williams, an important figure in the CAVEAT story partly because of who he was and largely because of his active promotion of Army aviation. Williams was important because, as a West Point graduate, an artillery officer, and a member of the "class before one," he combined the Cub spirit with the appropriate professional credentials. Insofar as his activities were concerned, he had been an early proponent of Army aviation while serving as a member of the test group for organic aviation and as Chief of the Flight Division, Department of Air Training, during most of World War II. Thus, he was in a position to serve a socializing function during a time of great expansion.

During the last years of World War II and immediately thereafter, Williams was a planner in the very area of Army-Air Force requirements which was the focus of interservice rivalry over air support. While it is reported that Williams was selected to make a comprehensive study of liaison aviation in an attempt on the part of officials in the Air Forces to be objective,[61] other evidence suggests that he was believed to be more of an aviator than an Army officer and was sympathetic to the soon-to-be-autonomous Air Forces' position.[62] In any event, the Air Forces empowered Williams to make an extensive trip through much of Europe, where he interviewed various Army Ground Forces and Air Forces officers in the field. His report, suggesting the retention of organic liaison aircraft by the Army, was greeted by a mixed reaction at the top Air Forces levels. Some officers—General Hoyt S. Vandenburg for example—felt that such an arrangement would permit the Army to convert its aircraft into close support fighter-bombers and airlift craft; others, such as General Lauris Nordstad, felt that the atomic bomb had rendered the Army essentially irrelevant.[63]

As in Williams's own case, his planning and staff group in G-3 was particularly active in providing support for the Army in its contests with the Air Force during this pentad. Besides providing support for the interservice battle, the G-3 team served as a focal point for bureaucratic activity within the Army. Recognizing the fragmented state of Army aviation, the team proposed several actions in a comprehensive four-year plan in November 1954.[64] The recommendations of this group included measures that would strengthen Army aviation vis-à-vis the Air Force, such as the assumption of depot maintenance and supply and the advancing of the Army's procurement authority. Three crucial intra-Army recommendations were made: the establishment of an aviation center at Fort Rucker, including an aviation test board; the development of career-aviator assignment authorization for G-1; and the establishment of an aviation division within the G-3.

By the time the proposal to establish an Army aviation center had been made, the first steps in this direction had already been taken. There had been several efforts in 1954 to remove the aviation school from Fort Sill. Such a move would be an acknowledgment of the growing importance of Army aviation in terms of both its need for physical facilities and its symbolic separation from the Artillery. Many locations were considered, each having its physical and political advantages as well as drawbacks. For instance, one effort to move to Fort Riley, Kansas, was negatively endorsed by an Army commander who had no interest in the school.[65]

Physically, Fort (then Camp) Rucker had four primary advantages: its Ozark Army Airfield had three 5,000-foot runways; buildings had been recently renovated; truck stands at the camp could be used as heliports; and large buildings could serve as helicopter maintenance hangers.[66] However, Rucker was really the most "expensive of all possible solutions in terms of new capital investment,"[67] and some later difficulties due to physical shortcomings seem to have been perceived in advance. Nevertheless, General Paul D. Adams, G-3 of the Army and supporter of the expansion of Army aviation, indicated that the goal was to get a foot in the door at Camp Rucker and expand the school and center from there.[68]

Department of the Army officials were not concerned with the planning of a post for such units as helicopter companies and fixed-wing transports.

101 / The Dynamics of Insurgency

Such matters were of great concern to Brigadier General Carl I. Hutton, the recently appointed Commandant of the Army Aviation School. Hutton's grand schemes for Camp Rucker were relayed to another supporter of Army aviation—Major General James M. Gavin, a subordinate of General Adams in the G-3 section of the Army. Gavin, who with his concerns for airborne warfare and sky cavalry had already developed a reputation as a visionary, was briefed at Camp Rucker on plans for the installation. Gavin, who urged the development of complete plans for a permanent installation, "was impressed by the comparative isolation of the post."[69] He recommended the construction of golf courses, athletic facilities, messes, and other accoutrements of a permanent post. He suggested that Hutton ignore mobilization plans that might bring forth demands for other activities that could reduce in importance the aviation activities at Camp Rucker. Gavin's encouragement confirmed Hutton's optimism, and the school's commandant then decided "to do my best to ruin the place for anything else but an aviation center."[70]

Gavin is an interesting figure in the development of CAVEAT. He had been concerned with aviation tactics for some time. He was both a heroic combat fighter, once described as the "prince of parachutists" for his noble exploits, and a strategic thinker of some note.[71] He was the youngest major general in the Army when he commanded the 82nd Airborne Division in World War II and had the appropriate credentials for the highest levels of military leadership, having been a West Point graduate, a protégé of General Ridgway, and a member of the "airborne club" that dominated postwar military organization. Gavin appreciated air mobility, but in its place—that is, as an aspect of strategy and tactics of the atomic battlefield. His point of view was too broad to be considered a reflection of the inner core of the bureaucratic social movement. He noted, for instance, that "there was almost as much reluctance to go into these new forms of air mobility in the Army as there was in the Air Force. Most of our senior Army officers had experience in combat with other than air mobile units and they looked with considerable skepticism on the enthusiasm of these zealots who were insisting, sometimes with considerable exaggeration, that everything in the Army had to fly."[72] He further stated that "there are those who would emphasize air mobility at the expense of everything else"[73] It is also worth noting that Gavin was not a skilled bureaucratic politician. Evidence for this observation includes his fitful departure from his post as G-3 of the Army in 1958 and reports of his undiplomatic outspokenness while in posts abroad.[74]

Army aviation also enjoyed the friendship of some members of the G-1 (personnel) section of the Army staff. The G-1 section had undertaken an Army aviation officer career program early in the Korean War, but his program had been lost in the confusion of personnel expansion during the war. In May 1955, a G-1 study revealed that most Army aviators were of low rank, with only 4 percent being above the grade of major.[75] As late as 1954, there were still fewer than 2,500 aviators in the Army. So, to advance the interests of Army aviation, it became necessary to increase the number and percentage of aviators who were higher-ranking officers.[76]

The G-1 and G-3 agreed that the G-1 would exercise within the career management division of the Adjutant General's Office central direction for any new career program. A new career program could have been useful in ironing out the problems of aviation officers who had to choose between branch and aviation assignments. Certain of the more senior aviators did not rotate to career-advancing duty in their basic branch until well after this period because they were required to supervise the flying activities of newly graduated pilots.

The rapid expansion of the Army during the Korean War created an additional hurdle for those attempting to rotate between ground and flight duty. At the end of the war, the turbulence caused by the additional personnel reflected the uncertainty of the days that preceded the establishment of an aviation division within G-3. The process of setting down recommendations for the future of Army aviation led to "some rather bitter infighting, as well as confusion of ideological lines."[77]

Certain elements of the Army advocated a separate aviation branch. The idea was that within the framework of a branch the Army aviators would have the leverage to promote their view of the Army's mission as well as the career well-being of the aviator. Opponents of this view who were supporters of Army aviation felt that the establishment of an aviation branch would lead to a situation analogous to that of naval aviation.[78] In this event, members of the Army aviation branch would be the only ones with access to aircraft and, in effect, a mini-, centralized air force would be created within the Army. Those who opposed this view felt that aviators could promote the Army's mission as well as their own careers by remaining with their own branch and promoting the aviation activities of that branch.

An important advocate of decentralized aviation was General Hutton. He wrote to Artillery, the Transportation Corps, and other interested officials, explaining to each how its own situation would be damaged by centralization (Figure 3).[79] Hutton was later called to a conference-room meeting of representatives from most headquarters and agencies having aviation, where, it was hoped, an agreement would be reached. General Paul Adams advised the conferees to remain until they reached consensus. Apparently, the majority of those in attendance preferred the aviation branch solution, while Hutton and some Transportation Corps and Artillery officers opposed it. The words exchanged were bitter and the discussion was reminiscent of disagreements between the old Air Corps and the Army more than a decade previously.[80]

Figure 3. Selected Postures Regarding Army Control of Army Air Support: Preamble, 1951-1955

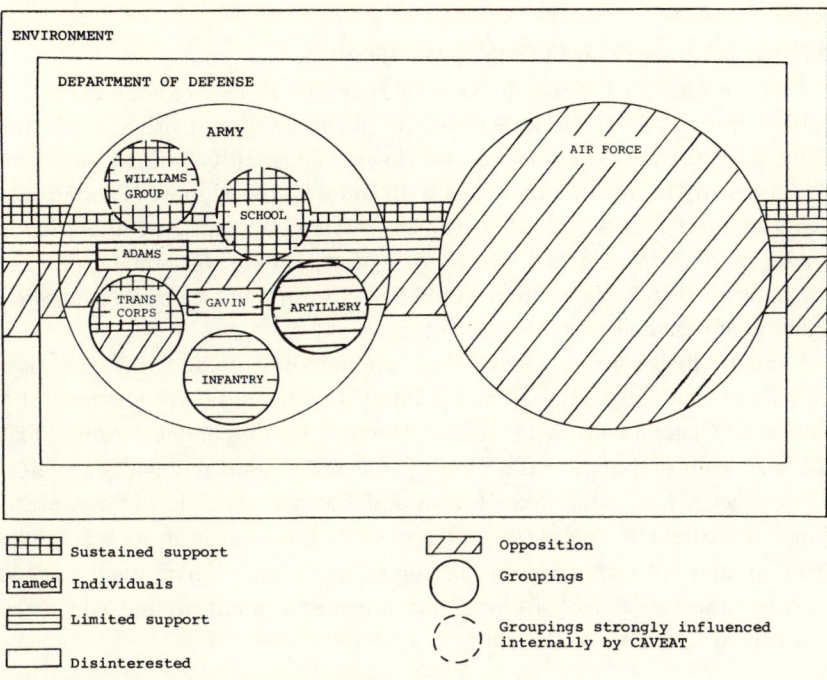

General Adams, a West Point graduate and later head of the XVIII Airborne Corps and the United States Strike Command, ordered Hutton to report to him on or about December 1, 1954. At that meeting, Hutton claimed, he was "told to shut up."[81] Adams informed Hutton that his (Hutton's) opposition and the letters he had written put the G-3 in an embarrassing position. Adams stressed centralization of career management as a necessary first step in the enhancement of Army aviation. As Hutton described it:

The scene was quite heated and at one time I removed my aviator's wings from my blouse and told General Adams that I wanted nothing to do with it. At this stage he left his office suddenly, I always believed to allow a cooling off period. In renewed discussion a few hours later, he told me he was going to establish an aviation division in the Department of the Army within G-3, headed by a Major General, who, he informed me, would not be Hutton.... He described the basic qualification required which was a great deal of Department of the Army General Staff experience so that aviation could protect itself in the clinches in the give and take of staff wrangles. The smoke of the battle at the time concealed the fact that I had won. Centralized career management was not established, and the handling of aviation matters was retained on the General Staff level.[82]

104 / The Army Gets an Air Force

It is with the naming of a director of Army aviation that we move into a new period.

PERIOD IV: AMALGAMATION, 1956-1960

Early in January 1956, Major General Hamilton H. Howze became the G-3 staff officer and later the director of the Army aviation division within the Army general staff. The selection of Howze, apparently brought about by the wishes of Gavin, who knew him well, and with the support of certain elements in the CAVEAT social movement, marked a significant alteration is the status of Army aviation. In the first place, Howze was a major general, which meant that Army aviation would have a formal advocate at a somewhat higher rank than had previously been the case.

Second, Howze was a part of the mainline elite of the Army: he was a West Point graduate, came from a military family, and was something of a protégé of General Gavin and General Maxwell Taylor (the new Army Chief of Staff). To his reputation as a "comer" was added some renown as a tactical theoretician. Thus, while like Hutton and Gavin he was deeply concerned with the battlefield implications of a possible European war, he was unlike them in that he had a reputation for undramatically going by the book.

Third, the creation of a directorate provided a point around which the members of CAVEAT could rally:

When it was first formed, that was the only real focal point in the Army's staff. General Howze was the first one. Army aviation was very small. There was, maybe, one officer in the personnel business and another one in the intelligence and another one in logistics, two or three. There weren't very many. And he was able to hold meetings periodically, get everybody together and say, "This is what I think we ought to do" and everybody'd say, "Oh, yeah, this is a pretty good idea," then they go back and under the table try to follow this general course of action towards the goal.[83]

Thus, the supporters of Army aviation gained the advantages of centralization without paying the heaviest costs.[84] Since the director was a staff officer rather than a commander, it was not expected that he would be ordered by superiors to restrain the activities of his men, who were not, in fact, his subordinates. His position was described by one officer in the following way: "Even though you didn't have authority you were, at least, running the meeting. You could, ordinarily, get a fair degree of consensus of what ought to be done and then you'd write your notes of the meeting so, informally, you sort of generated what passed for a program even though people wouldn't salute you and say, 'Yes, sir.' "[85] Further, while Howze could push for aviation interests from a strategic location, he was not so visible as to be a perpetual reminder to those who opposed Army aviation. Those who criticized Howze's activities had to direct their criticism at him, and thereby he became a "lightning rod" that attracted and dissipated much of the energy that could have damaged the aviation movement. Because Howze's main duties were such staff obligations as planning and theorizing, his personal rectitude tended to shield the more deviant behavior of the dispersed aviation enthusiasts.

Fourth, Howze got his wings only after he became involved in G-3 aviation planning. While there had been some precedent for bringing outsiders of fairly high rank into aviation matters, Howze's entry marked a major shift in personnel planning by the leadership elements of CAVEAT. The decision was taken to ensure the survival of Army aviation by recruiting high-ranking officers who were marked as future Army leaders in their own branches.[86] Some of the old aviators assisted in the selection process, though they themselves could have had their future careers damaged by such developments. For instance, Lieutenant Colonel J. Elmore Swenson, a World War II aviation leader and a member of P-1, the official first class of Cub pilots, aided in the talent search for Army aviation officers.[87] An example of a person admitted by this process was Lieutenant Colonel John J. Tolson, a distinguished World War II paratrooper and also a junior associate of General Gavin who, though not a pilot, had been a supporter of aviation for some time. After completing his flying course, Tolson became the assistant commandant of the aviation school. Tolson later became commanding general of the 1st Air Cavalry Division in Vietnam and later still was to be commanding general of the XVIII Airborne Corps at Fort Bragg, North Carolina.

The effort to get the onus of "fly-boy" off the backs of the Army aviators by putting the foot soldier into the air was enhanced by the senior-officer program. The marrying of the ground soldier and the Army aviators was symbolically consummated by bringing some of the brightest young colonels into the aviation program. Many of the majors and lieutenant colonels who had been Army aviators since World War II were shocked by this move. They realized that their potential for promotion would surely be limited by bringing in people from higher levels, particularly since so many of the aviators were reservists and, to some extent, aviation technicians.

The senior people who were recruited—that is, those "given the opportunity to volunteer for the program"—were selected by those who had "identified them as comers" in the Army, as

far thinking, far sighted people who were obviously going to be general material, who'd been identified at the War College level or by some special staff assignment as being outstanding people who had tremendous potential. And then they were point-blank asked if they would not volunteer for this with assurance implicit in this that they would become a real part of it. And, almost without exception, these people that did volunteer for the first few groups of senior officers got intensely involved with the program, stayed with the Aviation program, and have been a guiding force behind it.[88]

Thus, through word-of-mouth recommendations and the examination of records, a new component was added to the amalgam of Army aviation.

Concern that the older officers lacked the physical abilities to handle light aircraft competently was soon dispelled. "The senior officers turned out to be better at every stage of the course than regular students."[89] By taking senior officers, CAVEAT followed the path of naval aviation, which accepted older aviators, rather than that of the Air Force, which tended to initiate young officers into the fraternity of fliers.[90] Not only did the Army aviation school have a senior-officer course for training pilots, but it also initiated a senior-officer orientation course to further spread the word about Army aviation.[91] Thus, by 1959, a total of eleven Army generals had flight status.

This pentad also included a period of rapid technological development and experimentation with the armed helicopter. Such experimentation clearly suggested a logical process by which later developments would be well outside the limits on the Army under Department of Defense roles and missions policy. General Howze continued to publish material that did not include armed combat support as one of the functions of Army aviation,[92] but at the same time, experimentation that was aimed in that direction continued at the relatively isolated ranges of Fort Rucker, Fort Benning, the various arsenals, in Europe, and elsewhere. While Department of Defense officials continued to proclaim that it was not their desire to create a separate Air Force for the Army, they failed to realize that the strategy of Army aviation had fundamentally shifted and that prohibition of a separate aviation branch was therefore no longer relevant.[93]

General Howze and others struggled to gain exceptions to the roles and missions agreements while General Hutton and his successors used the school to socialize new supporters, train new pilots (including those of warrant officer rank), and experiment with new airmobile tactics and weaponry. During Hutton's tenure, Fort Rucker was raised to the status of an Army aviation center, and two additional schools for aviators were opened as well. By setting up a predominantly aviation-oriented post, CAVEAT benefited from a lively source of support—the political power of the local community. Senators Lister Hill and John Sparkman and Congressman George Andrews sought to assist the activities of Camp Rucker with "political pressure which apparently reached to the White House."[94]

Further, after the departure of General Hutton in 1957, the center became a dissemination point for limited public relations efforts as well as for diffusion of tactical innovations. Among themselves, the supporters of Army aviation became increasingly open as to their ends. The *U.S. Army Aviation Digest* contained a commandant's column in which General Hutton and his successors were able to express their views. While Hutton did become increasingly bold, he also followed a self-imposed censorship.[95] He, like General Howze, was well aware that if close air support were suddenly made an exclusive mission of the Army, Army aviation at that point in time would have neither the men nor the aircraft to accomplish the mission.[96] Some Air Force-supporting aviation magazines kept an eye on developments in the *Digest*. While the dissemination was wide, Hutton suggests that it probably received more attention behind the Iron Curtain than in high American military circles.[97] Still, it did stimulate thought and action among Army aviators and served as a testing ground for various doctrinal innovations.

In addition, the Army Aviation Test Board, later to become the largest board in the Army, was established at Fort Rucker with Colonel Williams, a symbol of the linkage of the West Point and Cub traditions, as well as the first master aviator, as its first president. The board was able to undertake legitimate experimentation in certain areas of Army aviation development.

This period was particularly important for the arming of the helicopter. Many of the new men had backgrounds in the infantry or cavalry. The armed helicopter was becoming more than the mobility device admired by theoreticians like Gavin, Howze, and Hutton. Its potential as a source of firepower made it especially attractive for those to whom "move, shoot, and communicate" was an axiom in which shooting was the chief element. Because it could move combat troops into battle and was able to serve as a gun platform, the armed helicoper became an emotional object for many of those who came in contact with it. Adding the excitement of flight to these other aspects, it is easy to understand how Army aviation converted and co-opted those who later later became its devotees.

Yet during this period CAVEAT remained a minority movement. It was particularly threatening to tankers and truckers, who feared that their functions would be partially usurped by helicopters. It was opposed by other officers and by many Defense Department civilians who found it too expensive and technically uncertain, and it was harshly opposed by the leaders of the United States Air Force. Yet by this time these forces were unable to mount the concerted effort against Army aviation that could have stunted or killed it in its formative years.

Part of the explanation for this failure lies in the entrance of the Army into the missile field. Missiles occupied the minds of high-ranking Army, Air Force, and Defense officials. Even the tension created by the Wilson Memorandum was due more to the Memorandum's impact on Army missile programs than to its restrictions on Army aviation.

One must also consider the significance of the combination of geographical dispersion with central motivation in the men of CAVEAT, who persistently advanced their views while proving an elusive target. This dispersal was especially effective in the promotion of a complex web of military-industrial contacts. Army aviators became accustomed to dealing with officials of important American industries. Such contacts not only enhanced the state of the armed helicopter but also established new sites for potential and actual political support. Such political support, like the technology which produced it, was still in a relatively early stage of development, but would prove useful as time passed.

Army aviation displayed other evidence of progress during this time period, including the establishment of an accident review board, the appointment of a director of safety, the assumption of depot maintenance and supply responsibilities, the enhancement of its procurement authority, and the addition of a special staff section of the Continental Army Command (CONARC).[98] Yet as late as 1960, when the Army Aircraft Requirements Review Board, headed by Lieutenant General Gordon Rogers, met at Fort Monroe to get at the problems of Army air power, inhibitions still persisted. As one officer stated: "The idea of the Army having an aerial combat capability was trying to break out into the open. It was on the minds of the men on the Board."[99] That idea was not pursued, however, because its supporters did not feel they could "get away with it."[100]

Air Force officials were not completely blind to the threat shown by the increased interest in Army aviation. The Air Force was particularly concerned about a build-up in the Army's interest in the jet. General Curtis LeMay offered a counterploy to this interest by stating that the Air Force would provide eleven support squadrons, with the Army selecting the kind of plane it preferred to have the Air Force fly.[101] Operation Menu, as this exercise was called, at first threatened to reinforce the enemies of CAVEAT to such an extent that the Army aviation movement could have been done great damage. Closer examination revealed that LeMay's offer was to be paid for out of the Army's fixed budget, thereby providing more pilot slots for the Air Force in a time of decreasing opportunity for flying due to the replacement of aircraft by missiles. At the same time, LeMay's proposal would cost the Army an amount equivalent to the expense of a division of troops.[102]

The aircraft included in the Air Force's offer ranged from the armed Mohawk to the most sophisticated experimental planes (including Navy fighters, to which the Air Force really had no access). When a demonstration was eventually held at Nellis Air Force Base in the Nevada, however, the offer turned out to be a "grand sales pitch for the F-105."[103] Moreover, the demonstration ended in tragedy as one of the pioneers of aviation, Colonel Wayne

The Dynamics of Insurgency

Figure 4. Selected Postures Regarding Army Control of Army Air Support: Amalgamation, 1956-1960

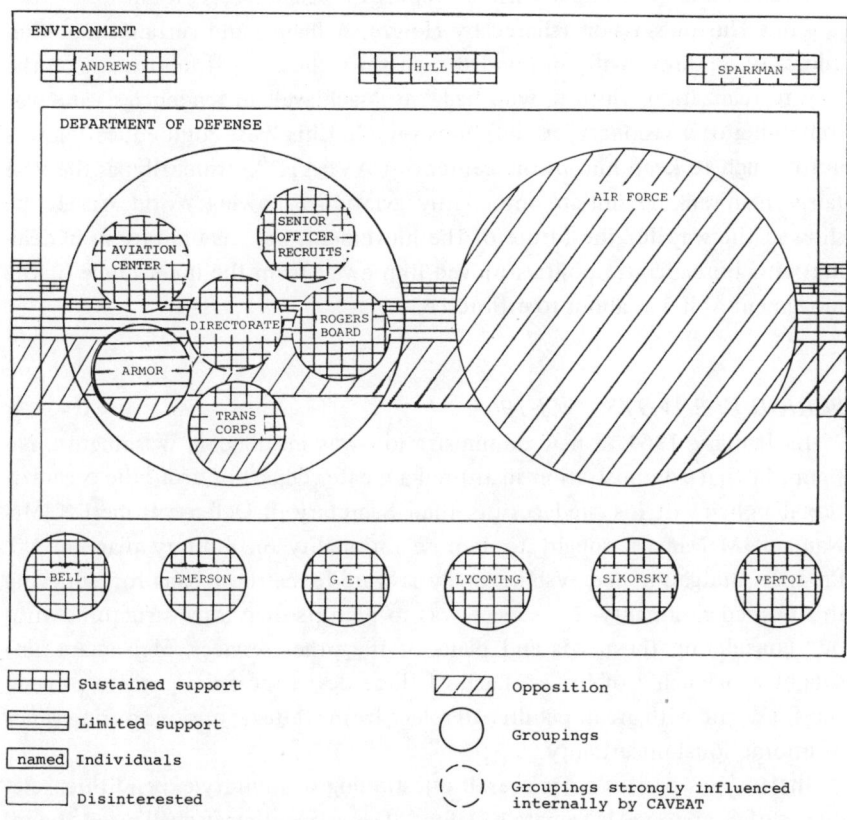

Downing, was killed when an Air Force H-21 helicopter crashed and one of its blades was propelled among the spectators.[104] Thus the Army aviators' grievances against the Air Force's ploy intensified.

At the beginning of this period, much of the Army aviation leadership was provided by World War II Cub veterans. By the end of the period, an amalgamation had taken place due to the infusion of certain officers, many of whom were members of the airborne club (Figure 4). It was a period of internal conflict, much in the manner of "Red versus expert" struggles.[105] Since it was not the airplane, but rather what such craft could do, that was essential, middle-ranking technicians were cut off in attempts to exalt the technology itself.[106] Assuming positions of leadership were upper-middle-ranking men from the generalist mainstream of Army life. Those who had significant "Red" credentials, such as a United States Military Academy

110 / The Army Gets an Air Force

diploma and paratrooper's wings, could obtain the minimum technical know-how to become quasi-experts while keeping the real experts on tap.

Thus Hutton's vision (shared by Howze, Williams, and certain other Cub pilots) of an Army with air-minded men throughout its structure was on the way to realization. Hutton, who had "no Machiavellian tendencies" and was something of a visionary, found, however, that his West Point education was not enough to keep him in the center of CAVEAT.[107] Ironically, as the first fairly high-ranking initiate into Army aviation following World War II, he showed the way for the future of the movement, but his limitations in dealing with bureaucratic politics moved him away from the inner circle of the movement as it was about to effloresce.

PERIOD V: ENVOYS, 1961-1965

In January 1961, a new administration was installed in Washington. No figure in that administration instituted a greater departure from the organizational policies of his predecessors than Secretary of Defense Robert S. McNamara. McNamara sought to impose rationality on military planning.[108] Program budgeting and systems analysis were to be the means for achieving this desired rationality. No service was to plan its own force structures without considering the needs and plans of the other services. McNamara also sought a balancing of forces. Each of these devices was designed to provide the President with greater ability to select from strategic options during times of international uncertainty.

In 1961, as part of their overall questioning of military expenditures, elements of Secretary McNamara's Defense Department staff challenged the requirement of aircraft for the Army. General Clifton Von Kann, who had become the director of Army aviation after being tapped for helicopter training, arranged for a briefing. McNamara indicated that the briefing helped him to see Army aviation in a new light and he requested additional paperwork. He was not totally satisfied with the documents that had reached his desk through the usual chain of command.[109]

During this time, certain officials in the Defense Department staff became allies of one military service or another. One official in systems analysis, particularly, became a supporter of Army aviation. His interest in and relation to the insurgents was "a cloak and dagger sort of thing."[110] Personnel in the Office of the Director of Defense Research and Engineering and Army staff officers dealing with tactical warfare combined with their supporters in the Office of the Controller (who were largely in the subsection concerned with systems analysis) and elsewhere to promote the cause of Army aviation. One analyst and one CAVEAT colonel prepared new paperwork for McNamara's eyes.[111]

The colonel also prepared a personal note from McNamara to Secretary of the the Army Stahr suggesting that he abandon his conservative approach and take a bold new look at the mobility situation by creating a special board from which a report, untrammeled by staff review, would go directly to the Secretary of the Army and the Secretary of Defense. Also prepared were a talking paper (which McNamara was reported to have "talked" to Stahr) and a document which included a list of potential board members.[112] Some of the wording later disseminated in Secretary McNamara's name was critical of the Army's failures to act, and therefore it became even more essential that the insurgents be concealed. Briefly, we have seen here how a soldier, supported by his allies, prepared words that were passed through a civilian and used by the Secretary of the Army to by-pass the Army hierarchy and establish a board to advance the cause of CAVEAT.

The relationship between the drafter of the documents and his civilian pipeline to Secretary McNamara was one of mutual interest, for in no sense was the civilian perceived as a member of the social movement by the inner circle.[113] Nevertheless, from this and other relationships, the Army Tactical Mobility Requirements Board, better known as the Howze Board, was created. The executive committee of the board was made up of twenty men (fifteen of them soldiers) who were supported by thirty staff officers plus other officers and their men.[114] This board was not impartial in terms of its basic evaluation of the utility of air mobility. All the military board members supported the concept of an airmobile Army and the civilians also tended to be affirmative.[115] Thus, the general thrust of the board's findings was virtually preordained.

The likelihood of dissent at the top level of the board was minimal, since members of the Army aviation social movement had their list of desired participants accepted as board members.[116] Further, no one who was untrustworthy was permitted access to the executive committee. Howze invited an Air Force liaison officer to be present for the tests, but he was not permitted to sit with the executive committee, because there was too much discussion on "what was wrong with the Army-Air Force interface."[117]

Though it was clear in advance that the board's findings would favor some form of air mobility, this did not mean there was no work to be done. Howze had only from May through September 1962 to conduct an incredible number of tests, devise new tactics and logistics, and surmount other organizational and mechanical difficulties. Hundreds of calls were made for advice. During a discussion of the size of the basic airmobile unit, one key officer in particular expressed the following viewpoint: "Don't fart around. Go big. Don't ask for battalions, ask for divisions."[118]

Various units of the 82nd Airborne Division had to be made available for the use of the board. Lieutenant Colonel J. J. Hennessey, who commanded most of these troops, had the difficult job of training his men to use helicopters while conducting tests to evaluate the concept of air mobility.[119] The helicopters were of an older vintage than those being considered for use in an airmobile division, and so the very vehicles that were important objects of planning had to be simulated through use of their obsolescent counterparts.

Several officers were pulled from their other activities to serve with the Howze Board, its staff, or its report-preparing groups for varying lengths of time. The work was especially difficult because it was fragmented by subject matter and geography. For example, separate military and civilian groups were to analyze the industrial as opposed to the Army theory of helicopter maintenance.[120] In the face of problems of distance, experiments were conducted at Fort Bragg, North Carolina; Fort Benning, Georgia; Fort Stewart, Georgia; and in the western mountains of Virginia. Simultaneously, research analysis groups organized war games at additional locations.[121]

Unexpected participation by individuals from other organizations also was a factor. When the time came to hang bombs on the Mohawk reconnaissance plane, the Army aviators were afraid to go to the Air Force for advice. Instead, they obtained from the Navy a pilot to teach the Army pilots how to bomb and some sailors (who were "not quite AWOL") to show them how to load bombs.[122]

Material was solicited from concerned industries, and documents came in to the Erwin School at Fort Bragg (the place designated as headquarters for the Howze Board because it offered an empty building during summer vacation). By September, a large room of that building was filled with documents that were "roughly knee deep on the floor."[123] A great deal was read, but given the hectic pace of events, much material obviously went unconsidered. "The lights at Erwin School burned past midnight every night, people over there arguing and writing things down."[124] Problems such as who should speak and for how long and deciding when enough testing had been done so that writing could begin contributed to the disorder. As one officer described it: "It's a nightmare of a job; you work all hours, you have large number of people you flew in from all over on these committees, very dedicated. As a matter of fact, during the Howze board many of us just ran ourselves into the ground; we worked so darned hard we almost couldn't think straight."[125]

Yet when it became necessary to pull the data together, the similarity of purpose must have been useful: there was general accord within the discord. As for serious dissent, "the only real skepticism was in some of the civilian analysts from DOD [Department of Defense] who kept pressing for quantification of things that we hadn't yet figured out how to quantify; and yet it was probably healthy that they were there because the thing might not have sold if we had done any less on it than we did. But we didn't do everything by any matter or means."[126] The still-secret final report contained thirteen chapters. In addition, there were a number of annexes and appendixes. Each chapter was prepared by a functional leader and his staff according to the group's division of labor. Howze himself did sufficient rewriting so that the stamp of his style and opinions was visible in the main report.

The amount of paper consumed by the report was staggering. Board members agreed to "restrict" their output by assembling no more than one footlockerload of paper each. Thus, 600 copies (600 footlockerloads of paper) were produced.[127] The value of the different sections varied greatly, but the report had been made, the work was on paper, and the bureaucracy's appetite for paperwork had been appeased.

There was, however, no guarantee that the work of the Howze Board would be continued. Having accomplished the extraordinary task of undertaking tests that tended to verify the need for large airmobile units and, remarkably, having a report prepared by a lieutenant general go directly to the Secretary of Defense without intervening editing by higher officials, CAVEAT was now faced with the necessity of maintaining its momentum. There was a period of delay after the tests which created discomfort for the supporters of Army aviation. At this time, the Air Force tried to counteract the effects of the Howze Board by forming a board of its own headed by General Gabriel Disosway, Vice-Commander of the Tactical Air Command.[128] The Disosway Board had very high-ranking members, and its recommendations, including the suggestion that the Air Force provide the support of additional fighter-bombers, were moderate and well-conceived.[129]

While some Army men derived a certain amount of satisfaction from the Disosway Board's findings, which seemed to promise Air Force support of Army ground troops, it was generally realized that Army aviation was not yet secure, despite the good wishes of Secretary McNamara. It was perceived that McNamara was supportive, but even after he expressed his desires, the recommendations of the Howze Board were "pretty much shelved."[130] Once again it became necessary to undertake an abbreviated version of the strategy that had been so effective in producing the Howze Board—that is, having men at the lowest levels coordinate the presentation of their views to their superiors so that their ideas would converge impressively at appropriate places in the chain of command. Plans were made so that it would appear that these suggestions and requirements were coming from unconnected places spontaneously. This would cause the top-level leadership to see a widespread trend or tendency throughout the Army which required action.[131]

McNamara was made aware that his affirmative wishes for Army aviation were being ignored in Army circles. He then provided the money and manpower for further tests of the recommendations of the Howze Board. (Even so, Army aviation was not one of McNamara's major concerns. He was far more interested in questions of deterrence, and even his non-atomic interests stressed intercontinental airlift aircraft.)[132] In January 1963, Army Chief of Staff General Earl Wheeler ordered Major General Harry Kinnard, a recently trained helicopter pilot with an abiding interest in airborne warfare, to create the 11th Air Assault Division. Kinnard busily scrounged for staff and troops with which to push beyond the experimental frontiers established by Howze.[133]

During this period there was still uncertainty on the part of certain officials as to the acceptability of an air assault division. Largely because of CAVEAT's missionary activities, its allies had grown in number and were increasingly well placed and effectively dispersed (Figure 5). The Commander of the Test Evaluation and Control Group at Fort Benning (and thus the evaluator of much of the activity of the 11th Air Assault Division) was Brigadier General Robert R. Williams. Further, many of the aviators' crucial test reports were prepared by Colonel James Brockmyer, an adept writer and one of the original Cub pilots. In fact, Fort Benning during this period became a way station for many supporters of Army aviation. For example, Colonel Del Bristol, one of the first Army aviators, became Commander of the 10th Air Transport Company supporting the activities of the 11th Air Assault Division.

The Air Force fought bitterly during this period to prove its superiority in matters of air support. For each Army test there was a more elaborate Air Force test. For example, Goldfire I was a combined Air Force-Army test which stressed the mobility of the Air Force's C-130 transport.[134] The test was conducted by the Strike Command, a unified command concerned with joint Army-Air Force mobility. The Commander in Chief of the Strike Command and the evaluator of its work was General Paul D. Adams, identified earlier as a supporter of Army aviation. Thus, the Air Force was in the position of being dependent upon the effectiveness of Army troops and the affirmative reaction of Army evaluators. The Army, on the other hand, could conduct its own tests. This set of circumstances ironically reversed the asymmetry of the relationship between the two services, for now the Air Force was dependent upon the Army.

There were additional factors in the testing of Air Force and Army air mobility. During this pentad the Army continued to produce more pilots of various ranks. Even more important, its colonels of the 1950s were becoming the brigadier and major generals of the 1960s. These men were able to continue to push for aviation, and to such an extent that the Air Force also was required to improve its tactical capabilities, thereby enhancing the general air support capabilities of the United States military forces.

115 / The Dynamics of Insurgency

Figure 5. Selected Postures Regarding Army Control of Army Air Support: Envoys, 1961-1965

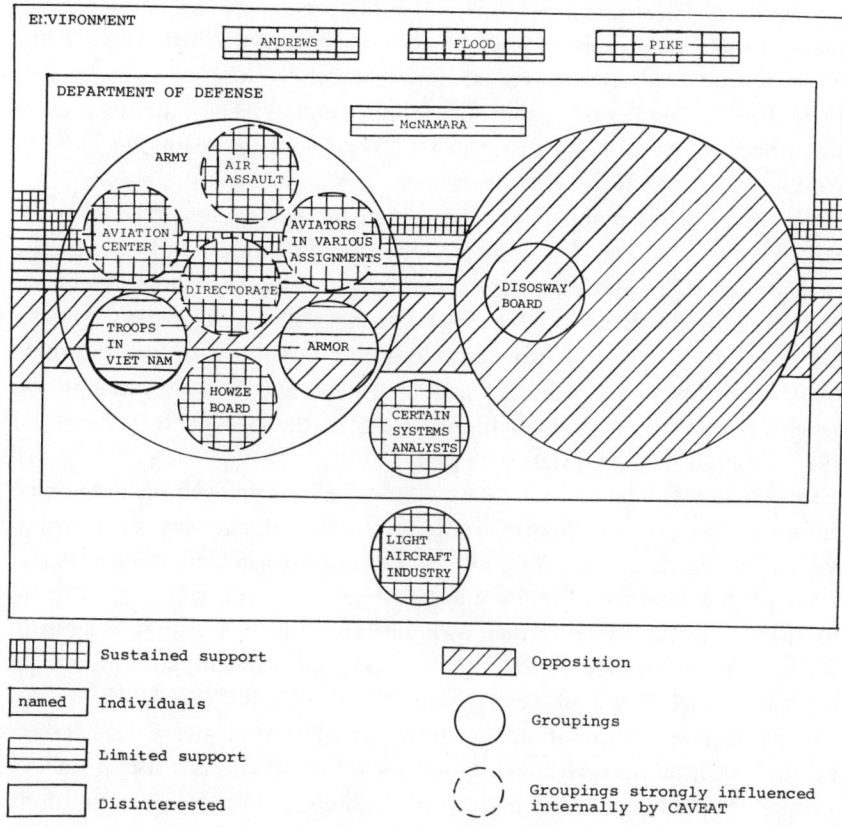

NOTE: Internal arrangement of subfigures irrelevant.

Nevertheless, as late as 1965, the possibility loomed that helicopters would be restricted to special units in each Army division and limited in number to just over a hundred per division. This type of organization was already in existence in the ROAD (Reorganization Objectives Army Division), and no one knew what impact Vietnam would have on the European-oriented Air Assault Division.

In the spring of 1965, initial moves were made to disband the 11th Air Assault Division. Some people became uneasy, but the members of CAVEAT continued to drive toward their goal. "A lot of the key officers were seeking reassignment orders, and then somebody revoked most of those."[135] In June 1965, the decision was announced that the 11th Air Assault Division was to be inactivated and its men and materiel transferred to the 2nd Infantry Division, with which it had mingled for the past two years.

116 / The Army Gets an Air Force

The changes did not stop there. The 2nd Infantry Division would exchange its colors with that of the 1st Cavalry Division, then stationed in Korea. The new 1st Cavalry Division would take on about six thousand additional men, many of them paratroopers, and several hundred new aviators. The 1st Brigade was to be airborne as well as airmobile, which meant that many men would have to undertake parachute training rapidly. The rapidity was required because, by early August, the 1st Cavalry Division (Airmobile) was to be on its way to the Republic of Vietnam.

Even the establishment of an airmobile division was not sufficient for the men of Army aviation. They wanted continued and improved support by the Air Force as well. Much of their effort was aimed at Congress. Earlier in this period Senator Barry Goldwater of Arizona, a strong supporter of the Air Force, was invited to Fort Rucker in an effort to familiarize him with helicopter hardware and capabilities and to win his support. No attempt was made to reduce his support for the Air Force; rather, it was hoped he would take an interest in Army aviation as well.[136]

In Congress as a whole, the men of Army aviation enjoyed the continuing support of Congressman George Andrews, the Fort Rucker area's representative, and other congressional figures. Some congressmen were influenced primarily by the presence of military installations in their districts, others by industrial supporters, some by their own outlook on tactical avaiation, and still others by a combination of these factors. One particular supporter was Congressman Daniel Flood of Pennsylvania, former Marine Corps officer who regularly received information that proved useful in congressional hearings as a tool for legislative oversight. Flood and others often made use of "spies" to reveal shortcomings that then became the basis for dramatic interrogations of witnesses.[137]

Another friend of Army aviation was Congressman Otis Pike, who chaired the 1965 close air support hearings during which witnesses told of the failure of the Air Force to support the Army in Vietnam combat. The attitude of Pike and other supporters is revealed in an exchange that took place between congressmen and counsel and General Delk McCorkle Oden, a former director of Army aviation, later an officer in Vietnam, and at the time the Director of Officer Personnel, Office of Personnel Operations, Department of the Army.

GENERAL ODEN: Yes. I don't mean to sound harum-scarum about the taxpayers' money which I contribute partly to, but I think any nation that can afford three strategic air forces can—
MR. BLANDFORD: Can have something to support the boys on the ground real close.
GENERAL ODEN: Whether it is this aircraft or something else.

117 / The Dynamics of Insurgency

MR. BLANDFORD: That is exactly right.
MR. PIKE: I couldn't agree with you more, General. Amen.
MR. GUBSER: Amen.
MR. PIKE: As you sit on the ground and you look up in the sky, you don't have any trouble finding aircraft which were designed for air superiority, do you, air-to-air superiority?
GENERAL ODEN: Yes.
MR. PIKE: And you don't have any trouble finding aircraft which were designed for these long-range interdiction missions, do you?
GENERAL ODEN: No, sir.
MR. PIKE: Can you find one that was designed for close air support?
GENERAL ODEN: Well, the experts, of course, Mr. Chairman, would tell you that they design for both.
MR. PIKE: General, I consider you an expert and I am asking you, once again, for your personal opinion.
GENERAL ODEN: No, sir; I don't think they are designed for close air support.
MR. PIKE: Mr. Evans, any questions?
MR. EVANS: No, I have no questions.
MR. PIKE: Thank you very much, General Oden. You have been most forthright and cooperative and I hope that—we will make the record abundantly clear that the testimony which you have given was your personal opinion and was dragged out of you most reluctantly.
GENERAL ODEN: Thank you very much, Mr. Chairman. I appreciate it.[138]

Indeed, it is the expansion of the Vietnam War which marks the next period in the development of Army aviation.

PERIOD VI: COMITY, 1965-1970

From 1966 to 1970, Army aviation grew at a rapid pace. Though it still had its detractors, Army aviation gave a distinctive character to the Vietnam War, which in turn gave Army aviation the ultimate legitimacy for a weapons system: proven combat effectiveness. By 1966, it was becoming apparent that the armed helicopter was to be an integral part of the Army's combat arsenal. Thus, on April 15 of that year General Harold Johnson, Chief of Staff of the Army, and General John P. McConnell, Chief of Staff of the Air Force, announced an agreement regarding the responsibilities of each service for the control and use of certain types of rotary- and fixed-wing aircraft.[139] The Army transferred the CV-2 (Caribou) and the CV-7 (Buffalo) to the Air Force as the latter service became responsible for intratheater fixed-wing tactical airlift. The Army became responsible for all helicopter support for intratheater movement, fire support, and supply of Army forces (and some Air Force troops as well). The Air Force retained some rotary-wing aircraft for search and rescue, administrative, and other limited functions. The Army and

118 / The Army Gets an Air Force

the Air Force continued their joint development of vertical takeoff and landing (VTOL) aircraft and made provisions for additional consultation on various problems.

This agreement brought a mixed reaction. Many of the members of CAVEAT felt that the Army was unnecessarily sacrificing fixed-wing capabilities for which they had fought so hard. Others were perhaps less sure about the decision but more satisfied that the Army now had a clear charter under which to operate all kinds of helicopters, including undisguised attack rotary-wing craft such as the Huey Cobra and the Cheyenne. Some of the discontent was traceable to misgivings about General Johnson's commitment to the cause of Army aviation. In Johnson's earlier years as commanding general of the Command and General Staff College, he is reported to have eliminated Army aviation departments within the school. Further, he is said to have felt burdened by having to defend the armed Mohawk for great lengths of time during apparently unrelated discussions with other members of the Joint Chiefs of Staff in the joint arena.[140] Johnson's distaste for the lengthy discussions in "the pit" about the armed Mohawk led him to call it the "barber pole of the air assault division."[141] The idea was that when one wanted a haircut, one looked for a barber pole; when one wanted an air assault division, one looked for the armed Mohawk. In fact, when the 1st Cavalry Division was deployed in Vietnam, its complement of between twenty-four and thirty armed Mohawks was deleted.

Nevertheless, Johnson was believed to have become something of an advocate of the Airmobile Division in general, preferring to negotiate the concept as opposed to dealing with specific aircraft such as the Mohawk and the Caribou. Johnson's views were hardly surprising. They epitomized the "top-politics" perspectives of members of the Joint Chiefs and some members of their Joint Staff Since 1958 it has become increasingly important in terms of promotion to be able to demonstrate the capacity for interservice cooperation. In fact, as early as 1955 there was evidence that the higher the position of an officer, the more likely it was he had a "broad, non-service point of view."[142] This was especially true with regard to officers working for the Joint Chiefs of Staff or in the Office of the Secretary of Defense. While the data are by no means conclusive, since it can be assumed that some official ideology was salient, they do suggest that the perspectives of men at the top or in certain functional posts differ from those of other personnel within the same service. Further, some type of joint duty had become a requirement for promotion to higher rank. It is not at all surprising, then, that military elites can act out their roles like other bargainers who have an overview of the requirements of their own organizations and can make trade-offs on the basis of some calculus appropriate to the pluralistic setting.

Figure 6. Selected Postures Regarding Army Control of Army Air Support: Comity, 1966-1970

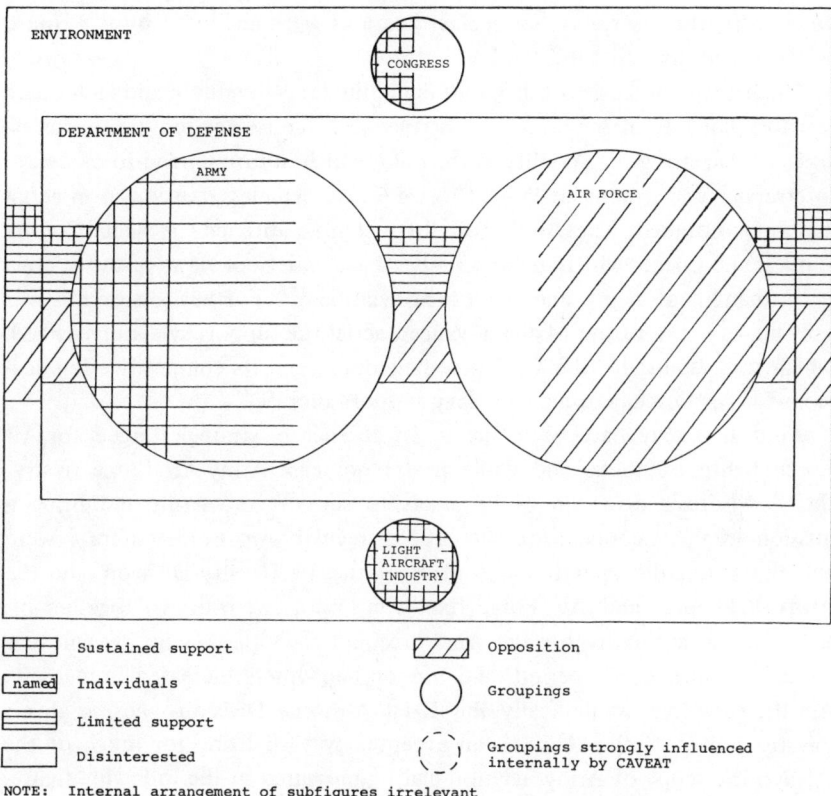

Johnson and McConnell ratified the combat-induced necessity for a major role on the part of Army aviation in Vietnam. The helicopter was so important that it is safe to say that without it there would have been no Vietnam War as we knew it.[143] In addition to the armed helicopter, the Air Force had relatively plentiful assets for support of the Army. Even the giant B-52 bomber was pressed into service in an effort to destroy Viet Cong and North Vietnamese Army targets. Fighter-bombers that were not used in attacks on the North were made available for support of ground troops, so much so, in fact, that an inquiry was held in 1967 in which great concern was expressed that the Tactical Air Forces were neglecting missions other than close air support: "The United States should obtain a proper mix of tactical aircraft to handle the . . . tactical missions; but we want to be assured that emphasis on the procurement of close support and interdiction type aircraft will not be achieved at the expense of a new and vitally needed air superiority weapons system."[144] Army aviation experienced additional difficulty in Congress over cost overruns and other problems associated with procurement of airframes for the light observation helicopter ("LOCH"). The implications were sufficiently serious that special hearings were instituted by the House of Representatives in 1967.[145]

Much as missionairies of different denominations in remote and forbidding territory come to understandings described as "comity," so too did the necessities of war bring on a comity in the field, which in turn tended to moderate interservice disharmony at home (Figure 6). Nevertheless, tensions over aerial support continued. The Air Force, for instance, initiated projects Corona Harvest and Checo, which included collecting a variety of views of the relative performances of Army and Air Force aviation.[146] Further, dissension was brewing over the future of the advanced aerial fire support system (AAFSS), which was essentially the Cheyenne helicopter, and its competitive implications for Air Force, Marine, and Navy support aircraft.[147]

Though it may have been due to an absence of strategic targets for Air Force fighter-bombers, and while it did not ease Army-Air Force rivalry, the Air Force's diversion of its assets to support the Army did bring a mission-oriented cooperation. In 1969, regular Air Force aircraft were actually under the operational control of the 1st Cavalry Division, and the Army helicopter and Air Force fixed-wing pilots were drawn together by their mutual antipathy for the Air Force and Navy pilots who lived in rear bases.[148] During this period, the use of helicopters increased immensely. Another division—symbolically the 101st Airborne Division—became an air cavalry unit. Aviation became an accepted way of living for much of the Army. The scope of Army aviation can be measured in the following figures (as of July 1969): "About 72% of the 3,500 U.S. helicopters in Vietnam are operational on an average day. And in any given month, this fleet will:—Log 30,000 flying hours. —Move 333,000 troops. —Haul 100,000 tons of supplies and equipment. —Evacuate 3,500 soldiers and civilians to hospitals."[149]

Thus as the period drew to a close, it appeared that CAVEAT had moved a great distance toward achieving its ends. But Army aviation still had its critics and opponents, and its apparent success in Vietnam did not guarantee its future in the post-Vietnam era American Army. It is to this future and the implications of the movement for bureaucracy in a democracy that we now turn.

Chapter 6 | **ARMY AVIATION
IN TOP POLITICS**

Events of the early 1970s ushered in a new era for Army aviation—the post-Vietnam era. It became increasingly apparent that the Nixon Doctrine of reduced American commitments abroad, including the Vietnamization of the Southeast Asian struggle (no matter how painfully slow), pointed toward a declining need for United States Army combat troops in Asia. Just what had been the role of Army aviation in Vietnam, and what did this role foreshadow for the future?

It is difficult to grasp the enormity of the impact of helicopters on the conduct of the American-Indochina War. Helicopters of all the American services flew more than thirty-six million sorties from 1966 to 1971.[1] In most parts of Vietnam, one observed helicopters in action several times a week. This is not an argument that all such use was correct or economical, or even that helicopters were essential to the conduct of *a* Vietnam war. Rather, it does suggest that helicopters were essential to the conduct of *the* Vietnam War, and that as such they are perceived as having an established utility. Thus Army aviation traveled from 1965, when several members of CAVEAT were concerned that aviation would be irrevocably damaged by the threatened breakup of the 11th Air Assault Division, to 1970, when the Army Chief of Staff, that ultimate Establishment figure, General William Westmoreland, received his own wings as a helicopter pilot with a fanfare of publicity.[2]

This is abundant evidence that Army aviation was well established by the 1970s. In 1970 the Army had about 12,000 aircraft.[3] Consider further the impact on the Army's personnel structure of the more than 24,000 aviators on active duty, more pilots than the Air Force had on active duty at the same time.[4] Perhaps most telling in terms of intraorganizational achievement is the

121

fact that by late 1972 approximately 36 generals and 230 colonels were drawing flight pay.[5] This permeation is not surprising when one considers that aviation has a role in each of the functions of land combat: command and control, logistics, reconnaissance, maneuver, and firepower.[6] Those who tried to restrict a machine so clearly applicable to certain functional requisites of the Army from being considered and experimented with in other functional areas on grounds of administrative or political convenience did not reckon with the reality of combat exigencies. While these areas might have been analytically separable in the minds of some defense planners, in practice, awareness of the utility of aviation crossed organizational boundaries.

Army officials found that they could not relinquish the chance to secure the ultimate attack helicopter, regardless of the trouble or the enormous expense involved. The notion of a highly sophisticated air machine with extraordinary avionics had captured them as surely as the Air Force had been captured by the need for higher-flying and faster-traveling electronically sophisticated fighter aircraft. From the rationale of seeking a simple device to meet the needs of its mission, the Army had in large part moved to an outlook dominated by technology.

The psychology of technology of the men involved in Army aviation seems to have varied with the amount of money involved in developing new aviation weapons. Even though the Cheyenne helicopter was first abandoned in 1969, when the Army canceled its contract with Lockheed, development continued and costs soared. This initial cancellation followed several delays in production of the 200-knot helicopter gunship and the death of a test pilot in a crash. By then the government had spent 86 million dollars, the Lockheed Corporation 80 million dollars, on the project. So the imperatives of investment and the strong desire for such an aircraft operated together to bring forth the possibility of a new billion-dollar-plus contract, with each chopper estimated at one point to cost about four million dollars if spare parts and pilot training were included in the overall funding. This was surely a far cry from the jerry-built gunships made of scrounged parts that were the hope of Army aviation supporters less than two decades previously.[7] By 1971 some estimates of the cost of one Cheyenne had gone to well above 5 million dollars.

This aircraft would have cost almost twice as much per copy as the fixed-wing international fighter F-5E, which is used by America's allies in the fighter role.[8] Perhaps even more striking is the fact that it would have had approximately the same price tag per aircraft as the newest fighter being added to the Air Force inventory, the F-16.[9]

Clearly, then, by the late 1960s the Army was increasingly manifesting the style of the Air Force in its weapons acquisition process, including the political aspects of the process. This was due in part to each service being reorganized along similar lines by Secretary of Defense Robert McNamara. As the Vietnam War wound down, interest in the old roles and missions questions began to increase. The pressures of combat no longer guaranteed interservice peace. During the period 1965-1969, interest in the future of close air support was not extinguished. Each service tended to look after its own house, but public interservice conflict became unfashionable in light of the need for a united front against antiwar forces, pressures to honor the Johnson-McConnell Pact, and the mutually accepted effectiveness of close air support in the theater of battle. As the Army acquired helicopters, Army aviation drew the attention of the concerned public and the scrutiny of political forces involved in supervision of or rivalry with the Army. This success thrust Army aviation squarely into the realm of top politics, where its very accomplishments stripped it of the protective cover of earlier days.

One further development, the open renewal of the attack on Army aviation by Air Force officials, seems to have been set in motion by the efforts to withdraw American troops from combat in Southeast Asia. Vietnamization, a device designed to bring peace to American military forces, ironically fueled the flames of interservice rivalry.

Vietnamization provided both a specific example and a general rationale for firing up the engine of competition. Operation Lam Son 719, beginning in February and ending in April 1971, was designed as an attack on North Vietnamese forces in their Laotian base camps which would give the ARVN (Army of the Republic of Viet Nam) a breathing space in which to reorganize and confidence to fight on, while also giving the American forces a breathing space in which to disengage and confidence that disengagement would not lead to instant Communist victory. No final analysis of Lam Son 719 has been made by United States military strategists, but none needed to be made for the soldiers of the ARVN, who were badly mauled in their enemy's lair.[10]

Specifically, the Air Force attacked the Army for the numerous helicopter losses over Laos (anywhere from 91 to over 200, depending on whom one choses to believe).[11] Such losses could be interpreted as evidence of the vulnerability of helicopters in a "mid-intensity" or "high-intensity" combat environment—one where there are authentic anti-aircraft weapons and trained soldiers to use them, unlike the situation in South Vietnam. In fact, the criticism was aimed at the Army's efforts to gain tank-killing attack helicopters for use in Central Europe. This criticism was the leading edge of the Air Force's general position on post-Vietnam military planning: in brief, as the services changed their focus from "counterinsurgency" in Southeast Asia to America's major commitment, opposing a Soviet incursion into Western Europe, the weapons should be commensurate with the task. For many airmen, it was axiomatic that Soviet anti-aircraft fire would demolish fighter helicopters. Army officials responded that changes in tactics and improved aircraft would reduce vulnerability to an acceptable level. Thus, the reduction of hostility on the battlefield corresponded to an increasingly open interservice bellicosity on the home front.

Another reason for the renewed conflict between the Army and Air Force was the failure to duplicate politically the effective integration of the services' performances in the skies over Vietnam. McNamara-initiated centralization was followed by both the Vietnam War and muted interservice rivalry. But it was the war, not the administrative adjustments, that promoted intensive cooperation. In the Army and the Air Force planning centers at the Pentagon and on Capitol Hill, concern was being expressed again as to who would perform close air support, and at what cost. The Army took the position that it was simply elevating the tactics and doctrine of the ground weapons system and giving it more firepower—in short, providing something like more tanks and machine guns.[12] Air Force officers, meanwhile, were with some reluctance seeking planes able to fly lower and slower—thus penetrating from above the same air space that the Army was evolving into from below. The graphic picture of congested air space suggested to planners and military officials did not have to be accurate, only energizing, for political considerations—matters of power, money, jobs, outlook, and identity—not technical ones, were crucial.

Close Air Support

There were a number of military tasks to be performed by close air support aircraft. Ideally they had to be able to attack moving targets beyond the range of direct-fire weapons; to concentrate fire on targets massed close to friendly ground forces and deliver this fire near friendly positions to weaken attacking armored forces before they came within range of ground anti-tank weapons; and to assault well-entrenched enemy with heavy ordnance.[13] The position of the Pentagon hierarchy, both military and civilian, was that one type of aircraft could not meet these diverse objectives.

This position was formalized by a position paper prepared by an ad hoc Defense Department committee, the Close Air Support Review Group. Approved by Secretary of Defense Melvin Laird, this top-politics device consisted of elements of various subinterests formed to study a problem under the direction of a high offficial seeking consensus. This review group, headed by Deputy Secretary David Packard, was established in February 1971 to examine close air support in general. It considered command and

125 / Army Aviation in Top Politics

control and logistics questions and roles and missions issues and analyzed military hardware. It used a variety of analytical and simulation techniques provided from several sources. It was, in essence, a collection of soldiers and civilians seeking solutions to apparently military questions that were, in fact, largely political. The group's very existence was political, yet it sought to describe its functions in military weapons systems terminology.

PARTIES INVOLVED

The makeup of the committee reveals much of the complexity of defense politics. Its members were David Packard, Deputy Secretary of Defense, Chairman; John S. Foster, Jr., Director of Defense Research and Engineering; Gardiner L. Tucker, Assistant Secretary of Defense (Systems Analysis); General William L. Momyer, Commander, Tactical Air Command, USAF; Vice-Admiral John P. Weinel, Director of Plans and Policy, Joint Chiefs of Staff; Lieutenant General Robert R. Williams, Assistant Chief of Staff for Force Development, USA; and Major General Homer S. Hill, Deputy Chief of Staff (Air), USMC.

Before such a report emerges from the bureaucracy, it normally involves several of the offices with an interest in its conclusions; elements of the report can be parceled out for preparation, or a basic working paper can be created, with opportunity provided for comment and revision. Coordination can be a challenge. In this case, the final product was assembled by the Office of the Assistant Secretary of Defense (Systems Analysis), with the summary and recommendations being developed primarily by the services and the Joint Staff and being coordinated among the services, the Joint Staff, and the Office of the Secretary of Defense.

The Close Air Support Review Group was largely a response to congressional wishes that the Pentagon's weapons requests be justified.[14] Its report provided an agenda for those concerned with the many problems related to close air support in the 1970s. In addition, it attracted commentary in military-oriented journals, the attention of weapons manufacturers, the interests of military-related congressional committees, the ire of a specialized congressional group—Members of Congress for Peace through Law (MCPL)—and the concern of the services themselves.[15]

ALLOCATION POLITICS

That the review group's work was to be directed at a congressional committee offers further insight into classic Washington politics. High-powered study groups are not spontaneously created in order to consider philosophical questions of military theory. Animating the work of the group was the very concrete question of the allocation of several billion dollars for research

126 / The Army Gets an Air Force

into, and development and production of, close air support weapons systems hardware. The three weapons systems under consideration were the Army's advanced aerial fire support system (AAFSS), also known as the Cheyenne helicopter; the Air Force's A-X close support, fixed-wing aircraft; and the AV-8 Harrier, vertical/short takeoff and landing (V-STOL) aircraft, already procured in small numbers for the Marine Corps.

The group's conclusions were essentially summarized in its recommendations:

1. Continue the Harrier procurement plan now before Congress.
2. Continue the A-X and Cheyenne development programs.
3. Execute tests to resolve the uncertainties found during this study so that the necessary information for decisions of production of the Cheyenne and the A-X and further procurement of the Harrier will be available.
4. Continue to refine the methodology for evaluation and comparing alternative close air support systems and arriving at procurement decisions. The results of present methods often require too many qualifications.[16]

In effect the men of Army aviation, represented in part by General Williams, a long-time aviation proponent, had become actively involved in allocation politics worked through at a high level. Top politics had succeeded insurgent politics, and the men of Army aviation became representatives of an established interest seeking its share of the pie. The group's recommendations were exactly that—a large pie filled with various kinds of fresh delights parceled out among the military diners.

CLOSE AIR SUPPORT HEARINGS

Congressional elements are important actors in top politics Washington style. Because they allow for expression of opinion, compile a record, and attract attention, hearings are a key part of the congressional political process. Thus the close air support study was of special significance because it provided the backdrop for the Close Air Support Hearings before the Special Subcommittee of the Senate Committee on Armed Services, which was to become a crucial arena in the struggle for close air support. Once the report was completed, hearings were arranged to consider the various questions of close air support. The hearings lasted several days, with Packard as the leadoff witness. Senator Howard Cannon of Nevada, although something of an Air Force partisan, allowed the hearings to be opened to several questions from various points of view. This liberality of leadership made for a somewhat disjointed exercise, with questions about esoteric hardware being intermixed with inquiries about grand strategy, military doctrine, and even that favorite topic on Capitol Hill, politics.

Much of the controversy vented in the hearings centered on technical capabilities and complexities of the various weapons systems under consideration. Advocates of the Army position stressed the past benefits of helicoper employment and how these would be enhanced by the addition of the Cheyenne to the Army's order of battle. One of the strongest arguments, that the Marine Corps and elements of the Air Force had been employing the helicopters in much the same way as the Army, even though they had their own fixed-wing attack aircraft, reinforced the contention that the armed helicopter was uniquely suited for certain functions.[17] The method of utilization, which differs from that of fixed-wing aircraft, is a crucial part of the armed helicopter's value:

The most feared capability of these helicopters is their ability to remain on target regardless of attempts to evade them. The minimum warning given before a helicopter attack contrasted in the minds of the enemy with the timely warning the FAC's (Forward Air Controller) presence gives before a fighter strike. Thus the helicopter gunship quickly catches on to a target and holds it while delivering its fire. Close air support fixed-wing aircraft provide the heavy punch. This is an essential distinction between the two.[18]

Timeliness of response to calls for support was particularly appealing to the soldiers. For example, in units with assigned attack helicopters, such as the 1st Cavalry Division (Airmobile), the average response time was twelve minutes, with more than 50 percent of the response times averaging ten minutes or less.[19] Optimally the rotary-wing aircraft lives close to the front, never gets very high into the air, and leaves the ground mainly to improve observation, mobility, and fields of fire. As such, its "roots are in the ground" and it is not a "true air vehicle."[20] Conjuring up the image of an olive-drab tactical vehicle, just slightly elevated from its sister vehicles—tanks, jeeps, and armored personnel carriers—may have been an accurate reflection of the views of the supporters of Army aviation, or it may have been a public relations ploy, but it left the Army in a vulnerable position because of an apparent paradox. If the aircraft was so insignificant an advance in the Army's way of doing things, why did a Cheyenne have to fly at speeds over 200 knots? Why did it need elaborate avionics and diving brakes? Why did it cost somewhere in the neighborhood of $5 million a copy?[21] If, on the other hand, it had all these extraordinary characteristics to improve its functioning, was it not then an inferior attack plane with a rotor? Then was it not too easily open to enemy attack? How did its designers still think that it would survive in the hostile environment of the land war in Europe for which it was targeted? Did any helicopter really have the capability to warrant its inclusion (at the cost of other forces or equipment) in the European battlefield? Could it deliver a lethal amount of ordnance against tanks? Could it live to fight another day against Soviet anti-aircraft weapons?

General William Momyer, Commander of the USAF Tactical Air Command, doubted the capability of a highly complex gunship in a "sophisticated" environment like Europe, North Korea, or North Vietnam. He argued that in a permissive environment (one without modern anti-aircraft weapons), simpler gunships than the Cheyenne could be used, while in a high-intensity environment, no gunship had the survivability or lethality to justify its cost.[22]

Top-Politics Rivalry

One more the relationship between the Army and the Air Force became asymmetric. Playing the politics of bargaining and compromise, Army officers strongly endorsed Air Force close support programs as necessary for the national defense. In selecting Momyer, the hard-line chief of its tactical forces to participate in the deliberations on the future of the Close Air Support Review Group, the Air Force picked a champion of its exclusivity doctrine: if it flies, we should fly it. Though as a member of the review group, Momyer, under the watchful eye of Secretary Packard, had endorsed continued testing of the Cheyenne (along with testing of the A-X and limited procurement of the Marine Harrier), when he responded to direct questions from friendly panel members, his answers left little doubt as to his continued hostility to fighter helicopters for the Army.[23]

In fact, the Army appeared to bend over backward to accommodate both the Air Force and the Department of Defense. Army officers affirmed their belief that air superiority, interdiction, and reconnaissance should have priority over close air support in the design of future Air Force combat support aircraft. In this way the Army sided with the traditional Air Force view of its mission, though there might have been a self-serving aspect to this: the Air Force might then neglect close support, thereby justifying later Army helicopter requests. It seems more likely that such friendliness was part of the line of accommodation projected by the Army toward a potentially pro-Air Force committee.[24] General Williams pointed to the joint training efforts of the Army and Air Force in the Strike Command's pre-Vietnam effort to achieve interservice cooperation.[25] He also defended the Department of Defense's efforts to coordinate capabilities requested by the various services. He praised the technique of the Area Coordination Papers used by the Department of Defense Research and Engineering Office, whose purpose is to identify duplication and coordination problems and assess alternative improvements.[26] Perhaps most revealing of the tactics used by the Army was the way in which Williams tried to fend off efforts by Senator

Thomas McIntyre of New Hampshire to give the whole close air support mission to the Army. After all the years of struggle, the men of CAVEAT were now in the position of defending the Air Force record, or at least of saying, "No hard feelings," and resisting McIntyre's futile efforts on their behalf to assign to them the close air support role.[27]

McIntyre's attempt to consider questions of roles and missions changes was a threat to the Army's tactic of not reheating the coals of interservice passions. In this regard, their approach was congruent with those of Secretary Packard and Admiral Moorer. Packard made it quite clear that he did not intend to address himself to the questions under study in terms of a change in roles and missions.[28] His mind would remain open, but he was not thinking analytically of roles and missions. He wanted to deal in allocations. Moorer indicated that helicopters do not affect the role of the Air Force in providing close air support. He tried to take the question out of the realm of passion and move it into the area of technology: it was a command and control problem.[29] But Senator Stuart Symington of Missouri, a former Secretary of the Air Force, and others would not let the issue remain under wraps. Like students of British history being reminded of the many written documents that comprise Great Britain's unwritten constitution, the witnesses time and time again were reminded by Air Force supporters of the documents—the National Security Act of 1947, the Key West Agreement of 1948, the Wilson Memorandum of 1956, in particular—that constitute the basic guidelines for Army-Air Force air support relationships.

The fourteen-year-old DOD directive 5160.22, which had been designed to clarify the roles and missions position expressed in the Wilson Memorandum, was canceled on March 21, 1971. The cancellation itself then became an issue: What did it reveal about the role and mission relationships? Army spokesmen tried to make light of the older arrangements: Exceptions to the old rules had been granted in the past, and many of the ideas stated in the documents were based on a technology that predated the modern helicopter.[30] Removal of weight limitations was presumed by some officials, oral statements of Secretary McNamara and others had confirmed this, and the Johnson-McConnell Agreement put helicopters in the hands of the Army in clear language. Still, the questioning went on. Senator Barry Goldwater of Arizona expressed his view: "So I don't agree with the statement made by Mr. Packard, 'Although considerable discussion in the past has focused upon the roles and missions, it became apparent quite early in the reviews this issue is secondary.' " Goldwater admitted that the Air Force had not stressed close air support in the weapons acquisition process, but he blamed McNamara's weapons policies, not the Air Force.[31] James Kendall, Chief Counsel for the Subcommittee, asked General Wiliams if the Army wanted any additional written authority to clarify the roles and missions issues. Williams's response typifies the Army's preference for process over paperwork when it comes to Army aviation:

> Roles and missions discussions and considerations are rampant throughout all of the services on a continuous basis. They have to be settled, and they are settled, on the basis of consideration in the budgetary and programming and approval cycles and authorization cycles as well as the DCP [Decision Coordinating Paper] at [D]efense level.
>
> If a system—if a service wants to develop a new system, any major system, it is required to go through a process in defense where a DCP is written, all the services comment on it and finally at each step it goes before the council of all the Assistant Secretaries, has to be approved by the Deputy Secretary of Defense. After that it has to come to this committee for authorization. It appears to me that this is the proper process . . .[32]

One can almost hear the political battle weariness in Williams's comment, "It is a question of determination of which of these weapons we need, not a question of roles and missions, which should be knocked out because a piece of paper said 20 years ago that one service had such a function."[33] Seek the answers in the administrative process, in bureaucratic politics. That should produce a rationality based on accomplishing the basic mission; after all, it had in the past. Now, however, Army aviation was established.

But Air Force perspectives on the letter of the law were quite different and, not surprisingly, so were the opinions of some of the lawmakers. Williams tried to concentrate on an older directive which was deemed rescinded by virtue of not having appeared in later lists of applicable directives. He tried to show that congressional and Defense Department actions had overruled DOD directive 5160.22. Yet one day it popped up again in the list of applicable regulations, and efforts had to be made to formally expunge it.[34] Someone else had learned to play bureaucratic politics.

Further, even after the recision of legislative actions and some executive arrangements, others remained on the books. Obedience to law was combined with two other basic Air Force military tenets to make opposition to the Cheyenne imperative. The Air Force and its supporters adhered strongly to the notion of the indivisability of air power. Army aviation meant giving up the flexibility inherent in centralization (as well as sharing pilot jobs with men in green suits). In addition, the Air Force wanted its tactical aircraft configured for maximum adaptability to several tasks. Preeminent among those tasks were those that required deep penetration into hostile territory. Such requirements call for large, expensive aircraft containing features such as complex avionics, countermeasures equipment, and fire control systems which are less necessary over friendly territory. Thus, as William D. White, Research Associate at the Brookings Institution, says, "The Air Force view seems to be that its tactical forces should concentrate on performing the tasks of which only the airplane is capable."[35]

So here is the Air Force standing for law and order, insisting that it be given the money and authority to control most, if not all, tactical aviation, yet faced with a doctrinal dilemma: the same mission sense that made it insist upon control of all aviation to assure its effective use in every realm, including close air support, required planes whose cost-effectiveness logic and doctrine made them uneconomic for close air support. How was this problem to be solved? The Air Force could acquire airplanes that were not multi-purpose, expensive weapons systems, but rather could be used only at or fairly near the battlefield. Thus one principle, multiple capability, would be sacrificed for the other, central control of tactical aviation missions. But this was inherently unsatisfactory to many Air Force enthusiasts. The real supporters of the A-X project were congressmen and those Air Force officers who felt that if nothing were done about close air support, the Air Force would lose this function and its accompanying weapons systems. Still the Air Force was reluctant to sacrifice other types of aircraft to put an A-X into its inventory.[36] But an economy-minded Congress, concerned about ground troops getting proper support, concerned about the letter of the law, and concerned about costs, found a friend in the A-X, which was projected to be vastly less expensive than multipurpose fighter attack aircraft that could perform close air support, and was considerably cheaper than the Cheyenne.[37]

Senator William Proxmire of Wisconsin, for example, a noted critic of the costs of defense, became an advocate of the A-X program and an opponent of the Cheyenne. Speaking for a "non-Hawk," bipartisan group of congressmen known as the Members of Congress for Peace through Law (MCPL), Proxmire advocated a solution to the close air support dilemma which was elegant in its simplicity and frank in its recognition of interservice distrust. He declared that assignment of the close air support function to the Air Force did not close the subjects of roles and missions. Rather, he suggested, the Army should be given the security of knowing that the A-X would be available to provide close air support. To insure this, Proxmire suggested that the Army continue to test, though not produce, advanced armed helicopters, and that Congress more closely monitor the Air Force's performance of close air support. Then, spurred on by potential competition and inspired by the probing eye of Congress, the Air Force would not neglect its least-attractive obligation, close air support. If this strategy were followed, money would be saved, each service would have what it needed to accomplish its mission, and a structure of trust would be built to insure effective air-ground cooperation. Structures of trust do not require that each side in a negotiation trust each other, only that they have trust-inducing mechanisms to insure arrangements.[38] Such structures are not built in a vacuum. Timeliness is one of the key variables that accounts for the effectiveness of such structure-building. Had someone made the MCPL proposal twenty years before, it might well have nipped the Army aviation movement in the bud. But by 1971, Army aviation had grown enormously and had many allies and an entrenched bureaucracy of its own. The Air Force might get the A-X, the Army might lose the Cheyenne, but the Army was in the armed helicopter business to stay.

With hindsight, it seems that Army aviation supporters simply overplayed their hand. Starting with a type of aircraft that had been rejected as unstable by fixed-wing aircraft pilots, helicopter aviators demonstrated that such vehicles could serve as gun platforms as well as troop carriers, reconnaissance vehicles, and command and control ships. But like a character in a novel who overcomes his origins, reaches success, and then overextends himself because he forgets who he is, the Army aviators lost touch with their antecedents while giving lip service to their background. From jerry-built low and slow air vehicles to the Cheyenne was more than just a technological advance along a straight line. For some it involved a change in the psychology of technology. Think of that little observation helicopter with the machine guns wired on hovering over a remote field at Fort Rucker, Alabama. Now consider this description of the Cheyenne:

The AH-56A incorporated a thermal imaging night vision system that requires no incident light and which can see through smoke and light fog; protection against (deleted) bullets; self sealing fuel tanks and redundant controls. It will be capable of carrying podded electronic countermeasure devices. A neodymium laser provided precise range data to the fire control system and can be used as a target designator for a variety of weapons. The laser rangefinder, used in conjunction with the self contained navigation system, enables the AH-56A to determine the precise location of enemy targets at standoff ranges of over 5000 meters.[39]

And diving brakes, no less.

Army planners went beyond the state of the art, counting on technological breakthroughs to provided for their exaggerated operational requirements. Other, somewhat less lavish helicopters competed for the Cheyenne's role, but when the AH-56A went down, it took its competitors with it.[40] Mission-born, combat-tested, bureaucratically entrenched Army aviation was here to stay, but not as an ersatz United States Air Force.

Procurement Politics

In essence, with the Cheyenne the Army clearly was inside the realm of big-time procurement politics. The distance from sophisticated avionics to sophisticated research and development politics is very short in Washington,

D.C. Delay, whether through inertia or dilatory tactics, is a significant element in this type of politics. Recalling that in April 1969 the Army had sent Lockheed a "cure notice" for failing to make satisfactory progress toward production, and that Lockheed's suggestion of a six-month's slippage in scheduling was followed by termination of the contract in May, one might be surprised to see the Cheyenne at the center of Army-Air Force rivalry in 1971. Here is what happened: Shortly after cancellation, Lockheed filed an appeal with the Armed Services Board of Contracts. Its disagreement with the Army was not resolved until January 1971, when the Army agreed to pay Lockheed $72 million in settlement of the canceled production contract and for research and development losses, and allowed Lockheed to keep another $54 million in "progress payments." Lockheed did not fare well either. It lost $75 million on the development program an additional $45 million in production costs. Yet somehow the project continued; though later efforts to bring the craft up to performance specifications fell short.[41]

Air Force partisans also had their procurement problems, especially disagreement among congressmen over the choice of aircraft. The Air Force case was frequently clouded by references to the A-7 attack craft (in its different models), the plane supported vigorously by Senator John Tower and (incidentally) produced by Ling-Temco-Vought (LTV) of Dallas, Texas.[42] Tower strongly opposed the termination of the relatively new A-7 and suggested that it be improved through modification (probably still cheaper than purchasing new airplanes).[43]

Professor James Kurth has argued that defense contract allocations for major weapons systems are subject to a follow-on imperative which stresses the pressure to keep production lines open.[44] LTV had only the A-7D and the A-7E in production after losing the freedom fighter competition to Northrup Corporation of California. LTV lobbied hard to keep the A-7 in production and sought to compete with the A-X at a fly-off. Proxmire pointed to the political pressure that had been brought to bear in behalf of the trouble-plagued F-111 produced by General Dynamics of Texas when its production line was scheduled to close. Concerned that this was a bad precedent for the A-7 matter, he recalled the resultant pressure on the Air Force to buy more F-111's. Proxmire did not oppose allowing the A-7 into the fly-off, but he did oppose the $68 million required to keep the line open until the competition occurred.[45]

Hearings Politics

Public utterance of these opinions brought forth the following exchange between committee member Tower and witness Proxmire, which reveals much about American politics in general and hearings politics as a variety of top politics:

TOWER: I want to know where the political pressure is coming from that kept the F-111 production line open. Would you like to identify who brought political pressure to bear?
PROXMIRE: General Dynamics.
TOWER: What is General Dynamics' great source of political power?
PROXMIRE: You and I have been in the—
TOWER: They lost the B-1 contract; they didn't get that.
PROXMIRE: I am not saying that when pressure is exerted it is always successful. I am saying that they did exert pressure.
TOWER: What is the source of GD's great political power?
PROXMIRE: General Dynamics—
TOWER: And who is it that exercises it in their behalf?
PROXMIRE: Senator Tower, I think you probably know a great deal more about that than I do for a number of reasons. First, you are on this committee and second you are from Texas.
TOWER: I might note that Senator Cannon, distinguished chairman of this committee, favored keeping the production line open. Are you saying the members of this committee are responsible?
PROXMIRE: Of course, I am not saying that. I am not saying they are the source of the political pressure. I am sure that most Senators, perhaps all of them, vote for something because they believe in it. What I mean by political pressure should be clear enough. You get it, and I get it constantly. I don't resent it at all. I think it is proper. We live in a political atmosphere. It occurs when we get a call from a constituent at home on the telephone saying, "I want this, we have to have it, we need it, how about helping us out," and if we can possibly do it we will.
TOWER: Is there some distinction between lobbying and political pressure? Obviously every munition maker lobbies.
PROXMIRE: I would say there is very little distinction between the two, yes.
TOWER: But what I want to establish is whether or not you are accusing certain of us here on the committee of bringing political pressure to keep this production line open?
PROXMIRE: Certainly not.
TOWER: Thank you.[46]

Hearings, then, can set the stage for expression of conflict. Egoism is etched into the pages of the close air support hearings—especially in the acid remarks of Senators Strom Thurmond and Stuart Symington. This fact highlights another feature of the hearings; instead of being impartial, some committee members had essentially made up their minds on many of the issues under consideration, and each used the hearings to express his point of view and those of his political allies. Thurmond neatly contrasted the deaths of the more than 40,000 soldiers in Vietnam with the low death rate of sailors and airmen. He further cooly exposed Proxmire's ignorance of large-scale Army order-of-battle experimentation that could have had an important effect on helicopter use.[47] Symington, for his part, provided historical and anecdotal evidence verifying the soundness of Air Force doctrine and ridiculed the notion of Army helicopters flying close air support.[48] Though their positions differed, Thurmond and Symington shared a willingness to take up the cudgels for their respective causes. Other senatorial behavior was noteworthy. Absence of many of the committee members was commonplace, even among those whose preferences were known. Some senators were never present. One senator, Thomas McIntyre of New Hampshire, was forever qualifying his pro-Army point of view with self-depreciating observations. "That is what I think," he once commented, "but the real trouble is that I am not smart enough and don't know enough to really be sure I am right."[49] Once when McIntyre tried to explain that he was not an expert, Cannon interjected, "You are not an expert."[50] Further, McIntyre missed much of the testimony and was scolded by Chairman Cannon: "The services don't even agree with you on that statement. So I hope you will be able to stay and listen to all the hearings, so you won't make your decision from a preconceived idea rather than from the testimony that is presented."[51]

Cannon apparently meant what he said about having an open mind, for when the subcommittee reported in the summer of 1972, a majority led by Cannon and including Tower supported an attack helicopter for the Army. This was to be the high-water mark of the pro-Cheyenne forces. Shortly thereafter, the entire Senate Armed Services Committee rejected the Cheyenne proposal.[52]

POLITICS OF LANGUAGE

Cheyenne's vicissitudes added to the confusion about close air support. Indeed, the confusion was compounded in no small part by the politics of language. On March 26, 1970, the Chiefs of Staff of the Army and Air Force had issued a joint memorandum which indicated the eight general tasks comprising combat air support, apparently in an effort to clarify the close air support issue. It hardly served that purpose. First of all, it did not clarify the relationship between combat air support and close air support. In fact, Admiral Thomas M. Moorer, Chairman of the Joint Chiefs of Staff, indicated that deciding which of those tasks constituted close air support was dependent upon the particular combat scenario.[53] The memorandum also failed to indicate which tasks belonged to which service. Ironically (though the specific tasks, which ranged from support of engaged troops to general support of the battlefield, need not concern us here) task six was omitted from the public record provided by the 1971 Close Air Support

Hearings.[54] Perhaps most important from the perspective of this work was the fact that *tasks* were mentioned while *purpose* was ignored. By concentrating on task and omitting or ignoring purpose, the top officials had once again managed to issue a document which did not come to grips with the important purposive aspects of mission, the significance of which has been woven throughout this narrative. Failure to face the basic issue meant more confusion, not less. But such a result has some appeal for administrative decision makers. The political costs of insistence upon specificity may be greater than officials are willing to pay. Ambiguity can yield a balm of hope and illusion to comfort the contending parties and soften the focus of political marksmen.

The confusion about close air support involved its very definition. Different definitions had been used in the past, with words themselves becoming political weapons. Because words have a variety of uses, they are often a top-politics device. There are many possible reasons for the power of words in the political realm. First the denotative meaning of words may establish certain bounds within which one must work. Second, words have legal power, which though open to interpretation has significant influence in a sphere where rules and their making and application are important. Third, words have powerful symbolic aspects, powerful enough to stir masses of men, or to lead them to quiescence (often in a situation which, if presented in a different light, would lead to concern and possibly action). Fourth, and related to their symbolic aspects, words can have a meaning for individuals which touches on their identities; a person might feel that "this definition does not indicate what I do, or why I do it. It does not reveal who I am." Fifth, the terminology may be employed (intentionally or unintentionally) for specifically political purposes—one man's imprecision is another man's obfuscation.[55]

Word use can range from euphemism to outright doublespeak in the Orwellian mold. One of the major functions of government seems to be to make things seem better than they are—a function which paradoxically secures and threatens a democracy. On the other hand, orderly democratic processes benefit from a certain evenness of citizen temperament. But on the other hand, the quality of participation required to maintain a viable democracy suffers from ignorance and numbness of spirit. Where a widespread flow of factual information is desirable, innumerable possibilities for the abuse of people exist through the abuse of language.

So wordsmiths do important work in governmental affairs. This is not less true for the lexicographers who produce the Department of Defense dictionary, known as "JCS Pub 1," appropriately the premier publication of the Joint Chiefs of Staff.[56] This lexicon provides an arena for conflict in the interservice realm. Close air support, for example, is defined as "air attacks against hostile targets which are in close proximity to friendly forces and which require detailed integration of each air mission with the fire and maneuver of those forces."[57] In addition, an eight-page addendum, Appendix C, deals with close air support and air interdiction.[58] Key CAVEAT operators were unsatisfied with this dictionary. One can imagine some of the reasons. First, the term "close air support" is an Air Force term describing one of the missions assigned to the Air Force in various documents over the years. Thus, use of the term "close air support" reminds the informed listener or reader of Air Force preeminence in the area. Second, there is no clear statement that the integration with ground fires is to be under the control of the ground commander, an ambiguity unpalatable to Army officers involved with aviation or with ground command. Third, Appendix C contained words generally associated with the Air Force-preferred method of close air support, a complex system requiring several layers of coordination between the Army and the Air Force, with aviation assets centralized for the high-level commander's use.[59]

The Army objected to the generality of definition on the grounds that the fires delivered by attack helicopters, light observation helicopters, and door gunners on troop-carrying helicopters were sufficiently distinct to require a special term. Terms to describe the helicopter's distinctive capability evolved from "suppressive fires" to "direct support" to "direct aerial fire support" and finally to "direct fires."[60] Part of the reason for the change in terminology was that various directives were aimed at preventing the Army from providing close air support. One way to avoid disobeying the letter of orders is to adopt a new term which superficially alters old activities. Yet the Army officials seemed to believe sincerely that the helicopter was providing something different in the way of air support. One method to express such uniqueness is to find new terms to describe the new phenomenon. In this case, however, the older general definition seemed quite adequate as English; where it failed was in the realm of action. Some Pentagon officials tried not only to inhibit the development of an attack Army aviation but also to prohibit the creation of terms which would describe such activity. In May 1971, shortly after the Wilson Memorandum of 1956 was rescinded by the Department of Defense, a Department of the Army message prohibited the use of the Army aviators' terminology.[61] Still, the Army preferred to think of its "direct fires" as a subcategory of close air support, even though utterance of the words was prohibited. Perhaps this prohibition was an aspect of the bargaining that followed the termination of the old Wilson Memorandum, though I have no evidence to support this notion. It appeared that the decision was one taken at the top in the general interest, and once again explicitness was sacrificed on the altar of conflict-easing ambiguity, an equivocation perhaps designed in part to mollify some members of Cannon's Subcommittee.

Trends in the Technopolitical Environment

While the Special Close Air Support Subcommittee seemed to be reacting to the testimony presented at the hearings, the broader panel, which rejected the Cheyenne, may well have been a more accurate barometer of changes in the technopolitical environment. Among these trends was a growing concern about the organization of the Army; a recognition that Soviet-made anti-aircraft weapons might prove fatal to Cheyenne helicopters using outmoded tactics; concern about defense expenditures that was serious enough to challenge the assumption that "nothing but the best was good enough for our military men"; and a fundamental reconceptualization of the nature of weapons acquisition. There is evidence that some of the supporters of Army aviation also perceived these tendencies, for in 1971 there was already some discussion of another armed-helicopter project.[62] But the product of this consideration was, at least partly by design, to be congruent with the drift of the above-mentioned factors.

ARMY REORGANIZATION

Among the Army's basic difficulties was the declining number of men in combat in proportion to the numbers in combat-support and logistical activities. Viewed differently, the very same situation seemed to favor a highly technical Army—the substitution of machines for men and a concomitant reduction in combat deaths—and suggested that enormous resources would be expended on fewer battle-ready troops. A huge logistical "tail" had created, as if by reverse regeneration, a military monster with an insatiable appetite for expensive hardware and all the comforts of home. Also, the "lean and mean" soldier was thought to have been replaced by the pot-smoking, disrespectful, clock-watching, and otherwise civilianized soldier—demoralized and noncomplaint. Finally, the very efforts of the Army, with its limited funds, to forgo equipment for combat armor and artillery units in order to obtain the Cheyenne, a highly praised sacrifice, might be look at differently by a front-line veteran, who might ask: "What is any Army if not its combat battalions?"[63]

There is in this the resonance of the old Army psychology of maintaining relatively small, decentralized groups, stressing individual initiative, and fighting under variable conditions in a heterogenous environment—a kind of anti-technology sense, if you will.

In 1973, Army Chief of Staff Creighton Abrams, himself a tanker and not an aviator, set in motion a major reorganization of the Army. Some headquarters were reduced in numbers while others were abolished. Headquarters personnel were assigned to newly created organizations or to combat units. The Army Aviation Directorate and its patron, the Assistant Chief of Staff for Force Development (ACSFOR), were disestablished, resulting in the distribution of aviation functions to the Army Materiel Command (AMC), the Training and Doctrine Command (TRADOC), and the Army Staff. Much of the work of TRADOC is now performed at the Army Aviation Center, Fort Rucker, Alabama. Aviation systems management and acquisition activities have been combined under the Deputy Chief of Staff, Research, Development, and Acquisition (DSCRDA).[64] Such reductions increased the significance of civilian technical employees in the new organizations as more officers moved into the field. As a corollary to the general reduction in the number of headquarters, an effort was made to reduce the number of general officers. Thus, some of the foremost leaders of Army aviation, including Lieutenant General Robert R. Williams, retired from active duty. Army aviation had become so widely accepted that it no longer needed as leaders those most closely identified with it. Rather, it sources of centrality were removed, its image was blurred, and its status became less distinctive. Aviation had succeeded in becoming commonplace in the Army.

AVIATION TACTICS AND COSTS

During this period a shift in tactical thinking also occurred. The new attack helicopter would be capable of nap-of-the-earth and pop-up flying. No dive bombing for this bird.[65] This was stated to be the tactic of the Cheyenne, but if it were, why was all the speed necessary? Hand-held antiaircraft missiles made high, slow flying a very hazardous maneuver. Further, the costs of the Cheyenne had become enormous, about $400 million.[66] Such costs brought public attention and political fire to Army aviation supporters. Part of the appeal of the A-X was that it was cheaper than the Cheyenne, and there was talk that the Air Force would have to procure practical rather than optimal fighter planes in order to get sufficient numbers to meet its tactical responsibilities—talk that became fact with the adoption of the F-16 to supplement the extremely expensive F-15.[67]

APPPROACH TO PROCUREMENT

Secretary Packard had made clear his displeasure with previous modes of weapons acquisition. His remedy for Department of Defense practices was a reversion to World War II methods. "Fly-before-buy" became the watchword of those who endorsed Packard's idea of "prototyping." Postwar weapons development had evolved into a complicated process requiring advanced engineering techniques to deal with perplexing problems of modern aircraft and their components. Efforts to coordinate the various aspects and phases of aviation research, development, testing, and production through systems engineering created many jobs for workers, who in turn generated enormous quantities of paperwork for executives who wanted studies of sufficient weight to support billion-dollar programs. In addition, the quest for continuity ("concurrency") in the process meant that some aspects of production would begin while testing of other parts was in progress.[68]

The result, in Packard's view, was high costs, weapons that often did not fit the needs of the service, and a dependence on paper which made the services rely on simulation rather than the actual performance of a prototype of the system to be purchased. Simply calling for prototyping did not remove all the complexity of modern weapons acquisition. It did, however, signal an uneven shift toward less paperwork, toward more latitude on the part of the contractor seeking to meet more general (and hence less detailed) requirements, and toward competitive "fly-offs" for final model selection. Added to this was an attempt to build weapons more within the state of the art—that is, requiring few, if any, costly efforts to achieve technological breakthroughs. In fact, design-to-cost was one method of procurement in which meeting cost specifications was supposed to be the paramount requirement to be met by a manufacturer.[69]

Such ideals do not correspond exactly to reality, for paperwork and simulations still exist. The manufacturers' latitude was severely restricted by the group most likely to lose from contractor discretion, the civilian technicians, whose role was to watch over development and production as part of teams stationed at work sites. Cost, on the other hand, became a crucial issue in the development of the Army's latest fighter helicopter, the advanced attack helicopter (AAH), under consideration since 1971. On August 10, 1972, the day the Army announced cancellation of the Cheyenne helicopter, it also announced the start of the AAH program. The process of moving toward the realization of a new fighter helicopter included procedures and paperwork—a series of transactions involving Army and Defense Department military and civilian officials and various aircraft manufacturers. The competition was narrowed to the YAH-63 helicopter produced by Bell Helicopter, a Textron Company, and the YAH-64 of the Hughes Helicopter Division of the Summa Corporation. These aircraft were flown for the first time in the fall of 1975, and were turned over to the Army for evaluation in May 1976. The decision made in November of that year was a winner-take-all victory for the YAH-64. Hughes' selection of John Kerr as its project director was symbolic: Kerr was there when "Hap" Arnold and "Dutch" Kindelberger initiated with a handshake the development of the P-51 fighter plane, a World War II success story in the tradition of contractor autonomy and development by prototyping.

Of course, today's industries have no such freedom. Daily telephone calls from the plants by members of the largely civilian Army-Department of Defense teams to their supervisors in Saint Louis circumscribe the latitude of the corporate developer. These technicians represent one aspect of a development which started with the calling in of Ramo-Wooldridge as consultants by the govenment to assist the Atlas missile program.[70] Very few, if any, military officers have the expertise to deal with the intricate technology of modern weapons development. It is the new cadre of Defense Department civilian experts who, by converting expertness into indispensibility, hold the balance of power between the uniformed services and the industrial suppliers. It has become a stable bureaucracy of relatively permanent specialists mediating between companies and services faced with unsettling personnel turnover.

An additional development should be noted. Helicopters have gone the way of both organization and equipment in the modern era: they have become increasingly specialized. Now there are in various stages of planning and development armed helicopters which cannot transport non-weapons-related cargo, a utility helicopter not meant for the attack role (UTTAS), advanced scout helicopters (ASH) designed for reconnaissance, and a hoped-for heavy-lift helicopter (HLH) for those tasks beyond the capacity of UTTAS. Much of the flying in these aircraft will have to be done by highly skilled technicians; in all probability many pilots will be warrant officers rather than commissioned officers. Now some new officers are expressing the desire for their own branch within the Army so that they will not have to be qualified in both aviation and a separate Army specialty.[71] One might anticipate that in the not too distant future one will observe rivalry between UTTAS helicopter pilots and ASH pilots and their respective supporters in the civil-military bureaucracy, and perhaps even in Congress. In fact, with the demise of the symbolically threatening Cheyenne, one might hypothesize reduced or contained Air Force hostility to Army aviation, with emphasis on interservice symmetrical bargaining relationships or joint activities. It may well be that the most intense rivalries will be neither interservice nor intraservice nor interindustrial, but rather intrabureaucratic, involving the increasingly potent civilian experts within each service.

The Future of the Army

We must tarry a bit longer to ponder the fate of the United States Army. It has been severely criticized for its conduct of the war in Southeast Asia.

Some of its most prominent middle-level officers, including Colonels David Hackworth, Anthony Herbert, and Edward King and Majors Josiah Bunting and Edward Deagle, have left the Army at mid-career—a decision made by men who would in many ways rather be in the service than on the outside. Some officers who have chosen not to exit—for example, Colonel William Hauser—have nevertheless exercised their option to voice their displeasure with the state of the Army.[72] Other complaints about the Army are well known: it is underdisciplined; its soldiers are mercenaries; and the officer corps has lost its morality in the mad scramble for promotion known as ticket punching, lost its credibility through cost overruns and the failure to produce victory, and lost its honor in tainted connections to the military-industrial complex, contacts secured through sinecures after retirement by the most useful or accommodating officers. So say the critics.

But as long as there is a mission to perform, it would, I suspect, be premature to pronounce the death sentence on the Army, despite the message of Colonel King's book, which is pointedly titled *Death of the Army: A Pre-Mortem*.[73] The missions of both the Air Force and the Navy have been threatened by technological developments and detente.[74] Ironically, air mobility and international developments, especially in the Middle East and Latin America, may merge to provide the Army with a modernized version of its traditional mission, land combat.[75] The combination of mission, outlook, and professional identity is, I believe, too deeply embedded to be expunged by a reversal, even one as serious as Vietnam. Even the contaminating effects of postwar policy-making duties and technological advances are not certain to exterminate the tradition of duty, honor, country. Long-held values and the attitudes they generate are hard to eradicate. With a return to either popular indifference or popular esteem, the Army may be sufficiently removed from external buffeting to get on with its business and be morally renewed, as it has been militarily reanimated by Army aviation.

The phenomena we have observed throughout this study suggest a particular pattern. What features of this pattern can we distinguish as regularities in organizational behavior and bureaucratic politics? And what do these developments mean for civil-military relations in a democracy? It is to these questions that we now turn.

Chapter 7 | **ANALYTIC RECAPITULATION**

At this point it seems appropriate to retrace our steps in order to further clarify our findings. The twentieth-century achievement of powered flight fundamentally altered the nature of weaponry available to military forces. When the Air Force, an American military service whose special province was aviation, became established, other services became clients or continued to control their own, previously secured aviation. The schism with the Air Force was viewed in certain quarters of the Army as an unnatural division. In the past, people had spoken of the mission of the various services. Now a technical function, flying, rather than control of the air, had become a mission for one service, the Air Force, thereby depriving the Army of control of a tool needed to accomplish its mission. Accomplishment of mission is no small consideration for institutions, and for the military institution, where failure could be a matter of national survival and life or death of comrades or self, the need for successful mission completion was especially intense.

At the moment of bifurcation, forces were unleashed which provided motive and opportunity for those who favored the Army's control of its own aviation. Earlier, the Artillery branch of the Army had begun to demonstrate the utility of Army aviation to those who would be receptive. These demonstrations continued, but were modulated because of several constraints placed on open opposition to the Air Force's virtual monopoly of aviation, a monopoly which, while it excluded the Navy and Marine Corps flying, included aircraft whose function was to support the Army.

There were a number of limits on manifest opposition: the power of the Air Force in presidential, bureaucratic, and congressional politics; the Air Force's technological supremacy in aviation matters; the inhibition of possibly jeopardizing national security (which, often though imperfectly, tended to reduce overt policy disagreements); the mixed performance by the

Air Force in support of the Army which was not sufficiently intolerable to induce open revolt; concern that the Air Force and others concentrated on aviation tasks other than close support, which produced a "who cares about us?" attitude; the acquiescence of certain Army leaders in the existing state of affairs; and the general lack of popular support for a significant change in the status quo, whether for reasons of apathy, ignorance, or acceptance of the Air Force's doctrine.

In such a situation, Army aviation became the province of a small group of pilots supported to varying extents by influential elements in the Army and buoyed up by the realization of fairly widespread dissatisfaction in the Army with the overall performance of the Air Force. During this period, the monopoly of the Air Force was broken, and a loose association of technicians committed to some kind of aviation for the Army, both to secure their positions and to better accomplish the Army's mission, was formed. But these aviators were indeed on tap, not on top. Their low position in the military hierarchy restricted some opportunities to promote their cause but enhanced others. It seemed implausible to many that a group of Artillery spotter pilots and liaison flyers could permanently alter the course of military events. Yet their presence served as a reminder to these same concerned Army officials of what might have been, had the Army controlled its own aviation. Further, each aviator was able to encourage such thinking, not by direct challenge, but by simply performing his duties. Most foot soldiers might not have cared about who flew the planes, but their resentment at not getting what they wanted in the way of support provided a matrix in which Army aviation could grow. By the end of World War II, enough aviators had been produced to provide a cadre for future use and to create in the other branches of the Army a desire for their own pilots. Yet the end of the war could have marked the end of this line of development of Army aviation.

As all parts of the Army were consolidated, many aviators left the service. Since the Army's only source of technological aviators was the Artillery branch, a concerted effort to stop the growth of aviation might have wiped these pilots out through discouragement and attrition. Such an effort would have required that the Air Force make a demonstrably serious effort to perform air support functions effectively. Demonstrated reassurances of air support might have reduced the opposition of those in power within the Army to the disestablishment or diminution of Army aviation. Further, the aviators constituted a distinct species of soldier; the career pattern they followed kept them from the generality of job assignments that permitted an officer to achieve high rank—it was a career pattern that at first located them conspicuously, hence dangerously, in the Artillery branch. Thus they had a sense of mission; a novel technique by which to advance their cause and the cause of their organization; and a distinctive identity, as well as a shared identity with other soldiers.

Despite the threats posed by Army aviation, its opponents did not obliterate it. The Air Force, for one, did not move in for the kill. Its very strength at the close of the World War II (enhanced enormously by the strategic implications of air-delivered atomic bombs) made some of its top officials view Army aviation as little more than an irritant not worth bothering with when considering global defense problems. Such division of attitude and deflection of concern allowed the few lingering aviators to set up their own relatively inconspicuous bases of operations. These small efforts seemed modest, but they provided the foundation upon which the aviation movement would be built. Through the National Security Act of 1947, the Army acquired the right to some aviation that was organic to its units and appropriate for its needs. Thus Congress granted a charter for Army aviation that could be removed only by legislative action or a willingness of high-level officers to give up something that was being given to them. Though some Army officers feared schismatic pressure from the new aviators, others could not turn down the chance for any asset that was of potential use in combat and in their struggle with the Air Force for resources. Further, certain aviators could exploit their new positions in the Pentagon for the advantage of Army aviators and Army aviation. These men were not typical soldiers. They risked the future of their careers by staying with aviation, since they were aware of the traditional generalist preference policy of promotion. Yet in some important ways they had little choice. Already closely identified with aviation, the chances for most of these technicians to advance were associated with the elevation of aviation to branch status, which would require high-level soldier-technicians.

One might discern here some evidence that the technological tide brought with it the wave of the future. The aviators' strategy was to further institutionalize Army aviation by obtaining places in the Army staff and by acquiring additional assets. Only a few envisioned the Army providing much of its own air support, and only a few preferred a non-branch organizational arrangement. It is not surprising that Robert R. Williams was one who was optimistic, since he had the West Point credentials to personally benefit from the expansion of aviation beyond a technical specialty. Further, as a West Pointer, he was acquainted with broader questions of military strategy and saw many of the combat potentialities of ground-commanded aviation. It is also not surprising that West Pointers Gavin and Hutton stressed aviation employment in this musings on the future of warfare. Yet it was not until the Korean War that the Army aviators had a chance to show their abilities in roles other than spotting and liaison—particularly in medical evacuation.

Efforts to resolve roles and missions questions between the Army and the Air Force continued at the top level. Since some Army leaders could see the possibilities of Army aviation and believed that roles calling for such potential should be theirs, air support appeared recurrently on the agenda. Top politics involved the exchange method: give the Army a little here, but limit them in another area. This was fine for bargaining-oriented officials, but it did not satisfy the aviators or some of their colleagues. As the Air Force continued to disappoint the Army in war, more supporters were created. Further, entrenchment in the Pentagon bureaucracy allowed pro-aviation thinking to "bubble up" on occasion into the upper councils of the Army.

Aviation resembled other "branches" in that it had close ties with some manufacturers and got congressional support from certain hometown congressmen who wanted more for their districts, and in 1957 it even became the raison d'être of a "backstop" interest group, the Army Aviation Association of America.[1] In addition, aviation had the ability to win the support of non-aviatiors, people who recognized that accomplishing the Army's mission was a public good.[2] This kind of thinking made aviation adaptable to other interests as well as an interest in and of itself. It was not an organization. It was a movement with several bases; aviators, who supplied the technological know-how and manpower, and thinkers, who saw the applicability of that power in resolving the nagging questions of close air support and mobility, were major early advocates. Some support was forthcoming from an elite that on the one hand feared and resisted the movement's potential, and on the other saw its possibilities. Further, in its manifest opposition to Air Force supremacy, CAVEAT struck a nerve not only with top political Army leaders but with aggrieved lower- and middle-participant soldiers. "Anything to help the G.I." was a popular theme—especially among GI's. Still, directives limiting the activities of Army aviation descended the bureaucratic stairs, and still, without contumacy, these activities were extended. A crucial question about this process must be asked: Why did the the Army leadership not quash or control aviation?

Let me suggest some answers: (1) At the top level of a joint hierarchy, yet under some civilian control, the Army elite was accustomed to operating on the bargaining principle. Extinction of opponents was left for the other type of battlefield. (2) Aviation had become part of the system. It is hard to dislodge long-standing system components. Like any organism, the system adapts to new realities, with new situations, new lines of communication, authority, and logistics, and new expectations being created in the process. (3) Aviation was useful. Generals enjoyed their little liaison Piper Cubs. (4) It was an asset with a quantifiable value. Like a "free" pedigreed puppy, one dwells on its value, not on what it will consume. (5) The aviation movement was diversified and had no organizational center. It continued to spread its influence, thereby making it harder and harder to root out. (6) Insurgents stayed low and were therefore a hard target to attack. They were low both in status in the hierarchy and in posture. (7) Many of the insurgents were aviation specialists. Their lengthy training made them difficult to replace, especially en masse, and their specialized skills and language functioned like a protective mantle. (8) Both top Army leaders and their Air Force counterparts spent much of their time and energy battling one another over missile allocations. Each elite was thereby significantly diverted from CAVEAT noncompliance.

Perhaps most important are the two remaining reasons for the failure to stop Army aviation. (9) Tenacity was essential for their success: insurgents are men of mission, persisters hard to dislodge. (10) There was a special advantage for the Army elite in maintaining Army aviation—aviation was a goad to the Air Force, and it could be a factor in rivalry situations. In the world of allocation politics, Army aviation could be a blue chip, if played astutely.

Opportunities change over time. The once-weak promoters of Army aviation made a tactical decision that must have been motivated by a strong sense of mission plus a keen political insight. It was a decision that rent the movement, but did not destroy it. In essence, some early pilots decided to yield much of the benefits to be derived from an enormously successful Army aviation to others in order to obtain aviation of grand magnitude. It was a painful decision; it was a political decision; it was a bureaucratic decision. It was not a predetermined decision. Had there been a successful effort to establish aviation as a branch, the qualities of a social movement would have given way to those of an internal bureaucratic interest group. Instead, its movement aspects were retained when they were most important—at the time when it passed the takeoff point of exponential growth.

Here, I would like to offer a biological analogy. There is an ecological theory which suggests that the numbers of species grew very slowly in the earliest period of life on this planet.[3] One species dominated the land. What was needed was some opening to provide a foothold to a species different from the dominant one. Once the minority species attained a tiny foothold and caught on, it began to expand. The resulting competition between species diversified the environment and ultimately changed it. It seems that internal movements in a bureaucracy might be thought of in this light. A species like Army aviation must take hold within an established bureaucracy over a long period of time before it can proliferate. One must not carry this analogy too far, however, for the Army was already diversified internally; moreover, its established values and procedures had been thrown into turmoil by post-

World War II events, creating the turbulent environment described in Chapter 3. I would hypothesize that the development of many movements follows the sigmoid curve often used to describe other population developments; that is, slow growth at first, quicker growth at a later point, then geometric growth.[4] Still later, populations reach a steady state and eventually decline (though they may not die, and thus each curve is not perfectly symmetrical). Much as in fighting the spread of a communicable disease, efforts to stamp out a movement have the highest probability of success when undertaken early, before the movement reaches it most rapid growth stage. After that it is too late.

This growth is not dependent on charisma. The Army aviators were by no means in the thrall of charismatic leadership; rather, they made good use of opportunistic, politically astute, and properly credentialed officers. In deciding to allow into the movement senior officers marked by others for positions of power, the direction of Army aviation was set. The probability of creating a separate Army aviation branch declined sharply as the up-and-coming star officers (and their constituencies) were co-opted into CAVEAT. These men would become emissaries deeply involved with aviation and powerful enough to do something for it and for themselves as aviators (though not willing to create a branch separate from their own component). Combining generalist and specialist credentials made for bureaucratic dynamite. Much as an older image of love depicted the woman yielding so that both she and her partner would benefit, many of the aviators subordinated themselves to the West Point-trained elite, allowing them to carry the cause forward by means of their own personal successes. Thus, when the civilian leaders were ready for Army aviation, Army aviation was ready for them. Its utility was to be tested by its supporters—surely a convenient device for assuring affirmative evaluation—but who else could test it? Aviation had the cream of the generalist and specialist elites. A super social circle sharing similar interests and ideas had become a super political circle with power in the Washington bureaucracy, on Capitol Hill, and in the Army itself.[5] Middle elites had become upper-middle elites. Hamilton Howze was the Establishment man *par excellence*. As Director of Army Aviation and head of the board that was to bear his name, his views were greeted with a certain amount of respect and consideration. The logic of the Howze Board's report was old; the political situation was new. The self-fulfilling prophecy of the 11th Air Assault Division's tests and McNamara's views on mobility (plus his insistence upon analytical systems quantification) merged in Army aviation.

CAVEAT could simulate with the best of them. Still, it took the ultimate test, combat, to finally establish the necessity for an Army with aviation support—a need which no one ever disputed but which was not met by the Air

Force. Filling the technopolitical vacuum, Army aviation found it had certain technical and political responsibilities. McNamara's requirement of centralization and quantification in weapons procurement removed much of the flexibility from technical development. The Army was largely dependent on civilian technicians to deal with sophisticated industrial suppliers. Politically it became appropriate for the Army aviation leaders to act like the top-politics officials they had become. Successful social movements must pay the price of success not only while ascending but at the top as well—congressional hearings, increased interest and scrutiny by civilian and military elites, tedious bargaining, and competition at various levels.

Here it was: Army aviation had moved from a mission-based insurgency to a competition-based establishment. It was an establishment at once too technical and not technical enough. Its technicality required specialist civilian technicians, who became extremely powerful in budget and other development decisions. It was not technical enough because the aviators' identity had become so diluted that many soldiers could become pilots, or so at times it seemed. Aviation moved beyond mere acceptance; it became chic. Then, like all fashionable things, it became almost passé. Its ultimate acceptance brought a nonchalance which made helicopters "no big thing" except as a budget item to be negotiated over, like tanks and trucks. While it was in vogue, many Army aviation supporters succumbed to the wiles of the Air Force psychology of technology. They too wanted bigger, faster, higher-flying, longer-range aircraft, and what they got was a dose of top politics and technological overreaching that ended with the termination of the long-desired Cheyenne and the abolition of the Army Aviation Directorate. Various aviation headquarters, those political hard points, were abolished, and aviation functions were dispersed.

There is an additional conceptual scheme one might use to gain a better understanding of the phenomena under scrutiny, a view from a different level so to speak. Think of the subelements of the movement as social circles.[6] By doing so, one is alerted to the intellectual connections and the questions raised by this aspect of modern social relations. Though this working definition may not fit our case perfectly, it may be thought of as an ideal type suitably heuristic to provide insights at this level of analysis.

A Social circle has three defining characteristics, two of which are positive and one, negative: (1) A Circle may have a chain or network of indirect interaction such that most members of a circle are linked to other members, at least through a third party. It is thus not a pure face to face group. (2) The network exists because members of the circle share common interest—political or cultural. (3) The Circle is not formal—i.e., there are: (a) no clear leaders, although there may be central figures; (b) no clearly defined goals for the circle, though it almost always has some implicit functions; (c) no definite rules which determine modes of interaction, though there are often customary relationships; and (d) no distinct criteria of membership.[7]

Perhaps it would be helpful if we were to conceptualize early aviators as a largely utilitarian social circle made up of people providing a service in exchange for status and income. This social circle was joined by a power circle, the West Point stars of the future who sought control of the apparatus of the Army and who, as they acquired the skill of the aviators, superseded them in the inner circle of the movement. A third circle, largely cultural, was made up of high-ranking military intellectuals who were drawn together by valuational and cognitive goals. A fourth major element of the movement was the integrative circle of those who shared the wartime experiences of less-than-adequate air support. Each of these circles actually has additional characteristics and hence is pure only as an analytical type. Furthermore, the circles overlap. But it is this overlapping that suggests how the groups sharing the sense of mission amalgamated sufficiently to form a super circle. Though there is relatively little evidence, I would like to continue speculating on how the circles were brought together through weak ties.

The strength of a tie is defined as "a (probably linear) combination of amount of time, the emotional intensity, the intimacy (mutual confiding), and the reciprocal services which characterize the tie."[8] One might suspect that social groups, like communities with strong internal ties, tend to keep such things as information and innovation within a relatively small group, while weak ties tend to serve as channels for diffusion, reaching a larger number of people and traversing a greater social distance. Likewise, political prospects can be strengthened by the "bridging" function of weak ties, leading from one inside group to an outside group with similar interests. Since weak ties such as those among soldiers changing assignments did not strengthen the internal cohesion of each group, one might expect that such groups would be very vulnerable to attack. Paradoxically, weak ties were used to disseminate information, attitudes, and innovations themselves, thereby providing reassurance of the existence of allies for the long struggle. Further, some who played bridging roles were important actors in the aviation movement. Thus, had the aviators not been required by personnel policy to go forth in different directions from aviation schools and to change duty stations, their social circle might never have developed into a social movement. Even differences in rank and status could be spanned by the values passed on through weak ties. Ironically, it was the aviators' very fragmentation, a policy later employed for the West Point initiates, that gave these circles the strength to coalesce enough to form a movement capable of a successful insurgency.

151 / Analytic Recapitulation

What I am suggesting is that there are "organizations" which are not organizations. In some ways they behave like organizations, yet in other ways they are distinct. They manage the tasks of promoting an idea, making contacts through weak ties, establishing commensal relationships with powerful hosts, and riding the roller coaster of internal bureaucratic politics.

It further suggest that Albert O. Hirschman's model of response to decline in organizations can be modified to include insurgency as well as exit and voice.[9] In an organization where people have a strong reason for not leaving, and where voice (outspoken complaint) is considered a violation of an important norm, interests may not be aggregated; rather, they may be diffused. Insurgents generally do not act in concert, under leadership, on a regular basis. Such behavior would constitute one tactic among many possible combinations that also include individualistic styles. Tactical variability is a characteristic of mission- and loyalty-motivated insurgency because it allows the organization that needs recuperation (the main object of exit and voice, according to Hirschman) to be resuscitated from within, but quietly, not loudly.

There are other types of bureaucratic movements, but because of their short duration they are not really social movments. Mutinies and strikes, though often similar to insurgency in their noncompliance behaviors, usually end quickly.[10] Insurgencies tend to persist. In considering the endurance of insurgency, one should keep in mind the notion of loyalty, a concept stressed by Hirschman in his discussion of exit and voice. Loyalty has about it an element of rational calculation; it is not blind faith. There is a chance to revivify the organization to which one gives one's loyalty. Hopelessness and loyalty are mutually exclusive terms.[11] Thus, when exit and voice are difficult, loyalty may be operative for those who care about the organization and its purposes. Additional signs of improvement through insurgency fuel the rational fires of expectation of advancement of cause and self. Some, like Billy Mitchell, make their case outside the organization. Some, like Hyman Rickover, seem to be solitary advocates. But there are times when a cause is more effectively advanced without heroes or publicity and only when the time is ripe. Insurgency requires no charismatic leader. Therefore, attempts to co-opt the charismatic leader in an effort to absorb protest in such situations are irrelevant.[12] The movement is so diffuse and so strongly motivated that it simply rolls on.

The Model

How may we make use of the insights obtained into the development of Army aviation? Earlier it was stated that distinctive aspects of the military set it apart from the civilian sphere; at the same time, similarities to many nonmilitary situations, especially in the public realm, suggest the analytical utility of a model derived from this study. The crucial factor regarding the military is its richly normative quality, which makes relevant for the individual officer the values of duty, honor, and country. When powerful ideals such as these are combined with the work activities of soldiers—activities which have an impact on their identity, if not on their very lives—a sense of mission is usually to be expected. When formal authority like that associated with the hierarchy in a military organization is asserted by those presiding in traditional ways over policies of declining utility, especially where a sense of mission is present, the potential for insurgent bureaucratic politics exists. Similar situations are conceivable in certain political, religious, journalistic, or even academic organizations characterized by a pronounced sense of mission.[13]

If such a structure contains a technically aware middle-level elite concerned about the future accomplishments of the organization's goals as they observe its failure to adapt to a turbulent environment, members of this stratum might well terminate their association, or complain about the course of events, or both. But if such actions were to have adverse consequences, these same members might try to change policy, promote organizational survival, and help themselves and others, perhaps especially those with skills similar to their own. When much of this activity takes place independently, it is often opposed by those in power. Occasionally in such cases, those who favor change seek out like-minded individuals or potential allies. Such insurgency therefore includes individual and combined action.

Driven by mission, yet restrained in certain cases by political sensitivity, these insurgents may have to undertake patiently the conversion of other individuals with whom they have often had no preceding attachments or only weak ties, but who share the activists' concern for the mission and welfare of the organization and its members. Such insurgent do not seek to overthow the system, but neither are they merely another elite seeking to "circulate" up to the position of greatest power. Rather, they are loyal insurgents trying to help their organization as they help themselves. Nevertheless, there are times when noncompliance must take precedence over the norm of obedience.

Usually those in positions at the top will endeavor to arrest insurgency, interpreting the activities as threatening to their power, position, and point of view. If the movement is small, the organization's formal leadership may try to punish or dismiss the insurgents. If it has grown to a certain size or performs some useful function, the elite may seek to corral it, preferably in an exposed position, perhaps by controlling its resources or numbers. If there

153 / Analytic Recapitulation

is a charismatic leader within the movement, the organizational elite may seek to co-opt him with a separate division for his followers and a share in the decision making for himself, thereby absorbing the protest. But a true bureaucratic social movement is not dependent on charismatic leadership. Though leadership is important, qualities such as tenacity and political skill ideally permeate into the nooks and crannies of the organization.

Finally, there may come a time when a movement is successful; the top elite is pursuing the goals of the movement, the organization is resuscitated, and several of the movement's members are in positions of prominence. One would anticipate that the tactics and strategy that served the insurgent movement would no longer be appropriate for those who have become established and have entered the realm of top politics. Perhaps the leaders of a successful movement who did not comply with the directives of their former superiors on the grounds that such regulations were based on bargains rather than on the authority of mission may now themselves become participants in the exchange process.

There is no guarantee of success for such a movement, though variables such as perseverance, bureaucratic adroitness, the need of the Establishment leaders for the talents of the insurgents, and so forth, bear on victory. It does seem, however, that containment of such movements once they are under way becomes increasingly difficult after a certain stage of growth is reached. Better later than never is not an applicable axiom when dealing with social movements.

An organization's division of labor by mission (in the sense of task alone) or function, process or product, is not the only crucial structural variable for this study. A more significant variable is how much structure is appropriate for certain kinds of complex organizations, especially large-scale government bureaucracies. Is the presence of a relatively unstructured bureaucratic social movement which aims at organizational revitalization and the self-promotion of its members a valuable thing? For example, does such a movement spur individual creativity or produce a societal good? And, if one is to make value judgments at all, one may as well ask the big questions: What is the relevance of bureaucratic social movements to democracy in general, and in this context particularly, to civil-military relations?

A bureaucratic movement by definition brings *movement* within the bureaucratic structure. Movement members seek organizational revitalization, self-aggrandizement, assistance to those of like interests, and mission accomplishment.

Organizational improvement seems to be a useful societal goal. All the effort poured into an organization in its creation and development might be seen as wasted effort if the organization were to wither. Nevertheless, why keep alive an organization whose time has passed? Why struggle to maintain an old organization if a new one might be more efficient in bringing about desired changes? Does not organizational resuscitation have an inherently conservative bias? Further, the choice of which organization is to be strengthened should in part determine the value of the effort: Most would not want to save organizations with noxious goals.

As for self-interest, the prevalence of the achievement ethic in America is widely recognized. But is personal gain to be founded on failure to comply with lawful regulation? Merit is surely to be based on some criterion other than, or at least in addition to, political acumen. Aiding similar colleagues is acceptable. The notion that elements of bureaucracy represent collectivities in the population could be raised to a moral imperative to include bureaucratic groupings. Perhaps the group basis of politics and social action in society as a whole is naturally carried over into the administrative mechanism. One might note, however, that bureaucrats are expected to have interests other than protection of group, and that time spent in such activity might be more productively spent on organizational goals, though, given the reality of politics, this scarcely seems a likely possibility. One may suggest, if not assert, that a "neutral" bureaucracy can hardly apply regulations evenhandedly if it is torn by internal groups, each with its own perspective.

Considerations about how to make a bureaucracy representative of some or all of the population are also intimately related to efforts to understand bureaucratic accountability. It is here that the notion of the accomplishment of mission strikes home and the concept of compliance comes into play. If organizations, especially public ones, are pursuing a policy that dooms the organization and perhaps even threatens the nation and its highest values, must not those who perceive the threat and have the means act to prevent disaster? How bleak life would be if despairing analysts were to be accurate in their forecast of a world dominated by an ever-expanding, ever-more-powerful, impenetrable, stolid bureaucracy ineluctably clearing a path through human rights with its implacable bulk. Caught up in its daily rituals, such a public bureaucracy would, in the name of economy and efficiency, order and rationality, rigidify everything it touched with its cold-as-death extremities.

What then of the alternative? Here recognizing large-scale complex organizations as requisites for modernity, one might hope that some life could exist within the bureaucracy, that functionaries could develop as persons, and that complex organization might become one of society's methods of adaptation to rapid change in the postmodern world. Bureaucracy itself could take the lead rather than follow political tutelage in moving to meet the challenges of the future.

Alas, this picture is tragically flawed. In the ideal republic, bureaucracy is supposed to be inert, a transmission belt applying the will of the people as manifested and legitimated by the legislative processes. This view denies that the bureaucracy or elements thereof can act for their own ends or for the ends which they, rather than legitimate political officeholders, deem appropriate. Soldiers' noncompliance with the orders of civilians challenges the very logic of civilian control of the military, a key principle of American democracy. Who is to say that one group's view of what is right can override the legitimate constitutional processes established for policy making?

When made by a technologically oriented core group, such decisions are especially threatening, for often such persons' view of their mission is inextricably linked to their technical bent. The mixture of mission authority and technological orientation has already emerged in at least one terrifying variation. Bertram Gross has considered the exploitation of Nazi Minister for Armaments and War Production Albert Speer's often blind devotion to his task.[14] Gross argues that had Nazi evil simply been banal, it would have been less potent:

Speer and his thousands of associates were like Eichmann in only one respect: they felt no moral responsibility for the consequences of their acts. They were also immensely different. They were *not* blindly obedient bureaucrats operating in accordance with civil service norms. Under Speer's brilliant guidance, they established new norms of collegial rather than bureaucratic decision making. They operated in an atmosphere of open discussion and debate (often referred to jokingly as "reintroducing the parliamentary system"), and of macrosystem interchange rather than closed-system hierarchy. Instead of blindly accepting orders, they opposed commands that interfered with war production and proposed new policies for all-out war mobilization, including the more efficient use of slave labor from conquered countries. *Their evil was not banal. In the "hurrah words" of modern management technology, it was creative, adaptive, and innovative.* If there had been more Speers in German society, Hitler's forces might have triumphed.[15]

Those who doubt the timeliness of these observation need only be reminded of the 1975 revelations of CIA technical officials' failure to follow presidential orders to destroy lethal and illegal shellfish toxin,[16] or of the 1974 noncompliance concerning the production of deadly nerve gases within the Army itself.[17]

There is another possible explanation for activities such as these. They may in fact be the result of enthrallment with technology without regard to mission. This fascination with technology is likely to be an enduring phenomenon. After all, technology is perceived by many to be the driving force in the American economy. Further, technology has become a panacea as military planners, seeking to replace men with machines, justify this automation as a life-saving device. In the not-too-distant future, soldiers may carry into battle miniaturized computers that will provide access to the means of movement, communication, and firepower. To what extent does this individual resemble a master of modern technology? To what extent does he harken back to the ancient soldier carrying his gods into the fray?

Technology, it seems, can be worshiped, enjoyed, respected, admired—even loved. It may provide job opportunities or reasons for not doing the job. As institutions face the confusions of the modern era, their leaders may find it easier to seek after a new bit of hardware rather than confront underlying problems. It is quite clear that many modern organizations find their attention dominated by gadgetry which by-passes considerations of mission or purpose. While in some cases the technology is appropriate, in others what develops is an inappropriate fixation on technology—technomania—with a corresponding technopathology contaminating administrative structures.

Why is this the case? What can be done about it? Technology is a means. In the business world the end is often productivity, which can be measured. In the public sector, however, the ends are more complex—the reduction or resolution of social problems. These goals are elusive, and facing them is difficult; it often requires reference to first principles or higher values. Bureaucracy is the organizational means for dealing with modern public dilemmas: complex organizations for complex problems. But the bureaucratic solution is to fragment the problem into manageable portions. Applying bureaucratic rationality to parts of problems may drive out the value-rationality that is needed if we are to see the whole problem in context. Experts in the bureaucracy become experts in smaller and smaller parts of the problem, often losing sight of ends. The natural attractiveness of technology comes to the fore for those who do not feel the need to overcome an injustice, master a hardship, pursue a mission. Values are fragile and intangible; hardware is tangible and offers challenges and a mystique. As the mission retreats, people seek control of the environment—but to what end? It is this loss of a sense of purpose, loss of willingness and ability to see the big picture, that is most distressing.

What can be done about the technological trivialization of our public organizations? Certainly no final solutions are available ("final solution" itself having an ominous technological resonance), but I offer the following suggestions: The place of values in education must be enhanced. People in positions of leadership should demonstrate a familiarity with value questions and humane concerns. Continuing education along broad perspectives is desirable. Consideration must be given to nonhierarchical forms of organization such as collegial or citizen participation structures. Frequent use of value-related material in evaluations is important. Periodic reconsideration of the purposes for which an organization was instituted should take place.

Politics should be exalted as a vocation, keeping in mind that policy leaders often come from outside the bureaucracy and should possess the characteristics of passion, patience, and perspective. Despite its potential dangers, citizenship training should be stressed. Personnel might be rotated more frequently, sacrificing some productivity for breadth of perspective. Tales of technopathology should be part of the educational process of every official and probably every citizen. A system of rewards should be sought that affirms the special utility of value perspectives.

It is important to remember that any program composed of some of the above elements would be experimental. Social and political problems often prove intractable, and methods in dealing with them must be given a chance to be evaluated. The very willingness to experiment in these programs provides protection against closed-mindedness in dealing with technology.

Thus we find that there are dangers in allowing technology to be influenced by the sense of mission if the goals of that sense of mission are evil. At the same time, we see that it is imperative that we not let technology function without regard to purpose, lest technology itself become an imperative.

Despite these insights, I do not want to leave the question quite yet. I linger for two reasons. First, the traditional democratic ideal may be changing, partly because political science research is beginning to describe and more or less endorse bureaucratic politics in democracy. Second, it is simply not satisfying to cease further consideration of the possible benefits that could accrue from insurgency. Pluck, valor, political adroitness, and vision must not be without meaning in modern organizations. These qualities are not restricted by nature to a wafer-thin upper strata in government or other organizations. An increasingly turbulent world environment suggests that ponderous organizations with plodding memberships will not adjust effectively in the interests of mankind. The basic values of law and regulation may not suffice to balance the scale of requirements for survival in the future. Perhaps in insurgency some may see that harbinger of future organizational developments wherein hierarchy will give way to new arrangements better suited to the needs of a given period.[18] For now, however, the tensions between bureaucratic regulation and the desires (in whatever form) for mission attainment and organizational renewal can be expected to persist.

Appendix 1 | **SELECTED MAJOR EVENTS IN THE HISTORY OF ARMY AVIATION**

Date		Event
1903	December 17	First flight of heavier-than-air, powered aircraft
1907		Aeronautical Division created in the Army Signal Corps
1914		Creation of Aviation Section in the Signal Corps
1917		Air Service established in the Army
1918		Air Service separated from the Signal Corps
1920		Army Reorganization Act passed by which the Air Service becomes a combat arm of the Army
1925		Court Martial of General Billy Mitchell begins
1926		Air Corps Act creates the Army Air Corps
1935		Creation of a General Headquarters Air Force commanded by an Army Air Corps officer
1939		Igor Sikorsky demonstrates a helicopter before Army Air Corps officials
1940	May	President Franklin D. Roosevelt calls for an Air Force of 50,000 planes
	August	Camp Beauregard, Louisiana, maneuvers in which light aircraft observe artillery fire
1941	February 18	William T. Piper, Sr., begins communication with Secretary of War Henry Stimson about the role of light aircraft
	Summer	Army obtains 20 light aircraft for ground-oriented missions
	June 20	Creation of the Army Air Forces
1942	June 6	Establishment of an organic Army aviation within the Army Ground Forces
1944	January 29	General H. H. Arnold sends a memorandum to General George C. Marshall requesting the discontinuation of organic Army aviation
1945	August	War Department allows five branches of the Army, in addition to Artillery, to have organic aviation
	December 7	Army Ground Forces Air Training School established
1947		National Security Act establishes the Air Force and guarantees an aviation component for the Army

Appendix 1

Date		Event
1948		Key West Agreement on roles and missions
1949		Defense reorganization
1950-53		Korean War spurs interest in helicopters
1951		G-3 section on Army aviation matters established in the Army staff
	October	First Pace-Finletter Agreement on roles and missions
1952	November	Second Pace-Finletter Agreement on roles and missions
1953		Defense reorganization
1954		First efforts to establish an Army aviation center at Fort Rucker under Brigadier General Carl I. Hutton
1954	November	Comprehensive Four-Year-Plan for Army aviation promulgated
1956	January	Major General Hamilton Howze becomes G-3 Staff Officer and later Director of the Army Aviation Division of the Army General Staff
	June	Lieutenant Colonel J. D. Vanderpool begins armed helicopter experimentation under the direction of General Hutton
	November	Secretary of Defense Charles Wilson's memorandum on roles and missions
1957		Sky Cav at Fort Benning
1960		Army Aircraft Requirements Review Board (the Rogers Board) appointed
1962		Air cav troop becomes part of the armored cavalry unit of the standard combat division
	May-September	Army Tactical Mobility Requirements Board (Howze Board) appointed
	October	Utility Tactical Transport Company goes to Vietnam
1963	January	Activation of the 11th Air Assault Division
1965	June	Conversion of the 11th Air Assault Division to the 2nd Infantry Division, then to the 1st Cavalry Division (Airmobile)
	August	1st Cavalry Division goes to Vietnam
1966	April	Johnson-McConnell agreement on the responsibility of each service for control and use of certain rotary- and fixed-wing aircraft
1969		First cancellation of the Cheyenne Helicopter
1970		Army has approximately 12,000 aircraft; Army Chief of Staff, William Westmoreland, receives his helicopter pilot's wings
1971	February	Operation Lam Son 719 calls into question the effectiveness of helicopters against modern anti-aircraft weapons
1971	February	Establishment of Close Air Support Review Group
1972	August 10	Army announces cancellation of Cheyenne and beginning of advanced attack helicopter program (AAHP)
1973		Army Aviation Directorate and Assistant Chief of Staff for Force Development (ACSFOR) disestablished in the midst of a major Army reorganization
1975	Fall	Rival prototypes of advanced attack helicopter tested
1976	Fall	Hughes YAH-64 selected as advanced attack helicopter
1978		Congressional struggle over consolidating Navy and Army undergraduate helicopter pilot training (UHPT)

Appendix 2 | **SELECTED AIRCRAFT SIGNIFICANT IN THE DEVELOPMENT OF ARMY AVIATION**

Designation	Nickname	Use	Type
Aircraft Used or Seriously Considered by the Army			
AH-1G	Huey Cobra	Gunship	RW
AH-56A	Cheyenne (AAFSS)	Attack (advanced aerial fire support system)	RW
ASH (proposed)		Advanced scout helicopter	RW
CH-37	Mohave	Medium tactical transport	RW
CH-47	Chinook, Hook	Medium-heavy tactical transport	RW
CH-54A	Sky Crane	Heavy lift	RW
CV-2	Caribou	Light transport	FW
CV-7	Buffalo	Medium transport	FW
G-91	Fiat Fighter	Light fighter	FW
H-13	Sioux	Observation, reconnaissance	RW
H-19	Chickasaw	Light tactical transport	RW
H-21	Shawnee	Light tactical transport	RW
H-23	Raven	Light tactical transport	RW
H-24	Choctaw	Light tactical transport	RW
HLH (proposed)		Heavy lift helicopter	RW
L-1	Grasshopper	Observation, reconnaissance	FW
L-2	Grasshopper Civilian "Challenger"	Observation, reconnaissance	FW
L-3	Grasshopper Civilian "Challenger"	Observation, reconnaissance	FW
L-4	Grasshopper Civilian "Cub"	Observation, reconnaissance	FW

Appendix 2

Designation	Nickname	Use	Type
L-5	Sentinel	Observation, reconnaissance	FW
L-6	Civilian "Cadet"	Observation, reconnaissance	FW
L-14		Observation, reconnaissance	FW
L-16	Champion	Observation, reconnaissance	FW
L-17	Navion	Utility	FW
L-18	Super Cub	Observation, reconnaissance	FW
L-19	Bird Dog	Observation, reconnaissance	FW
L-20	Beaver	Utility	FW
L-21	Super Cub	Training	FW
L-23	Seminole	Utility	FW
Model 309	King Cobra	Attack	RW
O-1	Bird Dog	Observation, reconnaissance	FW
OH-6	Cayeuse, Loch	Observation, reconnaissance	RW
OH-13	Sioux	Observation, reconnaissance	RW
OH-58A	Kiowa	Observation, reconnaissance	RW
OV-1	Mohawk	Observation, reconnaissance	FW
RH-12		Utility	RW
S-67	Blackhawk	Attack	RW
U1A	Otter	Utility	FW
UH-1A (HU-1, XH-40)	Iroquois (Huey)	Transport	RW
UH-1B	Iroquois (Huey)	Gunship	RW
UH-1H	Iroquois (Huey)	Transport	RW
XH-32A		Utility	RW
YAH-63	AAH	Alternative prototype advanced attack helicopter	RW
YAH-64	AAH	Alternative prototype advanced attack helicopter	RW
YH-32A		Prototype utility	
YUH-60A	UTTAS	Alternative prototype utility tactical transport aircraft system	RW
YUH-61A	UTTAS	Alternative prototype utility tactical transport aircraft system	RW

Non-Army Aircraft [a]

Designation	Nickname	Use	Type
A-7D	Corsair II	Attack	FW
A-7E (Navy)	Corsair II	Attack	FW
A-10	AX	Close air support	FW
AV-8 (Marines)	Harrier	Close air support	V/STOL
B-29	Superfortress	Bomber	FW
B-36	Peacemaker	Bomber	FW
B-52	Stratofortress	Bomber	FW
F-14 (Navy)	Tomcat	Fighter	FW
F-15	Eagle	Fighter	FW
F-16		Fighter	FW

Appendix 2

Designation	Nickname	Use	Type
F-100	Supersabre	Fighter-bomber	FW
F-105	Thunderchief	Fighter-bomber	FW
F-111	TFX	Fighter-bomber	MW
F-5E	Tiger	Fighter-bomber	FW
P-51	Mustang	Fighter	FW
R-5		Utility	RW
VS-300		Utility	RW
XR-4		Utility	RW
XR-6		Utility	RW

Note: FW=Fixed wing; RW=Rotary wing; V/STOL=Vertical/short takeoff and landing; MW=Movable wing (variable geometry).

[a] Air Force or Air Corps except where noted.

NOTES

Chapter 1

1. Colonel Wendell Blanchard and Colonel T. N. Dupuy, *The Almanac of World Military Power*, 2nd ed. (Dunn Loring, Va., and New York: T. N. Dupuy Associates and R. R. Bowker, 1972), pp. 8-15, 147-52.
2. William R. Corson, *The Betrayal* (New York: W. W. Norton, 1968), p. 81.
3. James Reston, "Divided Command in Saigon," *New York Times*, March 26, 1971, p. 39. Reston, like many other Americans, seems to be unable to differentiate between the Army and the Air Force: "Even within the ranks of the American expeditionary force, there are complaints of unequal sacrifices, for the burden is now falling on the U.S. Air Force, while the Army is holding the line and otherwise engaged in less risky assignments."
4. Drew Middleton's "Army Keeps Faith in Role of Copter," *New York Times*, March 11, 1971, p. 8, is striking because the *New York Times* in general did not indicate the service of the pilots who suffered most of the losses supporting the ARVN incursion into Laos.
5. Amitai Etzioni, *A Comparative Analysis of Complex Organizations: On Power, Involvement, and Their Correlates* (New York: Free Press, 1961), pp. 56-57. It will be interesting to observe the coercive aspects of military leadership as financial inducements rise in the all-volunteer American Army.
6. This seems to be a portion of the argument made by Samuel P. Huntington, *The Common Defense: Strategic Programs in National Politics* (New York: Columbia University Press, 1961), chap. 6.
7. Etzioni, *Complex Organizations*, pp. 56-57.
8. According to Charles J. Hitch, a former Defense Department Comptroller, "Virtually every attempt we have made to explain the inexorable logic of relating cost to military effectiveness seems to shatter on the argument–'Nothing but the best will do for our boys.'" *Decision Making for Defense* (Berkeley and Los Angeles: University of California Press, 1965), p. 43.
9. Rudyard Kipling, "Tommy," *Collected Verse of Rudyard Kipling* (Garden City, N.Y.: Doubleday, Page, 1920), pp. 37-38.
10. General Sir John Hackett, "The Armed Forces," in *Authority in a Changing Society*, ed. Clifford Rhodes (London: Constable, 1969), p. 152.
11. Seymour J. Deitchman has attempted such conflict-free analysis with mixed results. See *Limited War and American Defense Policy* (Cambridge: M.I.T. Press, 1964), p. vii.

166 / Notes to Chapter 1

12. Samuel P. Huntington, "Interservice Competition and the Political Roles of the Armed Services," *American Political Science Review* 55 (March 1961): 51, discusses the rise of proprietary issues as strategic issues declined during the fifties.

13. Ibid.

14. Harry Howe Ransom says that interservice rivalry has been "*the* prime characteristic" [italics added]. See, *Can American Democracy Survive Cold War?* (Garden City, N.Y.: Doubleday, Anchor Books, 1964), p. 79.

15. Michael Armacost lists his predecessors in *The Politics of Weapons Innovation: The Thor-Jupiter Controversy* (New York: Columbia University Press, 1969), pp. 4-5.

16. Ibid., Chap. 1.

17. Snow discusses the case of interpersonal rivalry between the two top science advisers to the British government, Sir Henry Tizard and F. A. Lindemann (Lord Cherwell). He elaborates on three major subcategories of closed politics—committee politics, hierarchical politics, and court politics. See *Science and Government* (Cambridge: Harvard University Press, 1960).

18. U.S., Joint Chiefs of Staff, *Dictionary of United States Military Terms for Joint Usage* (Washington, D.C.: Government Printing Office, August 1968), p. 138.

19. Since the name of the service that had primary responsibility for aviation changed during the period to be discussed, I have chosen names which I hope will be most clear.

20. Samuel P. Huntington, *The Soldier and the State: The Theory and Politics of Civil-Military Relations* (New York: Random House, Vintage Books, 1957), pp. 83-85.

21. Etzioni, *Complex Organizations*, p. 3.

22. The "congruent types" within which most organizations can be classified are referred to as predominantly coercive, predominantly utilitarian, and predominantly normative. See ibid., pp. 12-13, 87-88.

23. It would be well to note that there are significant examples of noncompliance in private and governmental (nonmilitary) settings. The following examples suggest the variety of possibilities.

Alvin Gouldner depicts the conditions in a gypsum mine where orders that interfered with the solidarity of the workers met with great resistance. While a new plant manager obtained compliance in the surface plant, his bureaucratizing rules were not obeyed underground, in the more dangerous mine. See *Patterns of Industrial Bureaucracy* (New York: Free Press, 1954).

Tyler Gatewood Kent, the U.S. Foreign Service officer assigned to the code room of the U.S. Embassy in London during the days preceding the fall of France, had access to the most secret messages exchanged between President Franklin Roosevelt and First Lord of the Admiralty, Sir Winston Churchill. Feeling that Roosevelt was trying to bring the United States into the war, a move Kent opposed, the young code room operative removed many copies of the most important documents in order to build a file on the Roosevelt-Churchill relationship. Kent "loaned" out pieces of his file to friends, and the information found its way into the hands of German intelligence. His exposure compromised the most secret Gray Code during the very weeks of the blitz into France. Kent insisted that his activities had nothing to do with espionage; he merely wanted to bring the papers to the attention of Congress in order to stop American participation in the European war. In governmental service, it appears that some noncompliance can approach treason. For the complete story see Ladislas Farago, *The Game of the Foxes: The Untold Story of German Espionage in the United States and Great Britain During World War II* (New York: David McKay, 1971), pp. 337-50.

24. Plato *Republic* 432A ff.

25. Machiavelli, *The Prince*, chap. 19.

26. Huntington, *The Soldier and the State*, p. 163.

27. Ibid.

28. Nicholas Harris Nicolas, *The Dispatches and Letters of Vice Admiral Lord Nelson, with Notes* (London: H. Colburn, 1845-46), 4: 308-9, cited in G. J. Marcus, *The Age of Nelson: The Royal Navy, 1793-1815* (New York: Viking Press, 1971), pp. 184-85.

29. Christopher Sykes, *Orde Wingate: A Biography* (Cleveland and New York: World Publishing, 1951), pp. 104-205.

30. Charles de Gaulle, *War Memoirs*, vol. 1, *The Call to Honor, 1940-1942*, trans. Joanthan Griffen (London: Collins, 1955), pp. 87-90.

31. The story is told in detail by Larry Collins and Dominque Lapierre, *Is Paris Burning?* (New York: Simon & Schuster, 1965).

32. For example, Richard Neustadt has devoted important parts of his *Presidential Power* (New York: John Wiley & Sons, 1960), pp. 123-46 *et passim*, to this matter while others, like John W. Spanier, have devoted entire volumes to the context and substance of the controversy. See Spanier's *The Truman-MacArthur Controversy and the Korean War* (Cambridge: Harvard University Press, Belknap Press, 1959).

33. "Banned Defoliant Ordered by Brass," *Nashville Tennessean*, November 22, 1970, sec. A, p. 2. "Orange," a mixture of equal parts of two widely used defoliants 2, 4-D (dichlorophenoxyacetic acid) and 2, 4, 5-T (trichlorophenoxyacetic acid), is discussed by Seymour Hersh, *Chemical and Biological Warfare: America's Hidden Arsenal* (Garden City, N.Y.: Doubleday, Anchor Books, 1969), p. 85.

34. "When the Landscape is the Enemy," *Newsweek*, August 7, 1972, pp. 24-26. "For bigger jobs, the U.S. turned to the 32-ton Rome Plow bulldozers. . . . As they ripped through the landscape, they piled precious top soil in heaps—leaving it to wash away with the next rain. Occasionally, moreover, the tractor operators exhibited a rather cavalier attitude toward the land. In Binh Long Province, some gouged a mile long image of the First Infantry Division's 'Big Red One' insignia into the earth."

35. "The Pressure of Command: Lavelle and His Raids," *Los Angeles Times*, October 1, 1972, sec. G, p. 5.

36. Dennis Wrong, "The Oversocialized Conception of Man in Modern Sociology," in *Sociological Theory: A Book of Readings*, ed. Lewis A. Coser and Bernard Rosenberg, 3rd ed. (New York: Macmillan, 1969), pp. 130-31.

37. "The Concept and Function of Ideology," pt. 1 of "Ideology," *The International Encyclopedia of the Social Sciences*, ed. David Sills 7 (1968): 66.

38. Ibid.

39. Huntington, *The Soldier and the State*, p. 61.

40. Ibid., pp. 63-74.

41. "Social Process and Power in a Medical School," in *Power in Organizations*, ed. Mayer Zald (Nashville: Vanderbilt University Press, 1970), pp. 13-14.

42. "Authority, Reason, and Discretion," in *Authority: Nomos I*, ed. Carl J. Friedrich (Cambridge: Harvard University Press, 1958), pp. 35-36.

43. "Max Weber's Missing Authority Type," *Sociological Inquiry* 37, no. 2 (Spring 1967): 231-40.

44. Max Weber, "The Three Types of Legitimate Rule," trans. Hans Gerth, in *A Sociological Reader on Complex Organizations*, ed. Amitai Etzioni, 2nd ed. (New York: Holt, Rinhart & Winston, 1969), pp. 6-15.

45. "Missing Authority Type," p. 235.

46. Dennis Wrong believes the last view is correct. See "Max Weber," in *Max Weber*, ed. Dennis Wrong (Englewood Cliffs, N.J.: Prentice-Hall, 1970), p. 41.

47. An example of this socialization effort may be seen in bayonet training when the instructor shouts to the ranks, "What is the spirit of the bayonet?" They respond forcefully, "To kill!"

48. See Huntington, *The Soldier and the State*, p. 73: "The military profession exists to serve the state." See also Ward Just, "Soldiers, Part II," *Atlantic Monthly*,

168 / Notes to Chapter 1

November 1970, p. 68: "The Defense Department lives in a world of menace, and the least of it in Southeast Asia. The principal menace is International Communism, on land, at sea, and in the air. There is a strategic nuclear threat, a general purpose forces threat, and an insurgency threat, all of them coming together under the general category of THE THREAT TO NATIONAL SECURITY."

49. Max Weber's notion of theodicy appears in "The Social Psychology of the World Religions," in *From Max Weber: Essays in Sociology*, ed. H. H. Gerth and C. Wright Mills (New York: Oxford University Press, 1946), pp. 274ff. It has been expounded on by Peter Berger in *The Sacred Canopy: Elements of a Sociological Theory of Religion* (Garden City, N.Y.: Doubleday, 1967), chap. 3, and in *A Rumor of Angels: Modern Society and the Rediscovery of the Supernatural* (Garden City, N.Y.: Doubleday, 1969), pp. 31-32.

50. Peter Berger defines a cognitive minority as a group that "forms around a deviant body of knowledge." See *A Rumor of Angels*, p. 7.

51. This idea of a "movement" was suggested by the notion of internal social movements as put forth in an unpublished paper by Susan M. Watson, "Social Movements in Large Scale Organizations" (Nashville: Vanderbilt University, 1966), prepared for and made available to me by Professor Mayer Zald.

52. For more on cabals see Tom Burns, "The Reference of Conduct in Small Groups: Cliques and Cabals in Occupational Milieux," *Human Relations* 8 (November 1955): 467-85.

53. Max Weber, "Politics as a Vocation," in *From Max Weber*, ed. Gerth and Mills, p. 115.

54. Donald R. Burgett, *Curahee!* (New York: Ballentine Books, 1968), p. 136.

55. Ward Just, "Soldiers, Part I," *Atlantic Monthly*, October 1970, p. 80.

56. Limited possibilities for career exit can play a part in the formation of cliques and cabals. See Burns, "Reference of Conduct." The implications of exit are explored by Albert O. Hirschman in *Exit, Voice, and Loyalty: Responses to Decline in Firms, Organizations, and States* (Cambridge: Harvard University Press, 1970), especially in chap. 2.

57. General Curtis E. LeMay, *Mission with LeMay: My Story* (Garden City, N.Y.: Doubleday, 1965).

58. Interview A. All interview citations have been coded in order to maintain the confidentiality promised interviewees. Additional information may be made available by the author to bona-fide scholars.

59. Jacques Ellul, *The Political Illusion*, trans. Konrad Kellen (New York: Alfred A. Knopf, 1967), p. 144.

60. Ibid., p. 143.

61. See, for instance, W. S. Robinson, "The Logical Structure of Analytic Induction," *American Sociological Review* 16 (1951): 812-18; and particularly S. Kirson Weinberg's comments on this article made in a letter to the *American Sociological Review*, ibid. 17 (1952): 494.

62. Such studies have been useful in the preparation of this particular work. For example, Graham T. Allison's *Essence of Decision: Explaining the Cuban Missile Crisis* (Boston: Little, Brown, 1971), helped to define some of the variables important in bureaucratic politics.

Chapter 2

1. Mayer Zald, *Organizational Change: The Political Economy of the YMCA* (Chicago: University of Chicago Press, 1970), p. 22.

2. U.S., *Statutes at Large*, vol. 32, pp. 775-80.

3. This was published by the Headquarters of the Army, Adjutant-General's Office, Washington, D.C., July 20, 1903, as General Order no. 107.

4. This was accomplished in the General Staff Act of 1903 (U.S., *Statutes at Large*, vol. 32, pp. 830-31). Root was cognizant of the differences between the German system of government and that of the United States and adjusted his plans accordingly. For discussions of the relationship between the President, the Secretary of War, and Congress, see Major Otto L. Nelson, Jr., *National Security and the General Staff* (Washington, D.C.: Infantry Journal Press, 1946), chap. 3; and Paul Y. Hammond, *Organizing for Defense: The American Military Establishment in the Twentieth Century* (Princeton: Princeton University Press, 1961), pp. 10-48.

5. The first balloon for military reconnaissance was used during the French Revolution. Union forces also utilized lighter-than-air craft to a limited extent in the American Civil War. But such experiences did not capture the imagination of numbers of military men in the way that heavier-than-air craft were to do. For a history of pre-1903 flight efforts see Hendrick de Leeuw, *The History and Future of Aviation* (New York: Vantage Press, 1960), pt. 1.

6. Vernon Pizer, *The United States Army* (New York: Frederick A. Praeger, 1967), p. 142, gives this figure. For a discussion of the primitiveness of the 1907-1914 period see Aaron Norman, *The Great Air War: The Men, the Planes, the Saga of Military Aviation, 1914-1918* (New York: Macmillan, 1968), chap. 2.

7. U.S., *Statutes at Large*, vol. 38, pp. 514-16.

8. Pizer, *The United States Army*, p. 143.

9. U.S., *Statutes at Large*, vol. 40, pp. 243-47.

10. Ibid., pp. 556-57.

11. I. B. Holley, Jr., *Ideas and Weapons: Exploitation of the Aerial Weapon by the United States During World War I: A Study in the Relationship of Technological Advance, Military Doctrine, and the Development of Weapons* (New Haven: Yale University Press, 1953), p. 47.

12. Ibid., p. 157.

13. Ibid.

14. Army Air Forces Historical Study no. 39, "Legislation Relating to the Air Corps Personnel and Training Programs, 1907-1939," December 1945, Army Air Force Historical Office, Headquarters of the Army Air Force.

15. U.S., War Department, Special Committee on Army Air Corps, *Final Report* (Newton D. Baker, chairman), July 18, 1934.

16. U.S., *Statutes at Large*, vol. 41, pp. 759-812, and vol. 44, pp. 780-90.

17. In his *Command of the Air*, trans. Sheila Fischer (Rome: Revista Aeronautica, 1958), Douhet stressed taking the offensive by attacking deep into the enemy homeland. Though he was not as specific as the theoreticians of American strategic air power about target selection, the theoreticians relied "heavily on his theories." See Perry McCoy Smith, *The Air Force Plans for Peace, 1943-1945* (Baltimore: Johns Hopkins Press, 1970), pp. 8, 28-29.

18. Ibid., pp. 22-25 and chap. 3. The effects of the absence of Air Force intraservice competition on technological development in areas that were not emphasized by prevailing doctrine are of prime importance in the later growth of Army aviation.

19. A dramatic telling of the tale is offered by Roger Burlingame, *General Billy Mitchell: Champion of Air Defense* (New York: McGraw-Hill, 1952), chap. 1. Congress authorized the test destruction of the heavily armored German battleship that had survived several hits at the Battle of Jutland. The battleship *Pennsylvania* was standing by to try to blow it to bits before a deadline some days hence. The contrast between the old sailors tearfully watching their most cherished beliefs follow the *Ostfriesland* to the bottom in twenty short minutes while the young flyer-bombardiers relished their triumph suggests melodrama. That the triumph was short-lived suggests why an internal bureaucratic political strategy is a useful adjunct to an external public relations campaign.

20. There were actually eight court martial specifications. Four were related to

Mitchell's famous statement of September 5, and four more grew out of a statement on September 9 in which he attacked Washington bureaucrats. See Burke Davis, *The Billy Mitchell Affair* (New York: Random House, 1967), pp. 218, 223-24, 247, 326.

21. Monro MacCloskey, *The United States Air Force* (New York: Frederick A. Praeger, 1967), pp. 28-29. The notion that this organizational arrangement was the outcome of a conscious decision on the part of Air Force officers is suggested by R. Earl McLendon in *The Question of Autonomy for the United States Air Arm, 1907-1945*, Air University Documentary Research Study (Maxwell Air Force Base, Ala., 1950), pp. 139, 172, 194-97.

22. German air power was one factor that influenced attitudes toward aviation. General H. H. Arnold commented that the *Luftwaffe* was the "unseen guest" at GHQAF conference. This apprehension of German air power was also manifested in the sending of Generals Spaatz and Kenney to observe air force procedures and equipment in Europe. See Wesley F. Craven and James L. Cate, eds., *The Army Air Forces in World War II*, vol. 3, *Europe: Argument to VE Day, January 1944-May 1945* (Chicago: University of Chicago Press, 1948), pp. 7, 8.

23. The struggle between the Army Air Force and the U.S. Navy flourished during the interwar years and persisted throughout World War II and beyond. Even the personal relations between King and Arnold were strained to the breaking point over the question of allocating bombers for convoy defense. See Kent Roberts Greenfield, *American Strategy in World War II: A Reconsideration* (Baltimore: Johns Hopkins Press, 1963), pp. 99-100.

24. There was, of course, a very complex network of interrelationships at the top level of the U.S. Government during World War II. No attempt is made to be comprehensive in this presentation. Rather, my purpose is to suggest how high-level politics operates and to offer some relevant information that will advance the reader's understanding of inter-Army policy processes. Much of the information in my discussion of the Army Chief of Staff is taken from the three-volume official biography by Forrest C. Pogue, *George C. Marshall: Education of a General, 1880-1939* (New York: Viking Press, 1963); *George C. Marshall: Ordeal and Hope, 1939-1942* (New York: Viking Press, 1965); and *George C. Marshall: Organizer of Victory, 1942-1943* (New York: Viking Press, 1973). The evolution of a Joint Chiefs of Staff is discussed by Demetrius Caraley in *The Politics of Military Unification: A Story of Conflict and the Policy Process* (New York: Columbia University Press, 1966), pp. 14-20. For an insider's view see William D. Leahy, *I Was There: The Personal Story of the Chief of Staff to President Roosevelt and Truman* (New York: McGraw-Hill, 1950).

25. Throughout his biography, Pogue places great stress on Marshall as an educator. Marshall clearly tried to change the direction of the military by influencing curriculum and pedagogy. The role of Army schools in political recruitment and socialization will be discussed in this and later chapters. Marshall's stay at the Infantry School was significant for several reasons. It was there that he observed and evaluated many of the men who were to be commanders in World War II. It was also there that he would stress combat realism in training that was to be very important during the early days of World War II. A man who shared Marshall's perspectives and who was to be one of his choices for an important leadership post was "Vinegar Joe" Stillwell. See Barbara W. Tuchman, *Stillwell and the American Experience in China, 1911-45* (New York: Macmillan, 1970), pp. 123-25.

26. In forming a picture of politics at the highest executive level one should not overlook the potential of Congress to intervene by altering the environment. Marshall, who had lived through the lean interwar years, knew full well the power of Congress and was careful to be on good terms with its leaders whenever possible.

27. Reorganization efforts continued after the 1939 consolidation mentioned above. On November 14, 1940, there was a shift away from centralized control and a

move toward insuring air support for ground operations. There was a reorganization when Marshall shifted GHQAF to the GHQ of the Army Field Forces. At the same time, Major General Arnold, who was Chief of the Air Corps, was also assigned the office of Deputy Chief of Staff for Air. In addition, Arnold was given a voice in the meetings of the War Council, where he sat while meeting with representatives of the Navy. There is some disagreement as to the significance of this change, since Arnold actually retained a very important decision-making position. Nevertheless, it was determined shortly thereafter that the Army's air arm was to have a single commander under a single civilian Assistant Secretary of War for Air. Arnold kept his position as Deputy Chief of Staff and Chief of the now-combined Air Force Combat Command (formerly GHQ Air Force and the Air Corps).

28. MacCloskey, *The United States Air Force*, p. 36.

29. John C. Ries, *The Management of Defense: Organization and Control of the U.S. Armed Services* (Baltimore: Johns Hopkins Press, 1964), p. 24.

30. Luther Gulick, "Notes on the Theory of Organization," in Luther Gulick and L. Urwick, eds., *Papers on the Science of Administration* (New York: Institute of Public Administration, 1937), p. 31. In a more recent interpretation, "staff" seems to refer to two different functions: (1) "in the sense of the General Staff, which is somewhat analogous to a Board of Directors that formulates policy and makes major decisions"; and (2) "in the sense of the management of support activities: i.e., the Medical Corps, the Supply Corps, the Ordinance Corps and the Signal Corps." See Gerald G. Fisch, "Line-Staff is Obsolete," *Harvard Business Review* 39 (September/October 1961): 67.

31. Ray S. Cline, *Washington Command Post: The Operations Division* (Washington, D.C.: Department of the Army, 1951), p. 93.

32. Pogue, *George C. Marshall*, 2: 292.

33. Although reorganization was needed, Marshall ran the risk of eliminating many of the diverse views that were likely to be valuable to a high-level executive of a complex organization with a multitude of tasks and responsibilities. This reorganization, implemented under Executive Order no. 9082, was adopted under the authority of the War Powers Act passed on December 18, 1941, which was similar to the War Powers Act that allowed for the general executive reorganization that separated the Air Service from the Signal Corps in World War I. There is nothing like a crisis to present an opportunity for the alteration of the political status quo through organizational readjustment. See U.S., *Statutes at Large*, vol. 55, pp. 838-39; and Pogue, *George C. Marshall*, 2: 295.

34. James MacGregor Burns, *Roosevelt: The Soldier of Freedom* (New York: Harcourt Brace Jovanovich, 1970), p. 85.

35. Robert E. Sherwood, *Roosevelt and Hopkins: An Intimate History* (New York: Harper & Bros., 1948), pp. 100-101.

36. Samuel P. Huntington, *The Soldiers and the State: The Theory and Politics of Civil-Military Relations* (New York: Random House, Vintage Books, 1957); pp. 317-19.

37. James MacGregor Burns, *Roosevelt: The Lion and the Fox* (New York: Harcourt, Brace & Co., 1956), p. 399.

38. Ibid., p. 365.

39. Sherwood, *Roosevelt and Hopkins*, p. 101.

40. Marshall's commitment to extracting the utmost benefit from air assets was epitomized by his insistence that his commanders fly on business when a time savings would result. Pogue indicates that those who refused to fly were relieved of duty. See *George C. Marshall*, 2: 82, 88.

41. Much of the information in this section may be found in Richard K. Tierney, "The Army Aviation Story, Part I," *U.S. Army Aviation Digest* 8 (June 1962): 2-25. The subject matter was also discussed at length in my interviews, especially in Interview C.

42. Tierney, "The Army Aviation Story, Part I," p. 15.

43. Efforts to establish the precise meaning of "organic" have become part of the struggle for Army aviation. See U.S. Department of the Army, Memorandum for the Secretary of the Army from the Office of the General Counsel, "Composition and Roles and Missions of Army Aircraft," April 30, 1971 (personal copy provided by an interviewee).

44. Major William W. Ford, "Wings for Santa Barbara," *Field Artillery Journal* 31 (April 1941): 232.

45. Tierney, "The Army Aviation Story, Part I," p. 18.

46. General McNair preferred organizing large units as task forces. To accomplish this he wanted to centralize each specialized force. For example, tactical aviation would be in a pool from which units could be drawn and assigned to a force for a specific task. But his Air Support Command did not succeed. A summary of McNair's thought can be found in Russell F. Weigley, *History of the United States Army* (New York: Macmillan, 1967), pp. 461-71.

47. This is the conclusion of Interviewee C, who related the story to me.

48. These men, who entered a program whose very existence was in question, set standards of career as well as of physical courage. The men in the early classes had no guarantee that they would perform the kind of service for which they were trained. In one case, early arrivals in Great Britain were snatched up as replacement ground officers for the 34th Division. By dint of circumstance, the pilots were later allowed to fly before they were lost in the personnel shuffle. Interview D.

49. Brigadier General William J. Maddox, Jr., "From Fabric to FLIR," *U.S. Army Aviation Digest* 18 (June 1972): 2.

50. The terrible losses suffered during the strategic bombing that was attempted before long-range fighter support aircraft were available is the central theme of the play *Command Decision*. The decision to continue bombing deep into Germany to strike at jet plane factories and thus win the war is challenged by Major General Kane, who was a leader in the movement to secure strategic-bombing forces for the Army. Kane must decide whether to abandon the important deep-bombing missions and risk terrible loss of life for the ground troopers or risk the destruction of the idea of strategic bombing. His dilemma reveals the extent to which deep-penetration bombing was under attack for the heavy losses sustained in 1943 and illuminates the attitudes of the separatists: "But the decision is at stake now. It isn't just a few losses this week, or even a lot in six months. The Germans are going to kill more of our people, of course. But they won't be any deader than all the ones who've been killed through the last thirty years to get us air power. You can worry about Germany . . . and you should. But I'm fighting the ground forces and the Navy and the Congress and the White House and the People and the press and our Allies. You think I don't know the boys call me Old Percent? You think I've enjoyed spreading this mug of mine around the press like a pregnant heiress? You think I don't know what they could do to me for the statistics I've juggled, the strike photos I've doctored, the reports I've gilded or suppressed. I know . . . and I'd do it all again! I've spent twenty years watching my friends killed and broken and disgraced and discarded for one single idea . . . to get our goddamned country Air Power!" See William Wister Haines, *Command Decision*, in *The Burns Mantle Best Plays of 1947-48*, ed. John Chapman (New York: Dodd, Mead, 1948), p. 118.

51. The Transportation Plan, which made railways a major target of strategic and tactical air attack, was in competition for resources with the effort to destroy German oil supplies. The Transportation Plan essentially won out, and it did provide some aid for the Normandy landings. See Stephen E. Ambrose, *The Supreme Commander: The War Years of General Dwight D. Eisenhower* (Garden City, N.Y.: Doubleday, 1970), pt. 2, chap. 3.

52. Ibid., p. 298.

53. Perry McCoy Smith, *The Air Force Plans for Peace* (Baltimore: Johns Hopkins Press, 1970), p. xi.

54. Kent Roberts Greenfield, Robert R. Palmer, and Bell I. Wiley, *The Organization of Ground Combat Troops*, p. 101, cited in James A Huston, "Tactical Use of Air Power in World War II: The Army Experience," *Military Affairs* 14 (1950): 166-85.

55. The War Department's Field Manual 100-20, *Command and Employment of Air Power* (July 21, 1943), superseded its Basic Field Manual 31-35, *Aviation in Support of Ground Forces* (April 9, 1942), which tended to emphasize the requirements of the ground commanders. See Thomas J. Maycock, "Notes on the Development of AAF Tactical Air Doctrine," *Military Affairs* 14 (1950): 186-200.

56. Such perceptions should not in any way impugn the record of courage wrought by the Army Air Forces in World War II. For instance, General James H. Doolittle points out that "no Eighth Air Force airplane was *ever* turned back from its assigned mission by enemy action." See his preface to *The Love and Fear of Flying*, by Douglas D. Bond (New York: International University Press, 1952), p. 8.

57. The "airborne club" is a somewhat derisive description of a group of men who served as parachutists in their Army careers. Belonging to an elite, such soldiers were often said to favor each other, as initiates of any fraternity might, in their business dealings. Members of this group served in a variety of high positions after World War II and include at least three Chiefs of Staff—Generals Matthew Ridgway, Maxwell Taylor, and William Westmoreland—as well as such powerful military intellectuals as Lieutenant General James Gavin and General Hamilton Howze.

58. Ross S. Carter, *Those Devils in Baggy Pants* (New York: Signet Books, 1951), pp. 71-72.

59. Huston, "Tactical Use of Air Power in World War II," p. 177.

60. Several of the documents pertaining to these matters retain a security classification. Later it seems to have become virtually standard operating procedure to classify documents relating to interservice rivalry.

61. General Henry H. Arnold, Memorandum for the Chief of Staff, "Liaison Aircraft in the Army Ground Forces," January 29, 1944. Personal copy provided by an interviewee.

62. General Lesley J. McNair, Memorandum for the Chief of Staff, U.S. Army (Attention: G-3 Division, Room 3A882, the Pentagon), "Liaison Aircraft in the Army Ground Forces," February 16, 1944. Personal copy provided by an interviewee.

63. One officer who had served in the Pentagon in a position concerned with Army aviation matters put it this way: "I never saw a general, I never went to a general officer for approval on any policy, '48 through '50. . . . In fact, we had very good cooperation, as I said, from the Lieutenant Colonel level down. It was only at the top level there would be any rumbling." Interview D, pp. 9-10.

64. Some of these Army aviators were not very concerned about receiving affirmative orders to go ahead with certain activities. Rather, they sought to avoid receiving a negative order that would require either a cessation of activity or the direct violation of a specific order. As one officer noted: "You should not push until you receive a no, since then you violate an order. You have to understand what you're trying to do, what to expect and what is expected. Keep the initiative without impatience." Ibid., pp. 2-5.

65. Ambrose, *The Supreme Commander*, p. 313.

66. Pogue, *George C. Marshall*, 2: 86.

67. Craven and Cate, eds., *The Army Air Forces in World War II*, 3: 716.

Chapter 3

1. When attempting to cope with an organization's environment, the researcher's eye is often directed to other organizations therein. In dealing with these complex organizations, he is faced with the danger of reifying the organizations under scrutiny. It is understood that organizations do not think or feel. Rather, in dealing with inter-

organizational relations, when speaking of organizations "doing" something, one refers to the aggregated attitudes of individuals.

At times I will use langauge that might, at first glance, suggest hypostasization of the organizations involved. This is a deliberate attempt on my part to avoid awkward phrasing and to stress the element of free will in interorganizational relations. In much the same way that I rejected the oversocialized notion of man in Chapter 1 (pages 10-11), here called into question is the assumption that environment creates ineluctable conditions that produce organizations whose leaders simply perform the tasks required of them by an overpoweringly deterministic and complex system.

2. James D. Thompson, *Organizations in Action* (New York: McGraw-Hill, 1967), especially pp. 22-51. Thompson borrows these three concepts from a 1961 study by Sol Levine and Paul E. White, "Exchange as a Conceptual Framework for the Study of Interorganizational Relationships," *Administrative Science Quarterly* 5 (March 1961): 583-601.

3. Thompson, *Organizations in Action*, pp. 28-29.

4. William R. Dill, "Environment as an Influence on Managerial Autonomy," *Administrative Science Quarterly* 2 (March 1958): 409-43. The notion of focal organization is expressed by William M. Evan in "The Organization-Set," in *Readings in Organization Theory: Open System Approaches,* ed. John G. Maurer (New York: Random House, 1971), pp. 33-45. Evan refers to the focal organization as the organization that is the "point of reference" (p. 35).

5. Dill, "Environment as an Influence," pp. 409-43.

6. William M. Evan, "An Organization-Set Model of Interorganizational Relations," in *Interorganizational Decision Making,* ed. Matthew Tuite et al. (Chicago: Aldine, 1973), pp. 35-63.

7. Ibid., pp. 34-35. The concept of role-set utilized by Evan was developed by Robert K. Merton in *Social Theory and Social Structure,* rev. ed. (Glencoe, Ill.: Free Press, 1957), pp. 368-80.

8. Haas and Drabek discuss some effects that the environment may have on the focal organization. See J. Eugene Haas and Thomas E. Drabek, *Complex Organizations: A Sociological Perspective* (New York: Macmillan, 1973), pp. 15-22.

9. Daniel Katz and Robert Kahn, *The Social Psychology of Organizations* (New York: John Wiley, 1966), pp. 9, 19-29.

10. F. E. Emery and E. L. Trist, "The Causal Texture of Organizational Environments," *Human Relations* 18 (February 1965): 21-31; see especially p. 22.

11. Thus, uncertainty becomes the dominant characteristic of organizations within these turbulent fields. For greater detail and clarifying examples see Shirley Terreberry, "The Evolution of Organizational Environment," *Administrative Science Quarterly* 12 (March 1968): 590-613. One example cited by Terreberry, for instance, is the turmoil brought about by the increasing influence of private foundations, national associations, and various bureaus of the federal government in the field of education, an influence which complicates the already intricate pattern of private and state and local authority.

12. Foster R. Dulles, *America's Rise to World Power* (New York: Harper & Row, 1954), offers a good description of the isolationist tradition, while William Reitzel et al., *United States Foreign Policy* (Washington, D.C.: Brookings Institution, 1956), detail some of the reasons for the break with tradition.

13. W. W. Rostow, *The United States in the World Arena* (New York: Harper & Row, 1960), pp. 172ff.

14. John L. Gaddis, *The United States and the Origins of the Cold War, 1941-1947* (New York: Columbia University Press, 1972).

15. John W. Spanier, *American Foreign Policy since World War II,* rev. ed. (New York: Frederick A. Praeger, 1962), pp. 31-33.

16. Rostow, *The United States in the World Arena*, pp. 226-27.

17. Such conclusions could be partially sustained by interpretations given in *United States Strategic Bombing Survey, Overall Report (European War) Sept. 30, 1945* (Washington, D.C., 1945), especially pp. 37-38.

18. Such conclusions could also be partially sustained by interpretations in *United States Strategic Bombing Survey*, especially pp. 11 and 139-46, where total armament production is reported to have increased in Germany until July 1944, and p. 95, where it is reported that the bombing campaign did not crack the will of the German people. In my view, it is important to remember that things got bad for the Germans only when they were being defeated in the air, on land, and at sea.

19. Demetrios Caraley deals with this period in great detail in *The Politics of Military Unification: A Study of Conflict and the Policy Process* (New York: Columbia University Press, 1966).

20. See U.S., Congress, House, Select Committee on Post War Military Policy, *Proposal to Establish a Single Department of Armed Forces: Hearings*, 78th Cong., 2nd sess., 1944.

21. Ernest S. Griffith has characterized much of the Washington scene as "government by whirlpools" in *Congress: Its Contemporary Role* (New York: New York University Press, 1951), pp. 37ff. For a more comprehensive treatment of this phenomenon see J. Leiper Freeman, *The Political Process: Executive Bureau-Legislative Committee Relations* (New York: Doubleday, 1955), especially chaps. 1 and 2.

22. Caraley, *The Politics of Military Unification*, p. 33.

23. U.S., Congress, Senate, Committee on Military Affairs, *Hearings on S. 84 and S. 1482*, 79th Cong., 1st sess., 1945, pp. 411-39.

24. Education was aimed especially at the newly inaugurated President Truman, who did not share Roosevelt's naval tradition. See James Forrestal, *The Forrestal Diaries*, ed. Walter Millis, with E. S. Duffiend (New York: Viking Press, 1951), pp. 46-47, 59-61.

25. U.S., Congress, Senate, Committee on Naval Affairs, *Unification of the War and Navy Departments and Post War Organization for National Security*, report prepared for the Honorable James Forrestal, Secretary of the Navy, 79th Cong., 1st sess., 1945.

26. Marshall specifically opposed the notion that national security can be provided for on a "piecemeal" basis. See the 1945 *Hearings on S. 84 and S. 1482*, p. 52. Use of this term ("piecemeal") suggests a difference of opinion over planning in a democracy between Marshall and the advocate of piecemeal social engineering, Sir Karl Popper. See Popper, *The Poverty of Historicism* (Boston: Beacon Press, 1957).

27. Charles E. Lindblom, "The Science of 'Muddling Through,'" *Public Administration Review* 19 (1959): 79-88.

28. See the 1945 *Hearings on S. 84 and S. 1482*, pp. 383-84.

29. Caraley, *The Politics of Military Unification*, p. 50.

30. The technocratic, apolitical bias of the large, hierarchical business organization is derived from Frederick W. Taylor, *The Principles of Scientific Management* (1911; New York: W. W. Norton, 1967). The implications of this arrangement for democratic government are analyzed by Emmette S. Redford in *Democracy in the Administrative State* (New York: Oxford University Press, 1969).

31. U.S., *Statutes at Large*, vol. 61, pp. 496-99.

32. The 1949 and 1958 reorganizations were by statute; see ibid., vol. 63, pp. 578-92, and vol. 72, pp. 514-22, respectively. The reorganization of 1953 was by executive order; see U.S., Congress, Senate, Armed Services Committee, *Reorganization Plan No. 6 of 1953 Relating to the Department of Defense*, 83rd Cong., 1st sess.

33. Samuel P. Huntington, *The Common Defense: Strategic Programs in National Politics* (New York: Columbia University Press, 1961), pp. 387-91.

34. Walter Millis, with Harvey C. Mansfield and Harold Stein, *Arms and the State: Civil-Military Elements in National Policy* (New York: Twentieth Century Fund, 1958), p. 178.

35. U.S., *Statutes at Large*, vol. 61, p. 501.

36. Ibid., vol. 64, p. 321.

37. Philip Selznick distinguishes between organizations and institutions. Organization "suggests a certain bareness, a lean, no-nonsense system of consciously coordinated activities. It refers to an expendable tool, a rational instrument engineered to a job." In contrast, an institution "is more nearly a natural product of social needs and pressures—a responsive, adaptive organism." Since becoming an institution requires the process of infusion with values, the reversal of this process suggests a decline in the significance of these precarious values. See Selznick, *Leadership in Administration* (Evanston, Ill.: Row, Peterson, 1957), pp. 5, 119-33.

38. These perceptive words of John M. Gaus were apparently spoken to one of his students, Charles O. Jones, who cited them in *An Introduction to the Study Public Policy* (Belmont, Calif.: Wadsworth Publishing, 1970), p. 5

39. Millis et al., *Arms and the State*, p. 497.

40. C. W. Borklund, *The Department of Defense* (New York: Frederick A. Praeger, 1968), pp. 57-58.

41. Huntington states that "after 1952, whatever the vicissitudes of budgets and strategy, the organizational existence of no service was threatened by another. An equilibrium had been reached" (*Common Defense*), p. 372. Unfortunately, this perspective does not deal with the *institutional* existence of each service nor does it deal with the perceptions of threats held by concerned officers.

42. Millis et al., *Arms and the State*, pp. 184-85.

43. This is not to say that a Chief of Service can relinquish his role as a service partisan entirely. As Paul Y. Hammond has pointed out: "A service Chief remains in effective control of his service only so long as he maintains its confidence; and nothing can cause the loss of that confidence faster than his abandonment of the role of service spokesman in the JCS. This situation is not unique with the office of service Chief, or with the Armed Services." See his *Organizing for Defense: The American Military Establishment in the Twentieth Century* (Princeton: Princeton University Press, 1961), p. 349.

44. Borklund, *The Department of Defense*, pp. 50-56.

45. Hammond, *Organizing for Defense*, pp. 375-89.

46. Harry S. Truman, *Memoirs* (Garden City, N.Y.: Doubleday, 1956), 2: 37-38.

47. For a general discussion see Warner B. Schilling, Paul Y. Hammond, and Glenn H. Snyder, *Strategy, Politics, and Defense Budgets* (New York: Columbia University Press, 1962).

48. General John B. Medaris, for example, advised that "it is far easier to justify a budget with the modern items that are popular and I would strongly recommend that you increase the amount you show in the budget for the production of missiles." See Medaris, *Countdown for Decision* (New York: G. P. Putnam's Sons, 1960), p. 65.

49. Borklund, *The Department of Defense*, p. 58.

50. Prior to the Korean War, the Tactical Air Command had no more than 150 men and was, in essence, inoperative. Interview S, p. 1.

51. Interview E, p. 47. The Air Force's decision to acquire the TFX fighter-bomber in 1959 confirmed for the soldiers their view that TAC was trying to become a junior SAC and was not really interested in close air support. See Robert J. Art, *The TFX Decision: McNamara and the Military* (Boston: Little, Brown, 1968), pp. 15-16.

52. In fact, many of these weapons were developed during the period from World War I to the 1930s, for example, the M-1 rifle and the Browning automatic rifle. See Russell F. Weigley, *History of the United States Army* (New York: Macmillan, 1967), p. 502.

53. James Gavin, *War and Peace in the Space Age* (New York: Harper & Bros., 1958), p. 112.

54. See Henry A. Kissinger, *Nuclear Weapons and Foreign Policy* (Garden City, N.Y.: Doubleday, 1957), p. 233, on the acquisition of the atomic cannon.

55. See Paul Y. Hammond, *Super Carriers and B-36 Bombers: Appropriations, Strategy, and Politics*, Inter-University Case Program, no. 87 (New York: Bobbs-Merrill, 1963).

56. Interview C, p. 2. According to the interviewee, the Army fought for the air evacuation mission during the Korean War. There was a terrible commotion when an Army warrant officer came in to pick up a casualty and an Air Force captain then landed and ordered the Army officer to remove the wounded man and put him on the Air Force chopper. A decision was later reached that medical evacuation was an Army function.

57. Morris Janowitz notes that "ten years after the end of World War II, professional officers who had participated in military operations had had time to reflect on their war-time experiences and the outcome of the post-war settlement. On the basis of their expressed attitudes, either in interviews or in public pronouncements, it was still possible to classify the more articulate ones as either Europe-oriented or Asia-oriented." See Janowitz, *The Professional Soldier: A Social and Political Portrait* (New York: Free Press, 1960), p. 288.

58. Interview C, p. 4.

59. Forrestal, *Diaries*, ed. Millis, pp. 389-94.

60. Ibid., pp. 476-79.

61. Richard E. Walton and John M. Dutton have gathered some evidence which suggests that task-related asymmetries between horizontally related organizational units may promote contention. "Symmetrical interdependence and symmetrical patterns on initiation between units promote collaboration; asymmetrical interdependence leads to conflict." See Walton and Dutton, "The Management of Interdepartmental Conflict: A Model and Review," *Administrative Science Quarterly* 14 (March 1969): 73-84.

62. This specified the two types of Army aircraft and suggested the ways in which the Army could improve and expedite ground combat procedures in the forward areas of the battlefield. Specific functions for the aircraft included: maintenance of aerial surveillance of enemy forward areas; aerial route reconnaissance; control of march columns; camouflage inspections of ground forces areas and installations; local courier and messenger service; emergency aerial evacuation; emergency wire laying; limited aerial resupply; and limited front line aerial photography. Of course, attack on the battlefield was excluded.

63. Major General E. M. Almond, Commander of the Army X Corps, who studied the problem closely, expressed his views in an interview entitled "Mistakes in Air Support Methods in Korea" in *U.S. News and World Report*, March 6, 1953, pp. 53-61.

64. The Air Force's position was expressed by Robert F. Futrell in *The U.S. Air Force in Korea, 1950-1953* (New York: Duell, Sloan & Pierce, 1961), pp. 658-63. In particular, Futrell rationalizes the more intense support given by Marine aviation to Marines (a source of conflict between the Army and the Air Force) and attacks "the fallacy of attaching 'penny pockets' of air power to ground units" (p. 661).

65. R. Earl McClendon has indicated that this "Memorandum of Understanding" has been called the Magna Carta of Army aviation because function was substituted for weight limitation. See McClendon, *Army Aviation, 1947-1953*, Air University Documentary Research Study no. 48 (Maxwell Air Force Base, Ala., May 1954), p. 23.

66. Interview C, pp. 2-3. As a result of the commotion over the air evacuation mission (see n. 56), the interviewee was told that the "big boy" wanted to see him. The interviewee and other aviation supporters worked forty-eight hours straight to produce their paper to make their case. The attitude was that they had to produce a signed agreement before election day so that it would not look like the government was putting off hard decisions because of politics. The result was the second Pace-Finletter agreement.

67. McClendon, *Army Aviation*, pp. 26-27.

68. Both the use of bargaining within the bureaucracy and the use of general language to reduce conflict are common practices in American bureaucratic life.

69. Memorandum for the Secretary of the Army, "Composition and Roles and Missions of Army Aircraft," April 30, 1971, p. 5, states that the document originally issued on October 1, 1953, was subsequently issued as DOD directive 5100.1 on March 16, 1954.

70. Interview E, p. 20.

71. "Wilson Memorandum Clarifying Roles and Missions," reprinted in U.S., Congress, House, Committee on Government Operations, *Hearings on the Organization and Management of Missile Programs*, 86th Cong., 1st sess., 1959.

72. Interview E, p. 13.

73. The 1st Cavalry Division (Airmobile), later the 1st Air Cavalry Division, then renamed the 1st Cavalry Division (Airmobile), included 449 helicopters ranging from miniscouts to large flying cranes. See John T. Wheeler, "Helicopters Make Difference in Vietnam," *Nashville Tennessean*, March 9, 1969, sec. B, p. 1.

74. Huntington, *Common Defense*, pp. 404ff. In stating that "each service (except the Marines) contributed something to each major function" Huntington should not be misinterpreted as suggesting an equilibrium.

75. James Alden Barber, Jr., "The Draft and Alternatives to the Draft," in *The Military and American Society*, ed. Stephen E. Ambrose and James Alden Barber, Jr. (New York: Free Press, 1972), pp. 208, 214-15.

76. For a comprehensive, though partisan, view of the UMT controversy, written by the former director of the National Council Against Conscription, see John M. Swomley, Jr., *The Military Establishment* (Boston: Beacon Press, 1964).

77. The idea of the pentomic division was that it could be highly mobile and, as a five-sided unit, face all directions at once. It was superseded by the Reorganization Objectives Army Division (ROAD) in the 1960s, which suggested a lessening of interest by the Army in nuclear warfare in Europe.

78. James M. Gavin, "Cavalry, and I Don't Mean Horses," *Harper's*, April 1954, pp. 54-60.

79. Adam Yarmolinsky, *The Military Establishment: Its Impacts on American Society* (New York: Harper & Row, 1971), pp. 194-233.

80. John W. Spanier, *The Truman-MacArthur Controversy and the Korean War* (Cambridge: Harvard University Press, 1959).

81. Huntington, *Common Defense*, pp. 394-98.

82. William S. White, "Carl Vinson Has Been Unified, Too," *New York Times Magazine*, September 10, 1950, p. 12.

83. For the enactment and effects of section 412 see Bernard K. Gordon, "The Military Budget: Congressional Phase," *Journal of Politics* 23 (November 1961): 689-710; and Raymond H. Dawson, "Congressional Innovation and Intervention in Defense Policy: Legislative Authorization of Weapons Systems," *American Political Science Review* 56 (March 1962): 42-57.

84. This may be inferred from Gordon, "The Military Budget."

85. Huntington, *Common Defense*, p. 399. The arsenal system was made up of "government scientists, engineers and technicians" who "were at times engaged in the in-house fabrication and assembly of military weaponry, as well as being participants in the research, development, and components development stages of weapons innovation." While providing a certain degree of stability, the arsenal system proved vulnerable to attack from those who preferred the system of contracting out research and development. See Michael H. Armacost, *The Politics of Weapons Innovation: The Thor-Jupiter Controversy* (New York: Columbia University Press, 1969), pp. 9, 155-63.

86. U.S., Congress, House, Committee on Armed Services, Investigations Subcommittee, *Hearings on the Employment of Personnel by Defense Industries*, 86th Cong., 1st sess., pp. 570ff., 739-44, 910-11.

87. Gavin, *War and Peace*, pp. 256-57.

88. For an evaluation of these techniques see John P. Crecine and Gregory W. Fischer, "On Resource Allocation Process in the U.S. Department of Defense," in *Political Science Annual: An International Review* vol. 4, ed. Cornelius P. Cotter (Indianapolis: Bobbs-Merrill, 1973), pp. 181-232. For Robert McNamara's own views see *The Essence of Security: Reflections in Office* (New York: Harper & Row, 1968).

89. Two classic works on planning-programming-budgeting systems (PPBS) are Fremont J. Lyden and Ernest G. Miller, eds., *Planning, Programming, Budgeting: A Systems Approach to Management* (Chicago: Markham Publishers, 1967), and David Novick, ed., *Program Budgeting: Program Analysis and the Federal Budget*, 2nd ed. (Cambridge: Harvard University Press, 1967). Less-affirmative studies are Alan Schick, "The Road to PPB: The State of Budget Reform," *Public Administration Review* 26 (1966): 243-58; and Aaron Wildavsky, "Political Economy of Efficiency: Cost-Benefit Analysis, Systems Analysis, and Program Budgeting," ibid., pp. 292-310.

90. Lawrence B. Tatum, "The Joint Chiefs of Staff and Defense Policy Formulation," *Air University Review*, May/June 1966, pp. 40-45, and July/August 1966, pp. 11-20.

91. See Gene M. Lyons, "The New Civil-Military Relations," *American Political Science Review* 55 (March 1961): 53-63.

92. Yarmolinsky, *The Military Establishment*, p. 115.

93. See Rudy Abramson, "Joint Chiefs: A Growing Influence in U.S. Policy," *Los Angeles Times*, August 27, 1972, sec. I, p. 1.

94. Yarmolinsky, *The Military Establishment*, p. 111.

95. The idea that preparing for war tends to bring on war is widely held. An advocate of this view is former Marine Corps Commandant David Shoup, who has stressed that the impact of interservice rivalry over readiness and deployment capabilities tends to escalate tense situations toward large-scale combat. See Shoup, "The New American Militarism," *Atlantic Monthly*, April 1969, pp. 51-56.

96. This was called the "Helicopter War" in the cover story of *Newsweek*, March 15, 1971, pp. 39-44.

97. U.S., Congress, Senate, Committee on Armed Services, *Investigation into Electronic Battlefield Program: Hearings before the Electronic Battlefield Subcommittee of the Preparedness Investigating Subcommittee*, 91st Cong., 2nd sess., November 1970.

Chapter 4

1. Jerome B. Wiesner, "Technology and Innovation" in *Technological Innovation and Society*, ed. Dean Morse and Aaron W. Warner (New York: Columbia University Press, 1966), p. 11.

2. Warner Schilling, "Technology," *International Encyclopedia of the Social Sciences*, ed. David Sills, 15 (1968): 589.

3. Interview F, p. 1.

4. Interview C, p. 5; also see Appendix 2 of this volume.

5. See Paul Y. Hammond, *Super Carriers and B-36 Bombers: Appropriations, Strategy, and Politics*, Inter-University Case Program no. 97 (New York: Bobbs-Merrill, 1963).

6. James M. Gavin, "Cavalry, and I Don't Mean Horses," *Harper's*, April 1954, pp. 54-60, deals with the concept of sky cavalry. For a discussion of the pentomic division see Chapter 3, p. 56.

7. Douglas D. Bond, *The Love and Fear of Flying* (New York: International Universities Press, 1952), p. 15: "Flying has long held a special place in man's thinking. It has been associated with aspiration and freedom from the restrictions of earth or of reality and has had strong religious connotations as well. Deeply rooted in man's mind is the idea that flying is a super-natural achievement."

180 / Notes to Chapter 4

8. Interview F, p. 2.
9. Interview G, pp. 83-85.
10. Ibid.
11. One of the main problems with deep-penetration daylight bombing raids without fighter cover over Germany was the ratio of pilots lost brought on by such tactics.
12. Francis R. Allen, "Influence of Technology on War," in *Technology and Social Change*, ed. Francis R. Allen et al. (New York: Appleton-Century-Crofts, 1957), p. 384.
13. Interview F, p. 1.
14. Interview H. It is further suggested that such patterns exist in management innovations from federal to state to local government levels.
15. Interview H, pp. 4-5.
16. See "Storm Brewing over Costly Chopper," *Nashville Tennessean*, April 20, 1969, sec. A, p. 12.
17. Merton Tyrell, *Pentagon Partners: The New Nobility* (New York: Grossman Publishers, 1970), pp. 70-71.
18. Such devices as the electronic battlefield and the Cheyenne assault helicopter may indicate a new attitude on the part of the Army with regard to weaponry. On the electronic battlefield see Raphael Littauer and Norman Uphoff, eds., *The Air War in Indochina*, rev. ed. (Boston: Beacon Press, 1973), pp. 151ff.; and Drew Middleton, "The Army is Developing Battlefield Computers and Detection Devices," *New York Times*, October 27, 1970, p. 12. On the Cheyenne see "Storm Brewing over Costly Chopper" and Tyrell, *Pentagon Partners*, pp. 57-59.
19. I. B. Holley, Jr., *Ideas and Weapons* (New Haven: Yale University Press, 1953), pp. 10-14.
20. See, for example, U.S., Army Infantry School, *Program of Instruction* (Fort Benning, Ga., n.d.), "Tactical Doctrine," Annex A1, p. 10.
21. Perry McCoy Smith, *The Air Force Plans for Peace, 1943-1945* (Baltimore: Johns Hopkins Press, 1970), pp. 29-33.
22. For the principles of war see U.S., Army Infantry School, "Tactical Doctrine."
23. According to Thompson's proposition 2.1, "Under norms of rationality, organizations seek to seal off their core technologies from environmental influences." See James D. Thompson, *Organizations in Action* (New York: McGraw-Hill, 1967), p. 19.
24. John Magee, "High Flight," in *Sunward I've Climbed*, ed. Herman Hagedorn (New York: Macmillan, 1942), p. 7.
25. John F. C. Fuller, *Machine Warfare: An Inquiry into the Influence of Mechanics on the Art of War* (Washington, D.C.: The Infantry Journal, 1943), pp. 61-62.
26. For a discussion of this see William F. Ogburn, "How Technology Causes Social Change," in *Technology and Social Change*, ed. Allen et al., pp. 14-15.
27. This difference in approach was later to animate the internal politics of Army aviation.
28. For a discussion of how equivalent inventions can be the outcome of the same social forces and hence can be substituted for each other see S. C. Gilfillan, *The Sociology of Invention* (1935; Cambridge: M.I.T. Press, 1970), pp. 137-39.
29. Clarence H. Danhof, *Government Contracting and Technological Change* (Washington, D.C.: Brookings Institution, 1968), pp. 53-56.
30. Ibid., p. 55.
31. Ibid., pp. 105-6.
32. This may well be an extension of the ideal typical distinctions between the Army and the Air Force. As Merton J. Peck and Frederic M. Scherer state: "Traditional philosophies and preferences of the organizations and groups involved in weapons programs are another influence on optimization decisions. That there are differences between groups in this respect is fairly widely recognized. . . . The various armed services, for instance, tend to place dissimilar emphasis upon the achievement of high

technical performance. The Air Force has probably tended to emphasize maximum performance, while the Army (at least, as exemplified by Army Ordnance) has generally stressed simplicity at the expense of some incremental performance." See Peck and Scherer, *The Weapons Acquisition Process: An Economic Analysis* (Boston: Harvard University, Graduate School of Business Administration, Division of Research, 1962), p. 478.

33. Tyrell, *Pentagon Partners*, pp. 70-72.

34. Danhof, *Government Contracting*, pp. 109-10. The implications of this for the military industrial complex will be explored in chapter 6.

35. Hanson W. Baldwin, "Defense Issue Crucial in the Budget Battle," *New York Times*, January 25, 1959, sec. E, p. 5.

36. Alain Enthoven, Address before the American Economic Association, Pittsburg, Pa., December 29, 1962, cited by David Novick, "The Department of Defense," in *Program Analysis and the Federal Budget*, ed. David Novick (Cambridge: Harvard University Press, 1967), p. 85.

37. Captain Stuard J. Evans, Harold J. Margulis, and Harry B. Yoshpe, *Procurement* (Washington, D.C.: Industrial College of the Armed Forces, 1968), p. 55.

38. Lockheed Aircraft Corp., *Development of the Helicopter* (Burbank, Calif.: Lockheed Aircraft Corp., 1966), p. 3.

39. Richard G. Hubler, *Straight Up: The Story of Vertical Flight* (New York: Duell, Sloan & Pierce, 1961), provides a useful history of early helicopter development.

40. Interview D, p. 19.

41. This appears in Charles O. Griminger and Aaron Rose, "Evolution of the Armed Helicopter and Future Design Requirements" (unpublished manuscript, 1968). This document, a looseleaf bound manuscript interspersed with photographs of various helicopter armaments, is in the U.S. Army Aviation Museum. It was apparently never finalized; instead, in 1971, a series of articles containing material taken in large part from the study was published in the *U.S. Army Aviation Digest*. The material was edited by Richard K. Tierney and appeared under the authorship of now Lieutenant Colonel Griminger. I will cite material from the articles where possible, thereby offering the reader easier access, and suggest which material, while not included in the *Army Aviation Digest* series, was relevant for this work.

42. Interview C, p. 4.

43. Ibid.

44. For example, Brigadier General Patrick W. Timberlake, Deputy Chief of Air Staff, Memorandum for Lieutenant General Hoyt S. Vandenberg, Major General Frederick L. Anderson, Jr., and Brigadier General Lauris Nordstadt, "Organizational Assignment of Aircraft Other Than to Air Forces," June 2, 1945: "General Arnold attaches a great deal of importance to the far-reaching subject and believes that once a policy is established it will carry over for the next fifteen years. This policy will affect Air Force appropriations, personnel to be carried on aviation duty, and the future relations between ground forces and Air Force." Personal copy provided by an interviewee.

45. R. Earl McClendon, *Army Aviation, 1947-1953*, Air University Documentary Research Study no. 48 (Maxwell Air Force Base, Ala., May 1954), p. 5.

46. This was in the form of two identical documents, Army Regulations 700-50 and Air Force Regulations 65-7, both titled *"Supplies and Equipment: Army Aircraft and Allied Equipment"* and issued on March 23, 1950.

47. Interview B, p. 1.

48. J. Pouget, "The Armed Helicopter," *Military Review*, March 1964, pp. 81-96 (translated from *L'Armée*).

49. For a general discussion of the role of the helicopter in Korea see Dario Politella, *Operation Grasshopper: The Story of Army Aviation in Korea from Aggression to Armistice* (Wichita, Kans.: Robert Longo, 1958); and Interview B, p. 1.

50. Colonel Spurgeon H. Neel and Major Roland H. Shamburek, "Medical Evacuation: The Army Aviation Story, Part IX," *U.S. Army Aviation Digest* 9 (February 1963): 38.

51. Richard K. Tierney, "The Army Aviation Story, Part VII: The War Years; Europe, Pacific, Korea," ibid. 8 (December 1962): 38.

52. Master Sergeant Thomas M. Lang, "Fixed Wing Aircraft: The Army Aviation Story, Part I," ibid. 8 (August 1962): 11.

53. Charles O. Griminger, "The Armed Helicopter Story, Part I: The Origins of U.S. Army Aviation," ibid. 17 (July 1971): 15.

54. Ibid.

55. Brigadier General Carl I. Hutton, "Without Trumpets and Drums: Recollections of Thirty-six Months with the Army Aviation School, June '54 to June '57" (unpublished manuscript), p. 148.

56. Ibid., p. 150.

57. Brigadier General Carl I. Hutton, "Air Mobility: Collected Papers, 1952-1956" (unpublished documents).

58. Griminger, "The Armed Helicopter Story, Part I," p. 16. Griminger says that Vanderpool was asked by Hutton to determine the feasibility of arming helicopters, but Vanderpool says he was "given the mission" of such a determination. See Colonel J. D. Vanderpool, "We Armed the Helicopter," *U.S. Army Aviation Digest* 17 (June 1971): 4.

59. Griminger, "The Armed Helicopter Story, Part I," p. 16.

60. *Army Flier* (Hartford, Ala.), August 2, 1957, p. 1.

61. The study known as the Fitzhugh Report is formally titled *Report to the President and the Secretary of Defense on the Department of Defense by the Blue Ribbon Defense Panel*, July 1, 1970 (Washington, D.C.: Government Printing Office, 1970).

62. Griminger, "The Armed Helicopter Story, Part I," p. 17.

63. Don Wagner, *Helicopter Armament Monograph, 1956-1958* (Fort Rucker, Ala.: USA Combat Developments Command, April 8, 1965), pp. 8-9.

64. "Wyman did not tell us to use armed helicopters, but neither did he tell us not to" (Vanderpool, "We Armed the Helicopter," p. 4). With such "approval" the experiments continued.

65. Griminger and Rose, "Evolution of the Armed Helicopter," p. 49.

66. Ibid., p. 50.

67. Thurlow Mayhood and Henry G. Benis, "Helicopter Armament," *American Helicopter Society Newsletter*, October 1960, p. 1. The G.E. kit was, in fact, delivered, but there were difficulties, both supply and mechanical, during its testing.

68. Charles O. Griminger, "The Armed Helicopter Story, Part III: Armed Helicopters around the World," *U.S. Army Aviation Digest* 17 (September 1971): 11.

69. Griminger and Rose, "Evolution of the Armed Helicopter," p. 63. This does not qualify as a "kit" and may mark the end of a simple line of development.

70. Vanderpool selected the Oerlikon as the most promising anti-tank rocket. See Vanderpool, "We Armed the Helicopter," p. 4.

71. USAAVNC (U.S. Army Aviation Center) History, 1954-1964, *Artillery Pilots* (Fort Rucker, Ala.: Adjutant General's Office, January 1, 1965). See especially pp. 2-3, 15-16, 53-54.

72. William Vance, "How the Army Got Its Shooting Helicopters," *National Guardsman* 17 (May 1963): 3-4.

73. Charles O. Griminger, "The Armed Helicopter Story, Part IV: Weapons Systems (Early Experiments)," *U.S. Army Aviation Digest* 17 (October 1971): 18.

74. Vanderpool, "We Armed the Helicopter," p. 5.

75. Ibid., pp. 5-6.

Notes to Chapter 4

76. Ibid., p. 29.
77. Griminger, "The Armed Helicopter Story, Part III," p. 12.
78. Griminger, "The Armed Helicopter Story, Part IV," p. 19.
79. Interview I, p. 1.
80. Ibid.
81. This and much of the following information is taken from Chief Warrant Officer James Ervin's diary, which he donated to the U.S. Army Aviation Museum in 1968. The diary, which is not paginated, was apparently kept at the request of then Major William Howell.
82. Griminger, "The Armed Helicopter Story, Part III," p. 13.
83. Ibid., p. 12.
84. Charles O. Griminger, "The Armed Helicopter Story, Part II: 'Vanderpool's Fools,'" *U.S. Army Aviation Digest* 17 (August 1971): 15-16.
85. This information is derived from the unpaginated scrapbook of the ACR Platoon which is on display at the U.S. Army Aviation Museum, Fort Rucker, Ala.
86. Charles O. Griminger, "The Armed Helicopter Story, Part V: Formal Development (Models XM-1 thru XM-50)," *U.S. Army Aviation Digest* 17 (November 1971): 18.
87. Ibid.
88. Ibid., p. 17.
89. Interview A, pp. 3-4.
90. It is particularly interesting to note how much of this assistance was based on company-sponsored initiatives, especially in the case of the Huey Cobra (AH-1G), which was to become the first exclusive attack helicopter. This aircraft was developed by Bell and, oddly enough, was not an object of excessive contention between the Army and the Air Force. It appears that the Air Force was preoccupied with the development of the Cheyenne attack helicopter, with which the Army was more currently involved. Interview J, pp. 69-71.
91. Interview I, p. 3.
92. Interview A, p. 3.
93. Interview I, p. 3.
94. Interview C, p. 4.
95. Griminger, "The Armed Helicopter Story, Part III," p. 22.
96. See, for example, Gavin, "Cavalry, and I Don't Mean Horses"; and Major General Hamilton H. Howze, "Soldiers with a Double Skill," *Army* 7 (January 1957): 30-34.
97. This phrase appeared in an undated and otherwise unidentified advertisement attached to a page of the ACR Platoon scrapbook.
98. See, for example, Brigadier General Bogardus S. Cairns, Speech to Fort Benning Chapter of the Military Order of World Wars, Fort Benning, Ga., February 20, 1958; and Brigadier General Carl I. Hutton, Presentation for National Security Commission of the American Legion Convention, Los Angeles, September 2, 1956.
99. USAAVNC History, 1954-1964, *Artillery Pilots*, p. 53.
100. Hutton, "Without Trumpets and Drums," p. 156.
101. Ibid. It is unclear whether the presence of unfriendly CONARC officials limited the ability of the Army aviators to communicate with the congressmen, or whether CONARC officials were reluctant to bluntly suggest to Congress noncompliance with roles and missions agreements.
102. The Association of the United States Army, like other backstop military organizations, contained potentially favorable elements as well as some opponents of Army aviation.
103. The selection of future leaders of the Army as persons especially to be impressed by the capabilities of armed helicopters is in keeping with the policy of carefully targeting elites for initiation into the fraternity of Army aviation, a strategy I will discuss more fully in Chapter 5.

184 / Notes to Chapter 4

104. The *Dothan* (Ala.) *Eagle*, July 6, 1957, p. 1.
105. *Columbus* (Ga.) *Inquirer*, July 30, 1957, p. 1.
106. "Army Flexes Missile Muscles for U.S. Leaders," *Stars and Stripes* (European ed.), July 2, 1958.
107. "Cavalry of Atomic Battlefield," *Army, Navy, Air Force Journal*, July 5, 1958, p. 1.
108. The presence of "Lieutenant General James M. Gavins [sic]" was noted in the *Army Flier*, August 2, 1957. The Army Flier also noted the attendance of General Edward Snedeker at a Fort Rucker demonstration (October 28, 1960). A detailed description of a tour by Secretary Brucker appeared in the May 4, 1959, *Dothan Eagle*, p. 1.

Chapter 5

1. Vincent Davis has aptly described a serious difficulty for those who are engaged in the analysis of innovation, the problem of creating a misleading impression of "good guys and bad guys." He states: "The advocates of innovation tend to be depicted as 'the good guys' who are 'intelligent' and 'progressive' whereas the opponents of innovation appear as 'the bad guys' who are 'cautious,' 'conservative,' even 'reactionary.' No such impressions are intended in this book.

"It is only with the benefit of hindsight that a critic can attempt to make such invidious distinctions. At the time when a decision is made within an organization with respect to initiating R & D on a proposed technological innovation, the opponents often have very sound arguments on their side. Indeed, unless one assumes that all innovative proposals are equally sound and worthy, the opponents serve the valuable function of filtering out the less worthy and less sound ideas. It is only when an innovation is in fact developed and adopted by an organization and then proves to be of great importance that one can look back and charge the opponents with having been excessively cautious, and even in these kinds of cases the charge is usually not warranted." *The Politics of Innovation: Patterns in Navy Cases*, Social Science Foundation and Graduate School of International Studies, Monograph Series in World Affairs, vol. 4, no. 3 (Denver: University of Denver, 1966-1967), pp. 4-5, n. 3.

2. It is interesting, though not central for our purposes, to consider the possible subtypes in the category of *acquiescers*. They might range from the classic amoral bureaucrats, the "good Germans" who did their duty, to the deeply committed "ends justify the means" types who acquiesed to Stalin's purges as necessary for advancing the economic well-being of the Russian people. Actors' perceptions of legitimacy should be distinguished from external analytical evaluations.

3. Noah Webster, *Webster's Dictionary of Synonyms* (Springfield, Mass.: G. & C. Merriam, 1942), p. 680.

4. See Clay Blair, Jr., *The Atomic Submarine and Admiral Rickover* (New York: Henry Holt, 1954).

5. Tom Burns, "The Reference of Conduct in Small Groups: Cliques and Cabals in Occupational Milieux," *Human Relations* 8 (November 1955): 480.

6. "Social Movements: Growth, Decay, and Change," *Social Forces* 44 (March 1966): 329.

7. Ibid.

8. "Social Movement," *Dictionary of the Social Sciences*, ed. Julius Gold and William Kolb, 1964.

9. "The Types and Functions of Social Movements," *The International Encyclopedia of the School Sciences*, ed. David Sills, 14 (1968): 439.

10. Ibid., p. 440.

Notes to Chapter 5

11. Ibid.
12. This acronym is used by the author for literary convenience and should not imply any such formal organization.
13. Interview J, p. 51.
14. Ibid.
15. Ibid., p. 70.
16. Interview F, p. 5.
17. Ibid.
18. Ibid.
19. See Chapter 3, pp. 47-48.
20. Interview D, p. 13.
21. Ibid., p. 2.
22. It must hardly have seemed inviting to travel to a remote range on a South Alabama Army post in July when one could sit in an air-conditioned office in Washington, D.C., or travel to its equivalent in, say, Old Point Comfort, Virginia, the home of CONARC. Even if one were so disposed, the physical isolation of the ranges could allow time for various preinspection alterations. In any event, high-ranking officers generally do not have the reputation of dropping in unannounced without proper preparations having been made for them and their aides.
23. Elton Trueblood, *The Validity of the Christian Mission* (New York: Harper & Row, 1972), p. 11.
24. "Slicks" are troop-carrying helicopters; "hooks" are CH-47 Chinooks; and "autorotation" is a method of safely landing a helicopter when the engine fails.
25. *Christian Mission*, p. 21.
26. *The Study of Man* (New York: Appleton-Century, 1936), pp. 113-14.
27. Interview E, pp. 10-11.
28. Interview G, pp. 75-76.
29. Interview G, p. 106.
30. Interview G, p. 108. On pp. 109-10 this interviewee indicates that such conduct is not essentially dishonest. Rather, small-scale experiments were conducted without asking permission. When larger sums of money were needed, "we had to come completely into the open and say what we wanted."
31. Interview K, p. 2.
32. "Bureaucratic Sabotage," *Annals* 189 (January 1937): 48-57.
33. Daniel P. Moynihan, *Maximum Feasible Misunderstanding: Community Action in the War on Poverty* (New York: Free Press, Arkville Books, 1969), pp. 66, 75-76. Query for Moynihan: What if it were a large group of people, with great endurance, who understood the problem rather well?
34. Interview E, p. 9.
35. *Modern Organization* (New York: Alfred A. Knopf, 1961), p. 24.
36. "Sources of Power of Lower Participants in Complex Organizations," *Administrative Science Quarterly* 7 (December 1962): 349-64.
37. See, for example, Karl W. Deutsch, *The Nerves of Government: Models of Political Communication and Control* (New York: Free Press, 1966), pp. 154-57.
38. See Chapter 2.
39. It should be remembered that on occasion such high-ranking officers with broad responsibilities as Generals Dwight Eisenhower and Mark Clark were at least somewhat supportive of Army aviation. See Chapter 2.
40. Information suggesting appreciation of the Cub pilots can be found in Richard K. Tierney, "The Army Aviation Story, Part VI: The War Years; North Africa, Sicily, Italy" *U.S. Army Aviation Digest* 8 (November 1962): 34-37; and idem, "The Army Aviation Story, Part VII: The War Years; Europe, Pacific, Korea," ibid. 8 (December 1962): 26-38.

186 / Notes to Chapter 5

41. This decision was based on an agreement between General Jacob L. Devers, Commanding General Army Ground Forces, and General Ira C. Eaker, Deputy Commander of the Army Air Forces. See R. Earl McLendon, *Army Aviation, 1947-1953*, Air University Documentary Research Study no. 48 (Maxwell Air Force Base, Ala., May 1954), p. 4.

42. At one point there were fewer than 500 pilots in Army aviation. Interview D, p. 9.

43. Interview B, p. 3.

44. Ibid. There is also evidence that during this period protective associations resembling cabals were formed. Interview I, p. 3.

45. Richard K. Tierney, "The Army Aviation Story, Part II; Academies and Training," *U.S. Army Aviation Digest* 8 (July 1962): 15.

46. Chapter 3, pp. 40-48.

47. Interview D, p. 8.

48. Ibid., p. 9.

49. Ibid.

50. Interview E, p. 2.

51. Ibid.

52. Interview D, p. 9.

53. Interview E, p. 7.

54. Ibid., p. 9.

55. Ibid., pp. 7-8.

56. Tierney, "The Army Aviation Story, Part II," p. 23.

57. Ibid., pp. 23-24.

58. James M. Gavin, *War and Peace in the Space Age* (New York: Harper & Bros., 1958), p. 109.

59. Interview E, p. 5.

60. Ibid., p. 6.

61. Perry McCoy Smith, *The Air Force Plans for Peace, 1943-1945* (Baltimore: Johns Hopkins Press, 1970), p. 99.

62. Interview C, p. 1.

63. Smith, *The Air Force Plans for Peace*, pp. 99-100.

64. This report was classified. I was able to gain access to some of its findings by reading portions of an unpublished and incomplete manuscript, "History of Army Aviation" (the specific material is located in chap. 8). This history, prepared by Major Donald Harrison, is on file at the Army's Office of the Chief of Military History in Washington. In order to gain access to original classified documents, one must receive a security clearance and then submit one's work for security review. I chose not to submit this draft to such a review. No disclaimer need be added, therefore, that my views are not the official line of any part of the government. The lack of access is especially unfortunate since interviewees told me that matters relating to interservice rivalry are routinely classified whether they contain defense information or not.

65. Brigadier General Carl I. Hutton, "Without Trumpets and Drums: Recollections of Thirty-six Months with the Army Aviation School, June 1954-June 1957" (unpublished manuscript on file at the U.S. Army Aviation Center Library, Fort Rucker, Ala., n.d.), p. 1.

66. Richard K. Tierney, "The Army Aviation Story, Part II," p. 19.

67. Hutton, "Without Trumpets and Drums," p. 2.

68. Ibid., p. 16.

69. Ibid., pp. 24-25.

70. Ibid., p. 25.

71. For a description of Gavin's achievements at Normandy see S.L.A. Marshall, *Night Drop* (New York: Bantam Books, 1962). This particular phrase is found in the pre-

187 / Notes to Chapter 5

face, written by Carl Sandburg, p. ix. Some of Gavin's ideas are put forth in his *Airborne Warfare* (Washington, D.C.: Infantry Journal Press, 1947).

72. James M. Gavin, *War and Peace in the Space Age* (New York: Harper & Bros., 1958), p. 110.

73. Ibid., p. 248.

74. Gavin's fitful departure from the Army is chronicled in the *New York Times* in a series of articles from the January 5, 1958, front page announcement of his intent to retire to the April 1, 1958, notation of his leaving. Gavin's quitting caused concern in Congress, as noted in a January 6, 1958, first-page article which stated that his departure would be studied by a Senate unit; in the White House, where Eisenhower was reportedly "irked" by the bargaining used to induce Gavin to remain (January 10, 1958, p. 9); as well as at the Department of Defense, where Wilson offered Gavin two major assignments with a chance of promotion (January 8, 1958, p. 1). Gavin's temperament is noted in Interview L.

75. Harrison, "History of Army Aviation," chap. 7, p. 8.

76. A 10 percent random sample was taken of all persons listed in the 1954 *"Who's Who" in Army Aviation* (Westport, Conn.: Army Aviation Publications, 1954). This compilation included not quite one-half of all Army aviators. The results were as follows: major general, 0; brigadier general, 1; colonel, 0; lieutenant colonel, 8; major, 15; captain, 37; first lieutenant, 22; second lieutenant, 4; warrant officer, Junior Grade, 7; sergeant first class, 3; sergeant, 4; corporal, 2; private first class, 5; private, 1; total, 109.

77. Hutton, "Without Trumpets and Drums," p. 130.

78. Ibid.

79. Ibid. Elements of the Transportation Corps were becoming interested in control of Army aviation. Thus, their opposition to an aviation branch had a different basis than that of Hutton.

80. Ibid., p. 131.

81. Ibid.

82. Ibid., pp. 132-33.

83. Interview J, p. 56.

84. The same data utilized in note 76 reveal that in 1954, of 109 soldiers sampled, no more than 10 were at any one location and 56 different places were represented.

85. Interview M, p. 4.

86. Ibid., p. 1.

87. Interview D, pp. 50-51, 54.

88. Interview E, pp. 33-34.

89. Hutton, "Without Trumpets and Drums," p. 50.

90. Ibid.

91. Such close attention was paid to the attitudes of the students that after one negative experience it was decided to welcome the newcomers with a cocktail party. Ibid., p. 53.

92. Major General Hamilton H. Howze, "The Last Three Years of Army Aviation," *U.S. Army Aviation Digest* 4 (March 1958): 16.

93. As Deputy Secretary of Defense Ruben H. Robertson, Jr., said of the Wilson Memorandum of 1956: "We're not going to set up an Air Force within the Army." See William H. Blair, "Wilson Restricts Army on Missiles and Air Program," *New York Times* November 17, 1956, sec. A, pp. 1, 22.

94. Hutton, "Without Trumpets and Drums," p. 172.

95. Ibid., p. 165.

96. Ibid., p. 164.

97. Ibid., p. 169.

98. Ibid., p. 144.

99. Interview A, p. 1.

188 / Notes to Chapter 5

100. Ibid.
101. Interview E, p. 22.
102. Ibid., p. 23.
103. Ibid., p. 24.
104. Ibid., pp. 25-26.
105. Unlike some members of the American military mainstream, the Soviet "Reds," in general, apparently did not have enough background or time to take on easily the status of experts. For a thorough study of Soviet managerial practices see Jeremy R. Azrael, *Managerial Power and Soviet Politics* (Cambridge: Harvard University Press, 1966).
106. Interview M, p. 1.
107. This assessment of Hutton's political adroitness is made by Interviewee E, p. 48.
108. See Chapters 3 and 4.
109. John R. Galvin, *Air Assault: The Development of Airmobile Warfare* (New York: Hawthorn, 1969), pp. 275-76.
110. Interview J, p. 60.
111. Ibid., pp. 60-61.
112. Ibid., p. 60.
113. Ibid., p. 62.
114. Galvin, *Air Assault*, p. 276.
115. By 1970, at least four of the members had been directors of Army aviation.
116. Interview E, p. 49.
117. Interview G, p. 90.
118. Interview A, p. 1.
119. Galvin, *Air Assault*, p. 276.
120. Interview G, p. 89.
121. Ibid., p. 88.
122. Ibid., p. 77.
123. Ibid., p. 89.
124. Ibid., p. 88.
125. Interview M, p. 15.
126. Ibid., p. 19.
127. Interview G, p. 86.
128. U.S., Department of the Air Force, Tactical Air Support Requirements Board, "U.S. Air Force Tactical Air Support Requirements Board Comments on . . . Report Army Tactical Mobility Board," 4 vols., Lietenant General G. P. Disosway, USAF, chairman (Washington, D.C.: 1962).
129. Interview N, p. 1; Interview G, p. 90.
130. Interview J, p. 65.
131. Interview E, p. 51.
132. For McNamara's own view of his priorities see *Essence of Security: Reflections in Office* (New York: Harper & Row, 1968).
133. Galvin, *Air Assault*, pp. 280-81.
134. Hanson W. Baldwin, "War Games Test Opposing Tactics," *New York Times*, November 15, 1964, sec. A, p. 80.
135. Interview J, p. 65.
136. Interview M, p. 9. Goldwater did become the friend of a key Army aviator.
137. Interview O, p. 1.
138. U.S., Congress, House, Committee on Armed Services, *Close Air Support: Hearings before the Special Subcommittee on Tactical Air Support*, 89th Cong., 1st sess., 1965, pp. 4779-80.
139. "Air Force, Army Agree on Roles, Missions," *Aviation Week and Space Technology*, April 27, 1966, pp. 26-27.

140. Interview E, p. 17.
141. Ibid., pp. 17-18.
142. Andrew F. Henry, John W. Masland, and Laurence I. Radway, "Armed Forces Unification and the Pentagon Officer," *Public Administration Review* 15 (1955): 178-80.
143. While the Howze Board performed some tests with Vietnam in mind, it is important to remember that the Airmobile Division was especially designed for European combat. Interview G, pp. 95, 114-15.
144. U.S., Congress, Senate, Committee on Armed Services, Preparedness Investigating Subcommittee, *Report on the Investigation of the Preparedness Program*, 90th Cong., 2nd sess., 1968, p. 4.
145. U.S., Congress, House, Committee on Armed Services, Subcommittee for Special Investigations, *Review of Army Procurement of Light Observation Helicopters*, 90th Cong., 1st sess., 1967.
146. Several documents on air support on file at the Air University Library at Maxwell Air Force Base, Ala., are stamped "Corona Harvest."
147. See Chapter 6.
148. Interview P.
149. David Lamb, "Copter Proves Itself as Vietnam Weapon," *Nashville Tennessean*, July 6, 1969, sec. A, p. 6.

Chapter 6

1. Raphael Littauer and Norman Uphoff, eds., *The Air War in Indochina* (Boston: Beacon Press, 1972), pp. 267-72. Military analysts might argue that this figure is not significant, because a sortie occurs each time an aircraft takes off and then lands; thus several tasks can be performed in one sortie. Further, the duration is relatively short for rotary-wing sorties, twenty-five minutes or half an hour, rather than the usual hour plus of fixed-wing flights. For our purposes (trying to assess the magnitude of the presence of helicopters) these distinctions are unimportant, considering that before Vietnam serious individuals had contended that the helicopter was inherently unstable and fragile, and thus useless in a combat zone.
2. Adding the helicopter badge to his airborne wings, Westmoreland himself symbolized the establishment of the airmobile army and suggests the eclipse of the fashionable airborne club. The paratrooper elite may be on its way out as the airborne mode is supplanted by air mobility as the most effective method of Army air combat. For a discussion of the abandonment of paratroop tactics, see Steven B. Patrick, "Combined Arms: Combat Operations in the Twentieth Century," *Strategy and Tactics* 46 (September/October 1974): 19.
3. Maureen Mylander, *The Generals* (New York: Dial Press, 1974), p. 188.
4. Lieutenant General John J. Tolson, "The New Challenge," *U.S. Army Aviation Digest* 18 (December 1972): 3.
5. Mylander, *The Generals*, p. 188.
6. Tolson, "The New Challenge," p. 3, fig. 1.
7. "Abandoned Craft Making Comeback: Cheyenne Copter Heads for Army Trials," *Los Angeles Times*, March 24, 1972, pt. 1, p. 3. Because of the many variables involved, I make no claim to expertness in identifying "real costs" of complex weapons systems and greet all such efforts with frank skepticism.
8. Harold D. Watkins, "At Northrup, Think Small Is the Motto," *Los Angeles Times*, September 1, 1974, pt. 5, p. 1.
9. "The DOD . . . subsequently established an average flyaway cost goal of approximately $3 million in 1972 dollars based on a production run of 300 aircraft at 100 per year." "Lightweight Fighter: The General Dynamics Approach," *Air International* 7 (August 1974): 60.

10. For a vivid depiction of the Battle of Laos, see "Scramble for Safety," illustrated by Mark Godfrey and Asihiko Okamua, *Life*, April 2, 1971, pp. 16-23; and John Saars, "An Ignominious and Disorderly Retreat," ibid., pp. 24-28.

11. U.S., Congress, Senate, Committee on Armed Services, Special Subcommittee on Close Air Support, *Close Air Support*, 92nd Cong., 2nd sess., 1971, p. 449.

12. Ibid., p. 108.

13. Ibid., p. 6.

14. Ibid., p. 3.

15. Ibid., p. 440. The MCPL is an example of a bipartisan congressional interest group. This group was responsible for the report prepared by three of its members—Senator Charles Mathias, Jr. (R-Maryland), Senator William Proxmire (D-Wisconsin), and Congressman John Seiberling (D-Ohio)—and their staffs, *Close Support Aircraft: The AX, Harrier, and Cheyenne*, which was presented to the Special Subcommittee on Close Air Support.

16. U.S., Senate, *Close Air Support*, p. 411.

17. Ibid., pp. 90, 274.

18. Ibid., pp. 91, 99.

19. Ibid., p. 167.

20. Ibid., p. 125.

21. Ibid., p. 445.

22. Ibid., p. 191.

23. Ibid., pp. 188, 220, 222.

24. For example, see ibid., p. 78.

25. Ibid., p. 138.

26. Ibid., p. 106.

27. Ibid., pp. 81-84.

28. Ibid., p. 11.

29. Ibid., p. 5.

30. Ibid., p. 84.

31. Ibid., p. 404.

32. Ibid., p. 136.

33. Ibid., p. 137.

34. Interview C, p. 2. Another regulation, which "simply appeared one day" and "resulted in some oil companies collecting hundreds of millions of dollars in actual or deferred price increases that they were not fairly entitled to," drew the ire of the *Los Angeles Times'* editorial staff, who wondered whether it was delivered by "the good fairy or the local drugstore or someone from the hierarchy of FEA [Federal Energy Administration]." "Double-Dipping with the Good Fairy," *Los Angeles Times*, September 29, 1974, pt. 5, p. 2.

35. William D. White, *U.S. Tactical Air Power* (Washington, D.C.: Brookings Institution, 1974), pp. 68-69.

36. U.S., Senate, *Close Air Support*, p. 386.

37. Bill Gunston, *Attack Aircraft of the West* (New York: Charles Scribner's Sons, 1974), p. 262.

38. U.S., Senate, *Close Air Support*, pp. 366-406 *passim*. For an extensive discussion of structures of trust, see Charles A. Zuzak, Kenneth E. McNeil, and Frederic Bergerson, *Beyond the Ballot: Organized Citizen Participation in Metropolitan Nashville* (Knoxville: University of Tennessee, Bureau of Public Administration, 1971), pp. 277-78.

39. U.S., Senate, *Close Air Support*, p. 125.

40. Ibid., p. 146. One estimate of the comparative unit costs for the Lockheed Cheyenne, the Sikorsky Blackhawk, and the Bell King Cobra was Cheyenne, $3,759,000; Blackhawk, $3,588,000; and King Cobra, $2,693,000.

41. Ibid., pp. 452-53.

191 / Notes to Chapter 6

42. Ibid., p. 397.
43. For example, see ibid., pp. 396-99.
44. James R. Kurth, "A Widening Gyre: The Logic of American Weapons Procurement," *Public Policy* 19 (Summer 1971): 390.
45. U.S., Senate, *Close Air Support*, pp. 372-73.
46. Ibid., pp. 399-400.
47. Ibid., pp. 383, 393.
48. Ibid., pp. 16-17, 191.
49. Ibid., p. 394.
50. Ibid., p. 82.
51. Ibid., p. 83.
52. Katherine Johnsen, "One Senate Unit Defends Armed Helicopters, Another Cuts Funds," *Aviation Week and Space Technology*, July 10, 1972, p. 15.
53. U.S., Senate, *Close Air Support*, p. 40.
54. Ibid., p. 99.
55. The employment of language may have widespread symbolic aspects as well as value in facilitating political bargains. See Murray Edelman, *The Symbolic Uses of Politics* (Urbana: University of Illinois Press, 1964). The potential absurdity of manipulated language was brought home quite humorously in a letter dated November 21, 1970, to the author from Professor John T. Dorsey, Jr.: "I have just read in the newspaper Secretary Laird's comically ponderous label, 'limited duration protective reaction air strikes,' for this morning's bombing in North Viet Nam. While on this subject, why don't we just label the war a 'strategic counterreactive operation of sub-globular and sub-nuclear dimension implemented to sanitize a proto-hostile, contra-indicated concentration of geopolitico-ideaologico-socioeconomic structures'? Thus it becomes merely a technical problem the solution of which involves dropping a few bombs, and who could object to that?"
56. For an interesting discussion of the role of "JCS Pub 1," see Argus J. Tressidder, "The Military Vocabulary," *Military Review* 52 (December 1972): 8-13.
57. Joint Chiefs of Staff, *Dictionary of United States Military Terms for Joint Usage* (Washington, D.C.: Government Printing Office, August 1968), p. 45.
58. Ibid., Appendix C, pp. 255-63.
59. The complexity of language alone suggests time-consuming coordination problems. Fred Harvey, *Air War-Vietnam* (New York: Bantam Books, 1967), p. 38, commented: "After furious attempts at concentration I can now tell you that the TACC is backed up by the DASC (Direct Air Support Center) and that the FASC is backed up by the FAC (Forward Air Controller) and that the FAC is backed up by the ALO (Air Liaison Officer) and THAT THEY ARE ALL ASSISTED BY THE TASS (Tactical Air Support Squadron) and the whole ball of wax is a JAGOS (Joint Air Ground Operation System). The TACC is composed of a staff of VNAF (Vietnamese Air Force officers) and their opposite numbers in the USAF (U.S. Air Force). So much for alphabet soup."
60. U.S., Senate, *Close Air Support*, p. 155. Sometimes users of jargon can get caught in their own verbal webs. According to one story, the Air Force applied the name F-110 to its essentially identical version of the Navy's F-4. Because they carried different designations, Secretary McNamara debated the merits of the two aircraft in public. When informed of the reality, he decreed that no piece of equipment was ever to have more than one name. Interview E, p. 26.
61. Interview E, p. 26. Efforts to stop the use of words by command action apparently are not uncommon. One person reported that at a company formation he was told never again to use the term "VOLAR," which had become the Army's vigorously promoted buzz word for the all-volunteer Army. When beer in the barracks and longer hair finally offended or threatened someone in authority, instant termination of the acronym became one method of changing the image of the volunteer Army. Interview R.

62. Interview Q.

63. U.S., Senate, *Close Air Support*, pp. 392-93.

64. Colonel William E. Crouch, Jr., "DA Happenings," *Army Aviation* 24 (July/August 1975): 8-9.

65. The Cheyenne was originally planned by Lockheed for the Air Force. It was to have a dive-bombing capability. The impact of the Army's possession of such a weapon on the Air Force's sense of mission must have been pronounced.

66. "Army Plans New Attack Helicopter Competition," *Aviation Week and Space Technology*, August 14, 1972, p. 21.

67. The cost of the F-15 had been estimated at $9,800,000. Even more expensive is the Navy's F-14A fighter, whose unit cost was planned to be $16,000,000; see White, *U.S. Tactical Air Power*, p. 47. A later estimate for this Navy craft was $19,900,000; see "Navy Hikes Estimated F-14 Cost," *Whittier Daily News*, September 16, 1975, p. 3.

68. "A Closer Look at the Utility Tactical Transport Aircraft System," *Government Executive* 4 (April 1972): 32.

69. Interview Q, p. 3.

70. Ibid. For an extended discussion of the development of the Ramo-Wooldridge organization, see Harvey M. Sapolsky, *The Polaris System Development: Bureaucratic and Programmatic Success in Government* (Cambridge: Harvard University Press, 1972), pp. 84-89.

71. Captain Charles F. Nowlin, "A Young Aviator Asks Some Questions," *Army Aviation* 24 (July/August 1975): 4.

72. Lieutenant Colonel William L. Hauser, USA, *American Army in Crisis* (Baltimore: Johns Hopkins University Press, 1973).

73. Edward L. King, *The Death of the Army: A Pre-Mortem* (New York: Saturday Review Press, 1972).

74. Interview C, p. 6. Also see, for example, Don Cook, "What Role for the Navy?" *Los Angeles Times*, September 28, 1975, pt. 5, p. 5: "In short, there is now grave doubt among those who study strategic problems as to whether the kind of sea power which has been traditionally pursued by the Western powers in the Mahan mold can continue to be exercised in the world."

75. "New Helicopter Roles Planned," *Aviation Week*, September 29, 1975, p. 53; and Interview C, p. 3.

Chapter 7

1. "The Army Aviation Association of America (AAAA) was formed in early 1957 by a small group of Senior Army aviation officers in the active Army, the Reserve forces, and industry. Following the incorporation of the AAAA as a membership corporation without capital stock under the laws of the state of Connecticut, this group took over control of the affairs of the AAAA from the incorporators on 18 April 1957.

"Modeled after several of the professional-technical societies in existence, the AAAA grew rapidly, receiving the membership support of the majority of those military and civilian persons having an interest in this segment of the Armed Forces." From "Objectives and Purposes," received with an application for membership in the AAAA, Westport, Connecticut.

2. *"Public goods* are defined as goods which are consumed by all those who are members of a given community, country, or geographical area in such a manner that consumption or use by one member does not detract from consumption or use by another member . . . . The distinguishing characteristic of these goods is not only that they *can* be consumed by everyone, but *that there is no escape* from consuming them unless one were to leave the community by which they are provided. The concept of public goods makes it easy to understand the notion that in some situations there can be

no real exit from a good or an organization so that the decision to exit in the partial sense in which this may be possible must take into account any further deterioration in the good that may result." Albert O. Hirschman, *Exit, Voice, and Loyalty: Responses to Decline in Firms, Organizations, and States* (Cambridge: Harvard University Press, 1970), pp. 101-2.

3. "Answer to Darwinian Riddle Seen in Modern Ecology," *Johns Hopkins Journal* 7 (Summer 1973): 2.

4. Rupert B. Vance, "The Development and Status of American Demography," in *Study of Population*, ed. Philip M. Hansen and Otis Dudley Duncan (Chicago: University of Chicago Press, 1959), p. 297.

5. See Charles Kadushin, "Power, Influence, and Social Circles: A New Methodology for Studying Opinion Makers," *American Sociological Review* 33 (October 1968): 692.

6. Ibid.

7. Ibid.

8. Mark S. Granovetter, "Strength of Weak Ties," *American Journal of Sociology* 78 (1973): 1361.

9. Hirschman, *Exit, Voice, and Loyalty*, chap. 7.

10. Cornelius J. Lammers, "Strikes and Mutinites: A Comparative Study of Organizational Conflicts Between Rulers and Ruled," *Administrative Science Quarterly* 14 (December 1969): 559.

11. "This intimation of some influence and the expectation that, over a period of time, the right turns will more than balance the wrong ones, profoundly distinguishes loyalty from faith." Hirschman, *Exit, Voice, and Loyalty*, p. 78.

12. Many aspects of the nonconforming enclave are similar to elements of a bureaucratic social movement. Methods of control of nonconforming enclaves within organizations are discussed by Ruth Leeds in "The Absorption of Protest: A Working Paper," in *New Perspectives in Organizational Research*, ed. W. W. Cooper, H. J. Leavitt, and M. W. Shelly II (New York: John Wiley, 1964).

13. Lee Sigelman, "Reporting the News: An Organizational Analysis," *American Journal of Sociology* 79 (1973): 133.

14. Bertram M. Gross, "Planning in an Era of Social Revolution," *Public Administration Review* 31 (May/June 1971): 284.

15. Ibid.

16. "Retired CIA Scientist Takes Blame for Keeping Poisons," *Whittier Daily News*, September 17, 1975, p. 6.

17. "The Army Gets Out of Line," *Los Angeles Times*, December 31, 1974, pt. 2, p. 2.

18. See, for example, Warren G. Bennis, "A Funny Thing Happened on the Way to the Future," *American Psychologist* 15 (July 1970): 595.

BIBLIOGRAPHY

Books

Abrahamson, Bengt, ed. *Military Professionalism and Political Power.* Beverly Hills, Calif.: Sage Publications, 1972.

Allen, Francis R. "Influence of Technology on War." In *Technology and Social Change*, edited by Francis R. Allen, Hornell Hart, Delbert C. Miller, William F. Ogburn, and Meyer F. Nimkoff, pp. 352-87. New York: Appleton-Century-Crofts, 1957.

Allison, Graham T. *Essence of Decision: Explaining the Cuban Missile Crisis.* Boston: Little, Brown, 1971.

Ambler, John Steward. *The French Army in Politics, 1945-1962.* Columbus: Ohio State University Press, 1966.

Ambrose, Stephen E. *The Supreme Commander: The War Years of General Dwight D. Eisenhower.* Garden City, N. Y.: Doubleday, 1970.

Armacost, Michael. *The Politics of Weapons Innovation: The Thor-Jupiter Controversy.* New York: Columbia University Press, 1969.

Art, Robert J. *The TFX Decision: McNamara and the Military.* Boston: Little, Brown, 1968.

Azrael, Jeremy R. *Managerial Power and Soviet Politics.* Cambridge: Harvard University Press, 1966.

Barber, James Alden, Jr. "The Draft and Alternatives to the Draft." In *The Military and American Society*, edited by Stephen Ambrose and James Barber, Jr., pp. 208-15. New York: Free Press, 1972.

Berger, Peter. *A Rumor of Angels: Modern Society and the Rediscovery of the Supernatural.* Garden City, N.Y.: Doubleday, 1969.

_____. *The Sacred Canopy: Elements of a Sociological Theory of Religion.* Garden City, N.Y.: Doubleday, 1967.

Blair, Clay, Jr. *The Atomic Submarine and Admiral Rickover.* New York: Henry Holt, 1954.

Blanchard, Colonel Wendell, and Dupuy, Colonel T. N. *The Almanac of World Military Power.* 2nd ed. Dunn Loring, Va., and New York: T. N. Dupuy Associates and R. R. Bowker, 1972.

Bond, Douglas D. *The Love and Fear of Flying.* New York: International Universities Press, 1952.

Borklund, C. W. *The Department of Defense.* New York: Frederick A. Praeger, 1968.

Boulding, Kenneth E. *Conflict and Defense.* New York: Harper & Bros., 1962.

Brodie, Bernard. *Strategy in the Missile Age*. Princeton: Princeton University Press, 1959.
Browne, Malcolm W. *The New Face of War*. Indianapolis: Bobbs-Merrill, 1965.
Bucher, Rue. "Social Process and Power in a Medical School." In *Power in Organizations*, edited by Mayer Zald, pp. 3-48. Nashville: Vanderbilt University Press, 1970.
Burgett, Donald R. *Curahee!* New York: Ballentine Books, 1968.
Burlingame, Roger. *General Billy Mitchell: Champion of Air Defense*. New York: McGraw-Hill, 1952.
Burns, James MacGregor. *Roosevelt: The Lion and the Fox*. New York: Harcourt, Brace & Co., 1956.
_____. *Roosevelt: The Soldier of Freedom*. New York: Harcourt Brace Jovanovich, 1970.
Caraley, Demetrios. *The Politics of Military Unification: A Study of Conflict and the Policy Process*. New York: Columbia University Press, 1966.
Carter, Ross S. *Those Devils in Baggy Pants*. New York: Signet Books, 1951.
Collins, Larry, and Lapierre, Dominique. *Is Paris Burning?* New York: Simon & Schuster, 1965.
Corson, William R. *The Betrayal*. New York: W. W. Norton, 1968.
Craven, Wesley Frank, and Cate, James Lea. *The Army Air Forces in World War II*. Vol. 3: *Europe: Argument to VE Day, January 1944-May 1945*. Chicago: University of Chicago Press, 1948.
Dallin, Alexander. *The Soviet Union and the United Nations*. New York: Frederick A. Praeger, 1962.
Danoff, Clarence H. *Government Contracting and Technological Change*. Washington D.C.: Brookings Institution, 1968.
Davis, Burke. *The Billy Mitchell Affair*. New York: Random House, 1967.
Davis, Vincent. *The Politics of Innovation: Patterns in Navy Cases*. Social Science Foundation and Graduate School of International Studies, Monograph Series in World Affairs, vol. 4, no. 3. Denver: University of Denver, 1966-1967.
Deitchman, Seymour J. *Limited War and American Defense Policy*. Cambridge: M.I.T. Press, 1964.
Deutsch, Karl W. *The Nerves of Government: Models of Political Communication and Control*. New York: Free Press, 1966.
Doolittle, General James H. Preface to *The Love and Fear of Flying*, by Douglas D. Bond. New York: International Universities Press, 1952.
Douhet, Giulio. *Command of the Air*. Translated by Sheila Fischer. Rome: Revista Aeronautica, 1958.
Dulles, Foster R. *America's Rise to World Power*. New York: Harper & Row, 1954.
Duncan, Donald. *The New Legions*. New York: Random House, 1967.
Ealy, Lawrence O. *Yanqui Politics and the Isthmian Canal*. University Park: Pennsylvania State University Press, 1971.
Edelman, Murray. *The Symbolic Uses of Politics*. Urbana: University of Illinois Press, 1964.
Ellul, Jacques. *The Political Illusion*. Translated by Konrad Kellen. New York: Alfred A. Knopf, 1967.
Etzioni, Amitai. *A Comparative Analysis of Complex Organizations: On Power, Involvement, and their Correlates*. New York: Free Press, 1961.
Evan, William M. "The Organization-Set." In *Readings in Organization Theory: Open System Approaches*, edited by John G. Maurer, pp. 33-45. New York: Random House, 1971.
_____. "An Organization-Set Model of Interorganizational Relations." In *Interorganizational Decision-Making*, edited by Matthew Radnor, pp. 35-63. Chicago: Aldine Publishing, 1972.

Bibliography

Farago, Ladislas. *The Game of the Foxes: The Untold Story of German Espionage in the United States and Great Britain During World War II.* New York: David McKay, 1971.
Forrestal, James. *The Forrestal Diaries.* Edited by Walter Millis, with the collaboration of E. S. Duffield. New York: Viking Press, 1951.
Freeman, J. Leiper. *The Political Process: Executive Bureau-Legislative Committee Relations.* Garden City, N.Y.: Doubleday, 1955.
Friedrich, Carl J. "Authority, Reason, and Discretion." In *Authority: Nomos I,* edited by Carl J. Friedrich, pp. 28-46. Cambridge: Harvard University Press, 1958.
Futrell, Robert Frank; Moseley, Brigadier General Lawson S.; and Simpson, Albert F. *The United States Air Force in Korea, 1950-1953.* New York: Duell, Sloan & Pierce, 1961.
Gaddis, John L. *The United States and the Origins of the Cold War, 1941-1947.* New York: Columbia University Press, 1972.
Galvin, John R. *Air Assault: The Development of Airmobile Warfare.* New York: Hawthorn, 1969.
Gaulle, Charles de. *War Memoirs.* Vol. 1: *The Call to Honor, 1940-1942.* Translated by by Jonathan Griffen. London: Collins, 1955.
Gavin, James M. *War and Peace in the Space Age.* New York: Harper & Bros., 1958.
Gilfillan, S. C. *The Sociology of Invention.* Cambridge: M.I.T. Press, 1970.
Goodrich, Leland. *The United Nations.* New York: Thomas Y. Crowell, 1959.
Gouldner, Alvin. *Patterns of Industrial Bureaucracy.* New York: Free Press, 1954.
Greenfield, Kent Roberts. *American Strategy in World War II: A Reconsideration.* Baltimore: Johns Hopkins Press, 1963.
Griffith, Ernest S. *Congress in Its Contemporary Role.* New York: New York University Press, 1951.
Gulick, Luther. "Notes on the Theory of Organization." In *Papers on the Science of Administration,* edited by Luther Gulik and L. Urwick, pp. 1-46. New York: The Institute of Public Administration, 1937.
Gunston, William. *Attack Aircraft of the West.* New York: Charles Scribner's, 1974.
Haas, J. Eugene, and Drabek, Thomas I. *Complex Organizations: A Sociological Perspective.* New York: John Wiley, 1966.
Hackett, General Sir John. "The Armed Forces." In *Authority in a Changing Society,* edited by Clifford Rhodes, pp. 140-71. London: Constable, 1969.
Haines, William Wister. "Command Decision." In *The Burns Mantle Best Plays of 1947-48 and the Year Book of the Drama in America,* edited by John Chapman, pp. 94-133. New York: Dodd, Mead, 1948.
Hammond, Paul Y. *Organizing for Defense: The American Military Establishment in the Twentieth Century.* Princeton: Princeton University Press, 1961.
_____. *Super Carriers and B-36 Bombers: Appropriations, Strategy, and Politics.* Inter-University Case Program no. 97. New York: Bobbs-Merrill, 1963.
Harvey, Fred. *Air War-Vietnam.* New York: Bantam Books, 1967.
Hauser, Lieutenant Colonel William L. *American Army in Crisis.* Baltimore: Johns Hopkins University Press, 1973.
Hersh, Seymour. *Chemical and Biological Warfare: America's Hidden Arsenal.* Garden City, N.Y.: Doubleday, Anchor Books, 1969.
Hirschman, Albert O. *Exit, Voice, and Loyalty: Responses to Decline in Firms, Organizations, and States.* Cambridge: Harvard University Press, 1970.
Hitch, Charles J. *Decision-Making for Defense.* Los Angeles: University of California Press, 1965.
Hittle, J. D. *The Military Staff: It's History and Development.* Harrisburg, Pa.: The Military Service Publishing Co., 1949.
Holley, I. B., Jr. *Ideas and Weapons: Explotation of the Aerial Weapon by the United States During World War I: A Study in the Relationship of Technological Advance,*

198 / Bibliography

Military Doctrine, and the Development of Weapons. New Haven: Yale University Press, 1953.

Hubler, Richard G. *Straight Up: The Story of Vertical Flight.* New York: Duell, Sloan & Pierce, 1961.

Huntington, Samuel P. *The Common Defense: Strategic Programs in National Politics.* New York: Columbia University Press, 1961.

_____. *The Soldier and the State: The Theory and Politics of Civil-Military Relations.* New York: Random House, Vintage Books, 1957.

Hurewitz, J. C. *Middle East Politics: The Military Dimension.* New York: Frederick A. Praeger, 1969.

Janowitz, Morris. *The Professional Soldier: A Social and Political Portrait.* New York: Free Press, 1960.

Jones, Charles O. *An Introduction to the Study of Public Policy.* Belmont, Calif.: Wadsworth Publishing, 1970.

Kahn, Herman. *Thinking About the Unthinkable.* New York: Horizon Press, 1962.

King, Edward L. *The Death of the Army: A Pre-Mortem.* New York: Saturday Review Press, 1972.

Kipling, Rudyard. "Tommy." *Collected Verse of Rudyard Kipling.* Garden City, N.Y.: Doubleday, Page, 1920.

Kissinger, Henry A. *Nuclear Weapons and Foreign Policy.* Garden City, N.Y.: Doubleday, 1957.

Kolkowicz, Roman. *The Impact of Technology on the Soviet Military: A Challenge to Traditional Military Professionalism.* Santa Monica, Calif.: Rand Corporation, August, 1964.

Krislov, Samuel. *Representative Bureaucracy.* Englewood Cliffs, N.J.: Prentice-Hall, 1974.

Lapp, Ralph. *The Weapons Culture.* New York: W. W. Norton, 1968.

Leeds, Ruth. "The Absorbtion of Protest: A Working Paper." In *New Perspectives in Organizational Research*, edited by W. W. Cooper, H. J. Leavitt, and M. W. Shelly II, pp. 115-35. New York: John Wiley, 1964.

Leahy, William D. *I Was There: The Personal Story of the Chief of Staff to President Roosevelt and Truman.* New York: McGraw-Hill, 1950.

Leeuw, Hendrick de. *The History and Future of Aviation.* New York: Vantage Press, 1960.

Lemay, General Curtis E. *Mission with Lemay: My Story.* Garden City, N.Y.: Doubleday, 1965.

Linton, Robert. *The Study of Man.* New York: Appleton-Century, 1936.

Littauer, Raphael, and Uphoff, Norman, eds. *The Air War in Indochina.* Rev. ed. Boston: Beacon Press, 1973.

Lyden, Fremont J., and Miller, Ernest G., eds. *Planning, Programming, Budgeting: A Systems Approach to Management.* Chicago: Markham Publishers, 1967.

MacCloskey, Monro. *The United States Air Force.* New York: Frederick A. Praeger, 1967.

Machiavelli, Niccolo. *The Prince.* Translated and edited by Thomas G. Bergin. New York: Appleton-Century-Crofts, 1947.

Magee, John. "High Flight." In *Sunward I've Climbed,* edited by Hermann Hagedorn. New York: Macmillan, 1942.

Marcus, G. J. *The Age of Nelson: The Royal Navy, 1793-1815.* New York: Viking Press, 1971.

Marshall, S.L.A. *Battles in the Monsoon: Campaigning in the Central Highlands, Vietnam, Summer 1966.* New York: William Morrow, 1967.

_____. *Night Drop.* New York: Bantam Books, 1962.

McNamara, Robert. *Essence of Security: Reflections in Office.* New York: Harper &

199 / Bibliography

Row, 1968.
Medaris, John B. *Countdown for Decision.* New York: G. P. Putnam's Sons, 1960.
Merton, Robert K. *Social Theory and Social Structure.* Rev. ed. Glencoe, Ill.: Free Press, 1957.
Millis, Walter; Mansfield, Harvey C.; and Stein, Harold. *Arms and the State: Civil-Military Elements in National Policy.* New York: Twentieth Century Fund, 1958.
Melman, Seymour. *Pentagon Capitalism: The Political Economy of War.* New York: McGraw-Hill, 1970.
Moynihan, Daniel P. *Maximum Feasible Misunderstanding: Community Action in the War on Poverty.* New York: Free Press, Arkville Books, 1969.
Mylander, Maureen. *The Generals.* New York: Dial Press, 1974.
Neustadt, Richard. *Presidential Power.* New York: John Wiley, 1960.
Nicholas, H. G. *The United Nations as a Political Institution.* London: Oxford University Press, 1959.
Norman, Aaron. *The Great Air War: The Men, the Planes, the Saga of Military Aviation, 1914-1918.* New York: Macmillan, 1968.
Novick, David, ed. *Program Analysis and the Federal Budget.* 2nd ed. Cambridge: Harvard University Press, 1967.
O'Connor, Raymond G., ed. *American Defense Policy in Perspective: From Colonial Times to the Present.* New York: John Wiley, 1965.
Ogburn, William F. "How Technology Causes Social Change." In *Technology and Social Change,* edited by Francis R. Allen, Hornell Hart, Delbert C. Miller, William F. Ogburn, and Meyer F. Nimkoff, pp. 12-26. New York: Appleton-Century-Crofts, 1957.
Peck, Merton J., and Scherer, Frederic M. *The Weapons Acquisition Process: An Economic Analysis.* Boston: Harvard University, Graduate School of Business Administration, Division of Research, 1962.
Pizer, Vernon. The United States Army. New York: Frederick A. Praeger, 1967.
Plato. *The Republic of Plato.* Translated with introduction and notes by Francis MacDonald Cornford. Oxford: Clarendon Press, 1941.
Pogue, Forrest C. *George C. Marshall.* Vol. 1: *Education of a General, 1880-1939.* New York: Viking Press, 1963.
──────. *George C. Marshall.* Vol. 2: *Ordeal and Hope, 1939-1942.* New York: Viking Press, 1965.
──────. *George C. Marshall.* Vol. 3: *Organizer of Victory.* New York: Viking Press, 1973.
Politella, Dario. *Operation Grasshopper: The Story of Army Aviation in Korea from Aggression to Armistice.* Wichita, Kans.: Robert Longo, 1958.
Popper, Sir Karl. *The Poverty of Historicism.* Boston: Beacon Press, 1957.
Ransom, Harry Howe. *Can American Democracy Survive Cold War?* Garden City, N.Y.: Doubleday, Anchor Books, 1964.
Rapoport, Anatol I. *Fights, Games, and Debates.* Ann Arbor: University of Michigan Press, 1960.
Redford, Emmette S. *Democracy in the Administrative State.* New York: Oxford University Press, 1969.
Reitzel, William ; Kaplan, Morton A.; and Coblenz, Constance G. *United States Foreign Policy, 1945-1955.* Washington, D.C.: Brookings Institution, 1956.
Richardson, Lewis F. *Arms and Insecurity.* Edited by Quincy Wright and Carl C. Lienau. Chicago: Quadrangle Books, 1960.
Ries, John C. *The Management of Defense: Organization and Control of the U.S. Armed Services.* Baltimore: Johns Hopkins Press, 1964.
Rostow, Walt Whitman. *The United States in the World Arena.* New York: Harper & Row, 1960.

Sandburg, Carl. Preface to *Night Drop*, by S.L.A. Marshall. New York: Bantam Books, 1962.
Sapolsky, Harvey M. *The Polaris System Development: Bureaucratic and Programmatic Success in Government.* Cambridge, Mass.: Harvard University Press, 1972.
Schilling, Warner R.; Hammond, Paul Y.; and Snyder, Glenn H. *Strategy, Politics, and Defense Budgets.* New York: Columbia University Press, 1962.
Scott, William A., and Witney, Stephen B. *The United States and the United Nations: The Public View, 1945-1955.* New York: Manhattan, 1958.
Selznick, Philip. *Leadership in Administration.* Evanston, Ill.: Row, Peterson, 1957.
Shelling, Thomas C. *The Strategy of Conflict.* Cambridge, Mass.: Harvard University Press, 1963.
Sherwood, Robert E. *Roosevelt and Hopkins: An Intimate History.* New York: Harper & Bros., 1968.
Smith, Perry McCoy. *The Air Force Plans for Peace, 1943-1945.* Baltimore: Johns Hopkins Press, 1970.
Snow, Sir Charles Percy, *Science and Government.* Cambridge: Harvard University Press, 1960.
Spanier, John W. *American Foreign Policy Since World War II.* Rev. ed. New York: Frederick A. Praeger, 1962.
──────. *The Truman-MacArthur Controversy and the Korean War.* Cambridge: Harvard University Press, 1959.
Swomley, John M., Jr. *The Military Establishment.* Boston: Beacon Press, 1964.
Sykes, Christopher. *Orde Wingate: A Biography.* New York: World, 1951.
Taylor, Frederick W. *The Principles of Scientific Management.* New York: W. W. Norton, 1967.
Thompson, James D. *Organizations in Action: Social Science Bases of Administrative Theory.* New York: McGraw-Hill, 1967.
Thompson, Victor A. *Modern Organization.* New York: Alfred A. Knopf, 1961.
Townley, Ralph. *The United Nations: A View from Within.* New York: Charles Scribner's, 1968.
Trueblood, Elton. *The Validity of the Christian Mission.* New York: Harper & Row, 1972.
Truman, Harry S. *Memoirs.* Vol. 2. Garden City, N.Y.: Doubleday, 1956.
Tuchman, Barbara W. *Stillwell and the American Experience in China, 1911-45.* New York: Macmillan, 1970.
Tyrell, C. Merton. *Pentagon Partners: The New Nobility.* New York: Grossman Publishers, 1970.
Vance, Rupert. "The Development and Status of American Demography." In *The Study of Population.* Edited by Philip M. Hausen and Otis Dudley Duncan. Chicago: University of Chicago Press, 1959.
Vatikiotis, Panajiotis. *Politics and the Military in Jordan: A Study of the Arab Legion, 1921-1957.* New York: Frederick A. Praeger, 1967.
Weber, Max. "Politics as a Vocation." In *From Max Weber: Essays in Sociology,* edited by H. H. Gerth and C. Wright Mills, pp. 77-128. New York: Oxford University Press, 1958.
──────. "The Social Psychology of the World Religions." In *From Max Weber: Essays in Sociology,* edited by H. H. Gerth and C. Wright Mills, pp. 267-301. New York: Oxford University Press, 1958.
──────. "The Three Types of Legitimate Rule." Translated by Hans Gerth. In *A Sociological Reader on Complex Organizations,* edited by Amitai Etzioni, pp. 6-15. 2nd ed. New York: Holt, Rinehart & Winston, 1969.
Weigley, Russell F. *History of the United States Army.* New York: Macmillan 1967.
White, William D. *U.S. Tactical Air Power.* Washington, D.C.: Brookings Institution, 1974.

Wiesner, Jerome B. "Technology and Innovation." In *Technological Innovation and Society*, edited by Dean Morse and Aaron W. Warner, pp. 11-26. New York: Columbia University Press, 1966.
Wrong, Dennis. Introduction to *Max Weber*. Edited by Dennis Wrong. Englewood Cliffs, N.J.: Prentice-Hall, 1970.
_____. "The Oversocialized Conception of Man in Modern Sociology." In *Sociological Theory: A Book of Readings*, edited by Lewis A. Coser and Bernard Rosenburg, pp. 122-32. 3rd ed. New York: Macmillan, 1969.
Yarmolinsky, Adam. *The Military Establishment: Its Impact on American Society*. New York: Harper & Row, 1971.
Zald, Mayer. *Organizational Change: The Political Economy of the YMCA*. Chicago: University of Chicago Press, 1970.
Zuzak, Charles A.; McNeil, Kenneth E.; and Bergerson, Frederic. *Beyond the Ballot: Organized Citizen Participation in Metropolitan Nashville*. Knoxville: University of Tennessee, Bureau of Public Administration, 1971.

Newspapers, Dictionaries, and Encyclopedias

"Abandoned Craft Making Comeback: Cheyenne Copter Heads for Army Trials." *Los Angeles Times*, March 24, 1972, pt. 1, p. 1.
Abramson, Rudy. "Joint Chiefs: A Growing Influence in U.S. Policy." *Los Angeles Times*, August 17, 1972, sec. A, p. 1.
"Army Flexes Missile Muscles for U.S. Leaders." *Stars and Stripes* (European ed.), July 2, 1958, n.p.
Army Flier (Hartford, Ala.), August 2, 1957, p. 1, and October 28, 1960, p. 1.
"The Army Gets Out of Line." *Los Angeles Times*, December 31, 1974, pt. 2, p. 2.
"Army's Copter Ability Witnessed by Brucker." *The Dothan (Ala.) Eagle*, May 4, 1958, p. 1.
Baldwin, Hanson W. "Defense Issue Crucial in the Budget Battle." *New York Times*, January 25, 1959, sec. E. p. 5.
_____. "War Games Test Opposing Tactics." *New York Times*, November 15, 1964, sec. A, p. 80.
Blair, William H. "Wilson Restricts Army on Missiles and Air Program." *New York Times*, November 27, 1956, sec. A, p. 1.
"Brucker Promises Gavin 4-Star Rank." *New York Times*, January 8, 1958, p. 1.
Columbus (Ga.) *Inquirer*, July 30, 1957, p. 1.
The Dothan (Ala.) Eagle, July 6, 1957, p. 1.
"Double-Dipping with the Good Fairy." *Los Angeles Times*, September 29, 1974, pt. 5, p. 2.
Drury, Allen. "Gavin's Quitting Will Be Studied by Senate Unit." *New York Times*, January 6, 1958, sec. A, p. 1.
"Gavin Retires, Backs Atomic Tests." *New York Times*, April 1, 1958, sec. A, p. 5.
Heberle, Rudolph. "The Types and Functions of Social Movements." *The International Encyclopedia of the Social Sciences*, edited by David Sills, 14 (1968).
"Insurgents." *Webster's Dictionary of Synonyms*. 1942 ed.
Lamb, David. "Copter Proves Itself as Vietnam Weapon." *Nashville Tennessean*, July 6, 1969, sec. A, p. 6.
Mayhood, Thurlow, and Benis, Henry G. "Helicopter Armament." *American Helicopter Society Newsletter*, October 1960, p. 1.
Middleton, Drew. "Army Keeps Faith in Role of Copter." *New York Times*, March 11, 1971, sec. A, p. 8.
_____. "The Army is Developing Battlefield Computers and Detection Devices." *New York Times*, October 27, 1970, sec. A, p. 12.
"Navy Hikes Estimated F-14 Cost." *Whittier Daily News*, September 16, 1975, p. 3.

202 / Bibliography

"The Pressure of Command: Lavelle and His Raids." *Los Angeles Times*, October 1, 1972, sec. G, p. 5.
Reston, James. "Divided Command in Saigon." *New York Times*, March 26, 1971, sec. A, p. 39.
"Retired CIA Scientist Takes Blame for Keeping Poisons." *Whittier Daily News*, September 17, 1975, p. 6.
Schilling, Warner. "Technology." *International Encyclopedia of the Social Sciences*, edited by David Sills, 15 (1968).
Schuster, Alvin. "Gen. Gavin, Missile Aide, to Quit; Criticized Joint Chiefs System." *New York Times*, January 5, 1958, sec. A, p. 1.
"Storm Brewing over Costly Chopper." *Nashville Tennessean*, April 20, 1969, sec. A, p. 12.
"Three Stars and Out: James Maurice Gavin." *New York Times*, January 9, 1958, sec. A, p. 17.
Valian, Preston. "Social Movement." *Dictionary of the Social Sciences*, edited by Julius Gold and William Kolb, 1964.
Watkins, Harold D. "At Northrup, Think Small Is the Motto." *Los Angeles Times*, September 1, 1974, pt. 5, p. 1.
"What Role for the Navy?" *Los Angeles Times*, September 28, 1975, pt. 5, p. 5.
Wheeler, John T. "Helicopters Make Difference in Vietnam." *Nashville Tennessean* March 9, 1969, B, p. 1.

Magazines and Journals

"Air Force, Army Agree on Roles, Missions." *Aviation Week and Space Technology*, April 27, 1966, pp. 26-27.
"Answer to Darwinian Riddle Seen in Modern Ecology." *Johns Hopkins University Journal* 7 (Summer 1973): 2.
"Army Plans New Attack Helicopter Competition." *Aviation Week and Space Technology*, August 14, 1972, p. 21.
Bennis, Warren G. "A Funny Thing Happened on the Way to the Future." *American Psychologist* 25 (July 1970) : 595-608.
Brecht, Arnold. "Bureaucratic Sabotage." *Annals* 189 (January 1937) : 48-57.
Burns, Tom. "The Reference of Conduct in Small Groups: Cliques and Cabals in Occupational Milieux." *Human Relations* 8 (November 1955): 467-86.
"A Closer Look at the Utility Tactical Transport Aircraft System." *Government Executive* 4 (April 1972): 32-34.
Crecine, John P., and Fischer, Gregory W. "On Resource Allocation Process in the U.S. Department of Defense." In *Political Science Annual: An International Review*, vol. 4, edited by Cornelius P. Cotter (Indianapolis: Bobbs-Merrill, 1973), pp. 181-232.
Crouch, Colonel William E., Jr. "DA Happenings." *Army Aviation* 24 (July/August 1975) :8-9.
Dawson, Raymond H. "Congressional Innovation and Intervention in Defense Policy: Legislative Authorization of Weapons Systems." *American Political Science Review* 56 (March 1962) : 42-57.
Dill, William R. "Environment as an Influence on Managerial Autonomy." *Administrative Science Quarterly* 2 (March 1958) : 409-43.
Emery, F. E., and Trist, E. L. "The Causal Texture of Organizational Environments." *Human Relations* 18 (February 1965) : 21-31.
Fisch, Gerald G. "Line-Staff Is Obsolete." *Harvard Business Review* 39 (September/October) : 155-69.
Ford, Major William W. "Wings for Santa Barbara." *Field Artillery Journal* 31 (April 1941): 232-34.

Gavin, James M. "Cavalry, and I Don't Mean Horses." *Harper's*, April 1954, pp. 54-60.
Godfrey, Mark, and Okamua, Asihiko. "Scramble for Safety." *Life*, April 2, 1971, pp. 16-23.
Gordon, Bernard K. "The Military Budget: Congressional Phase." *Journal of Politics* 23 (November 1961) : 689-710.
Granovetter, Mark S. "Strength of Weak Ties." *American Journal of Sociology* 78 (1973) : 1360-79.
Gross, Bertram. "Planning in an Era of Social Revolution." *Public Administration Review* 31 (May/June 1971) : 259-96.
"The Helicopter War." *Newsweek*, March 15, 1971, pp. 39-44.
Henry, Andrew F.; Masland, John W.; and Radway, Laurence I. "Armed Forces Unification and the Pentagon Officer." *Public Administration Review* 15 (1955) : 178-80.
Huntington, Samuel P. "Interservice Competition and the Political Roles of the Armed Services." *American Political Science Review* 55 (March 1961) : 40-52.
Huston, James A. "Tactical Uses of Air Power in World War II: The Army Experience." *Military Affairs* 14 (1950) : 166-85.
Johnsen, Katherine. "One Senate Unit Defends Armed Helicopters." *Aviation Week and Space Technology*, July 10, 1972, p. 15.
"Just Say It Was the Comancheros." *Newsweek*, March 15, 1971, pp. 39-44.
Just, Ward. "Soldiers, Part I." *Atlantic Monthly*, October 1970, pp. 59-98.
_____. "Soldiers, Part II." *Atlantic Monthly*, November 1970, pp. 59-90.
Kadushin, Charles. "Power, Influence, and Social Circles: A New Methodology for Studying Opinion Makers." *American Sociological Review* 5 (October 1968) : 685-99.
Kurth, James J. "A Widening Gyre: The Logic of American Weapons Procurement." *Public Policy* 19 (Summer 1971) : 373-404.
Lammers, Cornelius J. "Strikes and Mutinies: A Comparative Study of Organizational Conflicts Between Rulers and Ruled." *Administrative Science Quarterly* 14 (December 1969) : 558-72.
Levine, Sol, and White, Paul E. "Exchange as a Conceptual Framework for the Study of Interorganizational Relationships." *Administrative Science Quarterly* 5 (March 1961) : 583-601.
"Lightweight Fighter: The General Dynamics Approach." *Air International* 7 (August 1974) : 59-63, 88-89.
Lindbolm, Charles E. "The Science of 'Muddling Through.' " *Public Administration Review* 19 (1959) : 79-88.
Lyons, Gene M. "The New Civil-Military Relations." *American Political Science Review* 55 (March 1961) : 53-63.
Mechanic, David. "Sources of Power of Lower Participants in Complex Organizations." *Administrative Science Quarterly* 7 (December 1962) : 349-64.
"Mistakes in Air Support Methods in Korea." *U.S. News and World Report* 30 (6 March 1953) : 53-61.
Mohr, Lawrence B. "The Concept of Organizational Goal." *American Political Science Review* 67 (June 1973) : 473-74.
"New Helicopter Roles Planned." *Aviation Week and Space Technology*, September 29, 1975, pp. 53-55, 57, 59, 62.
Nowlin, Captain Charles F. "Something Is Clearly Wrong: A Young Aviator Asks Some Questions." *Army Aviation* 24 (July/August 1972) : 4.
Patrick, Steven B. "Combined Arms: Combat Operations in the Twentieth Century." *Strategy and Tactics* 46 (September/October 1974) : 5-7, 16, 19.
Robinson, W. S. "The Logical Structure of Analytic Induction." *American Sociological Review* 16 (1951) : 812-18.
Saars, John. "An Ignominious and Disorderly Retreat." *Life*, April 2, 1971, pp. 24-28.

Schick, Alan. "The Road to PPB: The State of Budget Reform." *Public Administration Review* 26 (1966) : 234-58.
Shoup, David. "The New American Militarism." *Atlantic Monthly*, April 1969, pp. 51-56.
Sigelman, Lee. "Reporting the News: An Organizational Analysis." *American Journal of Sociology* 79 (1973) : 132-51.
Simon, Herbert A. "On the Concept of Organizational Goal." *Administrative Science Quarterly* 9 (June 1964) : 1-22.
Terreberry, Shirley. "The Evolution of Organizational Environment." *Administrative Science Quarterly* 12 (March 1968) : 590-613.
Tucker, Robert W. "Professor Morgenthau's 'Theory of Political Realism.' " *American Political Science Review* 46 (March 1952) : 214-24.
Walton, Richard E., and Dutton, John M. "The Management of Interdepartmental Conflict: A Model and Review." *Administrative Science Quarterly* 14 (March 1969) : 73-84.
Weinberg, S. Kirson,. Letter. *American Sociological Review* 17 (1952) : 493-94.
"When the Landscape Is the Enemy." *Newsweek*, August 7, 1972, pp. 24-26.
White, Williams. "Carl Vinson Has Been Unified, Too." *New York Times Magazine*, September 10, 1970, p. 12.
Wildavsky, Aaron. "Political Economy of Efficiency: Cost-Benefit Analysis, Systems Analysis, and Program Budgeting." *Public Administration Review* 26 (1966) : 292-310.
Willer, David E. "Max Weber's Missing Authority Type." *Sociological Inquiry* 37 (Spring 1967) : 231-40.
Wright, Quincy. "The Nature of Conflict." *Western Political Quarterly* 4 (June 1951) : 193-209.
Zald, Mayer, and Ash, Roberta. "Social Movements: Growth, Decay, and Change." Social Forces 44 (March 1966) : 327-41.

Government Documents and Related Materials

ACR Platoon. Scrapbook. U.S. Army Aviation Museum, Fort Rucker, Ala.
"Armed Copters Show Army's 'Cavalry of Atomic Battlefield' at Project Ammo." *Army, Navy, Air Force Journal* 95 (July 5, 1958) : 1.
Army Aviation Association of America (AAAA). *Objectives and Purposes*. Westport, Conn., n.d.
Army Regulations 700-50 and Air Force Regulations 65-7, "Supplies and Equipment: Army Aircraft and Allied Equipment." March 23, 1950.
Arnold, General Henry H. Memorandum for the Chief of Staff, "Liaison Aircraft in the Army Ground Forces." January 29, 1944.
Cairns, Brigadier General Bogardus S. Speech to Fort Benning chapter of the Military Order of World Wars, Fort Benning, Ga., February 20, 1958.
Cline, Ray S. *Washington Command Post: The Operations Division*. Washington, D.C.: Department of the Army, 1951.
Dorsey, John T., Jr. Personal letter to Frederic Bergerson, November 21, 1970.
Ervin, Chief Warrant Officer James. Diary. U.S. Army Aviation Museum, Fort Rucker, Ala.
Fuller, John F. C. *Machine Warfare: An Inquiry into the Influence of Mechanics on the Art of War*. Washington, D.C.: The Infantry Journal, 1943.
Gavin, Major General James M. *Airborne Warfare*. Washington, D.C.: Infantry Journal Press, 1947.
Griminger, Charles O. "The Armed Helicopter Story, Part I: The Origins of U.S. Army Aviation." *U.S. Army Aviation Digest* 17 (July 1971) : 14-17.

205 / Bibliography

_____. "The Armed Helicopter Story, Part II: 'Vanderpool's Fools.' " *U.S. Army Aviation Digest* 17 (August 1971) : 14-19.

_____. "The Armed Helicopter Story, Part III: Armed Helicopters Around the World." *U.S. Army Aviation Digest* 17 (September 1971): 10-13, 21-25.

Griminger, Charles O. and Rose, Aaron. "Evolution of the Armed Helicopter and Future Design Requirements." Unpublished manuscript, 1968, U.S. Army Aviation Museum, Fort Rucker, Ala.

Harrison, Major Donald. "History of Army Aviation." Unpublished manuscript, n.d. Army Office of the Chief of Military History, Washington, D.C.

Howze, Major General Hamilton H. "The Last Three Years of Army Aviation." *U.S. Army Aviation Digest* 4 (March 1958) : 1-60.

_____. "Soldiers with a Double Skill." *U.S. Army Aviation Digest* 7 (January 1957) : 30-34.

Huston, James A. "Tactical Use of Air Power in World War II: The Army Experience." *Military Affairs* 14 (1950) : 166-85.

Hutton, Brigadier General Carl I. "Air Mobility—Collected Papers, 1952-1956." Bound unpublished document, U.S. Army Aviation School, Fort Rucker, Ala.

_____. Presentation for National Security Commission of the American Legion Convention. Los Angeles, Calif., September 2, 1956.

_____. "Without Trumpets and Drums: Recollections of Thirty-six Months with the Army Aviation School, June 1954-June 1957." Bound unpublished manuscript, U.S. Army Aviation Center Library, Fort Rucker, Ala.

Joint Chiefs of Staff. *Dictionary of United States Military Terms for Joint Usage.* Washington, D.C.: Government Printing Office, August 1968.

Lang, Master Sergeant Thomas M. "Fixed Wing Aircraft: The Army Aviation Story, Part III." *U.S. Army Aviation Digest* 8 (August 1962) : 9-19.

Lockheed Aircraft Corp. *Development of the Helicopter.* Burbank, Calif., May 1966.

Maddox, Brigadier General William J., Jr. "From Fabric to FLIR. " *U.S. Army Aviation Digest* 18 (June 1972) : 2-3.

Maycock, Thomas J. "Notes on the Development of AAF Tactical Air Doctrine." *Military Affairs* 14 (1950) : 186-200.

McLendon, R. Earl. *The Question of Autonomy for the United States Air Arm, 1907-1945.* Air University Documentary Research Study. Maxwell Air Force Base, Ala., 1950.

_____. *Army Aviation, 1947-1953.* Air University Documentary Research Study no. 48. Maxwell Air Force Base, Ala., May 1954.

McNair, General Lesley J. Memorandum for the Chief of Staff, U.S. Army (Attention: G-3 Division, Room 3A882, the Pentagon), "Liaison Aircraft in the Army Ground Forces," February 16, 1944. Personal file of interviewee.

Neel, Colonel Spurgeon H., and Shamburek, Major Roland H. "Medical Evacuation: The Army Aviation Story, Part IX." *U.S. Army Aviation Digest* 9 (February 1963) : 33-41.

Nelson, Major Otto L., Jr. *National Security and the General Staff.* Washington, D.C.: Infantry Journal Press, 1946.

Pouget, J. "The Armed Helicopter." *Military Review*, March 1964, pp. 81-96.

Tatum, Lawrence B. "The Joint Chiefs of Staff and Defense Policy Formulation." *Air University Review*, May/June 1966, pp. 40-45, July/August 166, pp. 11-20.

Tierney, Richard K. "The Army Aviation Story, Part I." *U.S. Army Aviation Digest* 8 (June 1962) : 2-25.

_____. "The Army Aviation Story, Part II: Academies and Training." *United States Army Aviation Digest* 8 (July 1962) : 10-31.

_____. "The Army Aviation Story, Part VI: The War Years; North Africa, Sicily,

Italy." *U.S. Army Aviation Digest* 8 (November 1962): 34-47.

———. "The Army Aviation Story, Part VII: The War Years; Europe, Pacific, Korea." *U.S. Army Aviation Digest* 8 (December 1962): 26-38.

Timberlake, Brigadier General Patrick W. (Deputy Chief of Air Staff). Memorandum for Lieutenant General Hoyt S. Vandenburg, Major General Frederick L. Anderson, Jr., and Brigadier General Lauris Norstadt, "Organizational Assignment of Aircraft Other Than to Air Forces." June 2, 1945.

Tolson, Lieutenant General John J. "The New Challenge." *U.S. Army Aviation Digest* 18 (December 1972) : 2-3, 15-17.

Tressidder, Argus J. "The Military Vocabulary." *Military Review* 52 (December 1972) : 8-13.

USAAVNC (U.S. Army Aviation Center) History, 1954-1964. *Artillery Pilots*. Fort Rucker, Ala.: Adjutant General's Office, January 1, 1965.

U.S., Air Force Research Studies Institute, Historical Division. "Legislative History of the AAF and USAF, 1941-1951." Air Historical Study no. 84. August 1954.

U.S., Air Training Command Headquarters. *Helicopter History and Aerodynamics*. ATC Manual 51-2. Randolph Air Force Base, Tex., January 1961.

U.S., Army Air Force Headquarters, Historical Office. "Legislation Relating to the Air Corps Personnel and Training Programs, 1907-1939." Army Air Forces Historical Study no. 39. December 1945.

U.S., Army Infantry School. *Program of Instruction*. Fort Benning, Ga., n.d.

U.S., Congress, House, Committee on Armed Services. *Close Air Support: Hearings Before the Sepecial Subcommittee on Tactical Air Support*. 89th Cong., 1st sess., 1965.

———, Committee on Armed Services, Investigations Subcommittee. *Hearings on the Employment of Personnel by Defense Industries*. 86th Cong., 1st sess., 1959.

———, Committee on Armed Services, Subcommittee for Special Investigations. *Review of Army Procurement of Light Observation Helicopters*. 90th Cong., 1st sess., 1967.

———, Select Committee on Post War Military Policy. *Proposal to Establish a Single Department of Armed Forces: Hearings*. 78th Cong., 2nd sess., 1944.

U.S., Congress, Senate, Committee on Armed Services. *Hearings Before the Special Subcommittee on Close Air Support*. 92nd Cong., 2nd sess., 1971.

———, Committee on Armed Services. *Investigation into Electronic Battlefield Program: Hearings Before the Electronic Battlefield Subcommittee of the Preparedness Investigating Subcommittee* 91st Cong., 2nd sess., 1970.

———, Committee on Armed Services, Preparedness Investigating Subcommittee. *Report on the Investigation of the Preparedness Program*. 90th Cong., 2nd sess., 1968.

———, Armed Services Committee. *Reorganization Plan No. 6 of 1953 Relating to the Department of Defense*. 83rd Cong., 1st sess., 1953.

———, Committee on Military Affairs. *Hearings on S. 84 and S. 1482*. 79th Cong., 1st sess., 1945.

———, Committee on Naval Affairs. *Unification of the War and Navy and Post War Organization for National Security*. Report prepared for the Honorable James Forrestal, Secretary of the Navy. 79th Cong., 1st sess., 1945.

U.S., Department of the Air Force, Tactical Air Support Requirements Board. "U.S. Air Force Tactical Air Support Requirements Board Comments on . . . Report Army Tactial Mobility Board." 4 vols. Lieutenant General G. P. Disosway, USAF, chairman. Washington, D.C., 1962.

U.S., Department of the Army. Memorandum for the Secretary of the Army from the Office of the General Counsel, "Composition and Roles and Missions of Army Aircraft." April 30, 971.

Bibliography

U.S., Department of Defense. *Report to the President and the Secretary of Defense by the Blue Ribbon Defense Panel, 1 July 1970*. Washington, D.C.: Government Printing Office, 1970.

U.S., *Statutes at Large*, vols. 32, 38, 40, 41, 44, 53, 55, 61, 63, 64, and 72.

U.S., War Department, Special Committee on Army Air Corps. *Final Report* (Newton D. Baker, chairman). Washington, D.C.: Government Printing Office, July 18, 1934.

United States Strategic Bombing Survey, Overall Report (European War) Sept. 30, 1945. Washington, D.C., 1945.

Vance, William. "How the Army Got Its Shooting Helicopters." *National Guardsman* 17 (May 1963) : 2-4.

Vanderpool, Colonel J. D. "We Armed the Helicopter." *U.S. Army Aviation Digest* 17 (June 1971) : 3-6, 24-29.

Wagner, Don. *Helicopter Armament Monograph (1956-1958)*. Fort Rucker, Ala.: USA Combat Developments Command, April 8, 1965.

Watson, Susan M. "Social Movements in Large Scale Organizations." Paper prepared for Professor Mayer Zald, Vanderbilt University, 1966.

"Who's Who" in Army Aviation, 1954. Westport, Conn.: Army Aviation Publications, 1954.

Williams, Major General Robert R. Presentation for Army Scientific Advisory Council, Fort Rucker, Ala., May 12, 1969.

"Wilson Memorandum Clarifying Roles and Missions." 1956. Reprinted in U.S., Congress, House, Committee on Government Operations. *Hearings on the Organization and Management of Missile Programs*, 86th Cong., 1st sess., 1959.

INDEX

AAFSS (advanced aerial fire support system). *See* Cheyenne
Able Buster, 72, 73
Abrams, Creighton, 139
Adams, Paul D., 100-103, 114
Advanced attack helicopter (AAH), 140
Advanced scout helicopter (ASH), 141
"Airborne club," 34, 101
Air cavalry, 22, 57
Air Corps Act of 1926, 23
Aircraft: costs of, 122, 133, 139; production of, 26
Air Force, 1, 14; autonomy of, 23, 27, 43, 44; and National Security Act, 47, 48; support of Army by, 5, 16-17; technology of, 63, 64, 66. *See also* Disosway Board; Rivalry, interservice
Airmobility, 4, 71; congressional support of, for the Army, 116; Gavin's view of, 101; and the Howze Board, 111; testing of, 72-78, 93, 111-15
Air power, 22-25; demonstrations of, 79-80; in Korea, 71; language of, 135-36; post-Vietnam, 124-26, 130-32, 139; pre-World War II, 22-25; and psychology of technology, 63; strategic, 29-33
Allocation, politics of, 3-4, 125-26
Andrews, Frank, 26
Andrews, George, 106, 116
Armacost, Michael, 4
Army, 1, 4, 44; airborne forces in, 95, 101, 110, 116; air support requirements of, 99-105; Artillery Branch of, 29, 35, 143; future of, 141-42; mission of, 14-17, 19, 20; organization of, 33, 74-75, 77, 115; and psychology of technology, 62-64, 66; rank within, 121-22
—reorganization of, 41, 56; and Army aviation, 95-99; in 1942, 27; prior to World War II, 21, 24, 26; relation of, to National Security Act of 1947, 43-50; and Vietnam, 138-39
Army Air Force(s), 24, 25, 33-34. *See also* Air Force
Army Air Service, 22, 23, 93-94
Army aviation, 18, 102-6, 132, 145-46; centers for, 100, 104; civilian employees' impact on, 110-11, 112; and Congress (*see* Congress); Directorate of, 104-5; movement for (*see* Bureaucratic social movement; CAVEAT); organic status of, 30, 31, 35, 70, 95; restrictions on, 53-54; scope of, 70, 120, 121; training for, 29-32
Army Aviation Association of America, 146
Army Aviation School, 72, 76-77
Army aviators, training of, 96, 98, 101, 105-6
Army Ground Forces, 27, 99, 100; in World War II, 35-36. *See also* CONARC Rivalry, interservice
Army Reorganization Act of 1920, 23
Army Reserve system, 21
Army Signal Corps, 21-22; Aeronautical Division of, 21, 22

Arnold, Henry H., 25, 69, 146; battle of, with McNair, 35, 36, 37; demonstration of helicopter for, 70; early career of, 26, 28
Arsenal systems, 67, 74
ARVN (Army of the Republic of Viet Nam), 123. See also Vietnam
Ash, Roberta, 84
Atomic Energy Act, 47
Atomic weapons, 37-38, 56, 63
Authority: charismatic, 11-12, 148, 153; and compliance, 6, 7, 152; ideological, 11-12; and mission, 15, 16; rational-legal, 11-12; traditional, 11-12; value-rational, 11-12, 85
Autogiro, 69
A-X, 126, 131

Baker Buster, 72, 73
Bell Helicopter Company, 75, 76, 97-98, 140
Brecht, Arnold, 91
Bristol, Delbert L., 32, 114
Brockmyer, James, 114
Brucker, Wilbur, 81
Bucher, Rue, 12
Budget: the Air Forces' problems with, 108; and interservice rivalry, 2; post-World War II military, 51; role of Office of Secretary of Defense in preparing, 59; and technology, 67-68; as a tool of legislative oversight, 57
Buffalo (CV-2), 117
Bureaucracy, 17, 154-57; authority within, 13; goal structure within, 14
Bureaucratic adaptation, 19
Bureaucratic politics, 1, 3, 5, 15
Bureaucratic sabotage, 91
Bureaucratic social movement: characteristics of, 84-87; as a cognitive minority, 15; conditions for development of, 18; ecological theory of, 147-48; geographical dispersion of, 108; meaning of success for, 153, 146, 149-51. See also CAVEAT

Cairnes, Bogardus S., 80
Cannon, Howard, 126, 135
Career, military, 16, 101-2, 144, 145
Carentan, Battle of, 16
Caribou (CV-7), 55, 90, 91, 117
Carter, Clarence J., 78
Carter, Ross, 34

Case, Tom, 30
CAVEAT: Gavin's relationship to, 101; Howze's relationship to, 104-6; Hutton's relationship to, 110; perseverance of, 85-87; as a social movement, 107; success of, 129; tactics of, 111, 113, 115
Central Intelligence Agency, 155
Chaffee, Adna, 30
Charisma, 148, 153. See also Authority, charismatic
Cheyenne (AH-56A): and allocation politics, 126; contract for, cancelled, 122, 140; development of, 64; and Johnson-McConnell Agreement, 118; and psychology of technology, 132-33
Chidlaw, Benjamin W., 30
Civilian aviation: in Germany, 24; in the Soviet Union, 24
Civilian support groups, 57
Civil-military relations, 2, 3; and complex organizations, 153-56; models of, 6; and noncompliance, 7, 9
Clark, Mark W., 25, 28, 29
"Class before one," 32, 99
Close air support, 124-28; Air Force's involvement in, 33-34, 93; and the armed helicopter, 4; and bureaucratic insurgency, 15-16; congressional hearings on, 126-28; in the Korean conflict, 52; in Vietnam, 119
Close Air Support Review Group, 124-28
Closed politics, 4
Cold War, 41-43, 95-99
Combat: impact of, on society, 2; and the momentum for air power, 22; and sense of mission, 13, 14, 60
Comity, 117-20
Complex organizations, 5; and civil-military relations, 154-57; and domain, 39, and noncompliance, 6
Compliance, 6, 7, 9, 14
CONARC (Continental Army Command), 73, 80, 98, 108
Congress: as arena for air power debate, 22-24; close air support hearings in, 126-35; and domain, 57-58; hearings politics in, 120; and military reorganization, 43-46; and National Security Act of 1947, 47-49, 145. See also House Appropriations Com-

mittee; House Armed Services Committee; Select Committee on Post-War Military Policy; Senate Armed Services Committee; Senate Military Affairs Committee
Constitution, U.S., 7
Continental Army Command Training Memorandum 13, 73
Conventional weaponry, 51-52
Core technology, 65
Costello, Norman A., 78
"Cub spirit," 88, 94

Danford, Robert M., 30-31
de Bothezat, George, 68
Decision making, 4, 45-46
Defense Department, 4, 19, 59, 110-11, 124-26. *See also* McNamara; Packard; Secretary of Defense, Office of
de Gaulle, Charles, 8
Democracy, 153-57
Dick Act, 21
Disosway, Gabriel, 113
Disosway Board, 113
Doctrine, 15, 64-66
DOD directive 5160.22, 129
Domain: of the Air Force, 5; of the Army, 60; controversy over, 39-61; defined, 39; and military reorganization, 47
Douhet, Giulio, 23
Downing, Wayne, 108-9

Eberstadt, Ferdinand, 45
XVIII Airborne Corps, 95, 103, 105
82nd Airborne Division, 98, 101, 111
Eisenhower, Dwight D.: and Army aviation, 25; defense policy of, as president, 54; on interservice cooperation, 37, 45; and the Louisiana maneuvers, 30, 31
11th Air Assault Division, 114-15, 121
Ellul, Jacques, 17
Emery, F. E., 40
Erwin, James P., 75, 76
Etzioni, Amitai, 6
Exit, 16, 151. *See also* Albert O. Hirschman

Field Manual 100-20, 34
Finletter, Thomas K., 54
1st Air Cavalry Division (1st Cavalry Division [Air Mobile]): under John J. Tolson, 105; and Sky Cav, 77; and Vietnam, 116, 118, 120, 127
Flood, Daniel, 116
Ford, William W., 30, 32
Foreign policy, 2, 59-61
Forrest, Frank, 69
Forrestal, James V., 45, 49
Fort Benning, Ga., 75-76, 110, 114
Fort Bragg, N.C., 110
Fort Rucker, Ala., 72-75, 76-77, 100, 104
Friedrich, Carl J., 12
Fuller, F. C., 65

Gavin, James: on air mobility, 101; at Fort Rucker, 81; and Hamilton Howze, 104; on interservice rivalry, 59; as military thinker, 79, 98, 107, 145
General Accounting Office, 67
General Dynamics Corporation, 133
General Electric Corporation, 73, 78
General Headquarters Air Force, 24
Generous, Harry, 76
Goldfire I, 114
Goldwater, Barry, 116, 129
Goodwin, F. C., 73
"Grasshopper Squadron," 31
Gross, Bertram, 155
Grumman Corporation, 90

Hackett, Sir John, 3
Halsey, William "Bull," 45
Hardy, Jack, 73
Harrier (AV-8), 126
Haynes, Tommy, 69
Hearings politics, 133-35
Heavy-lift helicopter (HLH), 141
Heberle, Rudolph, 85
Helicopters: as air cavalry, 55, 56-57; armed, 4, 16, 69-78, 107, 117, 127; loss rate of, 1; and medical evacuation, 52; and technology, 62-81; testing of, 98-99; vulnerability of, 123-24, 127-28. *See also* Advanced scout helicopter; Advanced attack helicopter; Cheyenne; Heavy-lift helicopter; Huey Cobra; LOCH; UH-1; Utility tactical transport aircraft system
Hennessey, J. J., 111
Hill, Lister, 106
Hiller Corporation, 75
Hirschman, Albert O., 151. *See also* Exit

212 / Index

Hitler, Adolph, 8
Hopkins, Harry, 28
House Appropriations Committee, 58
House Armed Services Committee, 57
Howell, William A., 75
Howze, Hamilton, 79, 104, 105, 106, 110-14, 148
Howze Board (Army Tactical Mobility Requirements Board), 111-14, 148
Huey (UH-1), 78
Huey Cobra (AH-1G), 118
Hughes Helicopter Division, 140
Hull, Cordell, 28
Huntington, Samuel, 11, 55
Hutton, Carl I., 110; as advocate of decentralized aviation, 102-3; as commandant of the Army Aviation School, 106, 107; and the development of Fort Rucker, 101; as a military scholar, 145; and Sky Cav, 72-73

Identification with unit, 16
Identity, professional, 12
Incentives, 2
Industrial rivalry, 58-59
Industrial supporters: as backstop interest groups, 146; and CAVEAT, 108; and the Louisiana maneuvers, 30-31; and Sky Cav, 75-76; and Vanderpool, 73; and weapons demonstrations, 80-81
Innovation: and insurgency, 16, 85-86; and invention, 78-81; and noncompliance, 91; and technology, 19
Insurgent bureaucratic politics, 15, 18; and Army aviation, 31, 149; conformity of participants in, 16; dynamics of, 82-120, 152; persistence in, 151; and Sky Cav, 72. *See also* Bureaucratic social movement; Rivalry, intraservice
Interest groups, 4. *See also* Industrial supporters
Invention, 68-81

Jenkins, Reuben, 71
Johnson, Harold, 117-18
Johnson-McConnell Agreement, 117-20, 123, 129
Joint Army-Air Force Adjustment Regulations 5-10-1, 53
Joint boards, 21, 49

Joint Chiefs of Staff: on the armed Mohawk, 118; development of, 49-50; on "mission," 4, 53; role of chairman of, 47, 50
Just, Ward, 16

Kendall, James, 129, 130
Kennedy, John F., 59
Kerr, John, 140
Key West Agreement, 55
Key West Conference of 1948, 53
King, Ernest J., 25
Kinnard, Harry, 114
Kipling, Rudyard, 2
Korean conflict, 99-104; Army aviation during, 71, 145-46; domain controversy during, 52; MacArthur's role in, 8
Kurth, James, 133

Laird, Melvin, 124
Language, politics of, 135-38
Laos, 1, 123
Lavelle, John D., 9, 84
"Leaning approach," 86
Legislative oversight, 58. *See also* Congress
Leich, Robert, 96
LeMay, Curtis, 17, 108
Light aviation, 30, 31. *See also* Helicopters; Piper Aircraft Corporation
Light observation helicopter. *See* LOCH
Linton, Robert, 89
LOCH (Oh-6A), 120
Lockheed Aircraft Corporation, 122, 133
Lovett, Robert: as Secretary of Defense, 54; as Assistant Secretary of War, 15, 31
Lycoming Company, 78

MacArthur, Douglas, 8, 45, 52, 57
McConnell, John P., 117, 119. *See also* Johnson-McConnell Agreement
Machiavelli, 7
McKinley, William, 21
McIntyre, Thomas, 129, 135
McNair, Lesley J.: association of, with Marshall, 28, 29; and battle with Arnold, 35-36; death of, 34; on air power, 25, 31, 32

McNamara, Robert S.: and airmobility, 110-11; budgeting approach of, 59, 67; and the Howze Board, 113-14; military reorganization by, 123; weapons procurement approach of, 149
McNarney, Joseph T., 27
Marine Corps, 5, 49, 90, 126
Marshall, George C.: and Army aviation, 32, 36; and Army reorganization, 27, 43; key political relationships of, 28-29, 36-37; and top politics, 25, 26
Mayhood, Farrell T., 73
Mechanic, David, 92
Members of Congress for Peace through Law, 125, 131
Military Construction Authorization Act of 1959, 58
Military education, 23, 26
Military organization, 37, 123; role of international politics in, 21
Military politics, 3
Military reorganization, 44-50. *See also* National Security Act of 1947
Missiles, 107
Mission, 4-5, 136, 153; and the Army's future, 142; assignment of, 87-90; authority of, 12-15; and bureaucratic insurgency, 149-52; commitment to, 18; and the employment of air power, 22-23; the Navy's view of, 44; and technology, 66, 156-57. *See also* Roles and missions
Missionaries, 5, 88-89
Mitchell, William, 84, 85; court martial of, 24; on the employment of air power, 22; outspokeness of, 72, 151; as a student of Marshall, 26
Mohawk (OV-1), 90, 112, 118
Momyer, William, 128
Montgomery, James, 74
Morgan, John E. P., 30
Moorer, Thomas M., 135
Motivation, 10-11
Moynihan, Daniel "Pat," 91

National Security Act of 1947, 46-50, 70, 96, 145
Naval aviation, 53
Navy: vs. the Air Force, 63; vs. Billy Mitchell, 23, 24; and unification of the armed forces, 44-46; roles and missions of, 5
Neeley, Robert, 97
Nelson, Horatio, 7
"New Look," 54
Newport Conference of 1948, 53
Nimitz, Chester, 45
Nixon, Richard M., 9
Nixon Doctrine, 121
Noncompliance, 6, 9; and compliance, 6; effect of, on roles and missions decisions, 90-91; historical examples of, 7, 8, 9; insurgents' style of, 86, 152; and the sense of mission, 4, 5, 155
Nordstad, Lauris, 100
North American Aviation Corporation, 77
Nuclear war, 9, 56-57, 63. *See also* Atomic weapons

Oden, Delk McC., 116-17
Officers, military, 11
101st Airborne Division, 120
Operation Ammo, 81
Operation Lam Son 719, 123
Operation Menu, 108-9
"Orange" (defoliant), 9
Organic aviation. *See* Army aviation
Organizational analysis, 3, 39, 82, 153-54
Organizational environment, 47, 58-59; types of, 39, 40, 48
Organizational legitimacy, 83-84
Organizational structure: high-level participants in (*see* Top politics); low-level participants in, 5, 6, 19, 29-32, 92-93; role of middle-level participants in, 6, 9, 93
Organization-sets, 40, 47
Ostfriesland Affair, 24, 79
Outlook, 11; and goals, 13, 14, 44; and norms, 12

Pace, Frank, Jr., 54
Pace-Finletter agreement, 54
Packard, David, 124, 126, 128, 139-40
Panama Canal, 21
Paperwork, 110-11
Patton, George, 35
Persistence, 18, 87. *See also* Insurgent bureaucratic politics

214 / Index

Petroczy, Stefan, 68
Pike, Otis, 116-17
Piper, W. T., Sr., 30, 31
Piper Aircraft Corporation, 29
Plato, 7
Policy making, 17, 18, 83-84, 156-57
Powell, Herbert B., 75
Power, 16
PPBS (planning-programming-budgeting systems), 59. *See also* Budget
President's Council on Juvenile Delinquency and Youth Crime, 91
The Prince. See Machiavelli
Project Checo, 120
Project Corona Harvest, 120
Project Sally Rand, 71
Prototyping, 139-40
Proxmire, William, 131, 133-35
Psychology of technology, 62-64, 122, 138, 149
Public administration, 45-46, 154-57
Public officials: soldiers as, 3
Public relations, 58, 146; through demonstration, 79-81
Public support, 57

Ramo-Wooldridge Corporation, 67, 141
Rank, military, 93, 101-2, 105
Research and development, 64
Reston, James, 1
Richardson, James O., 44, 45
Rickover, Hyman, 84, 85, 151
Ridgway, Matthew, 54, 99, 101
Rivalry, interservice: and Arnold, 35-37; and CAVEAT, 143-49; and close air support, 134-38; and the concept of mission, 5; and the Howze Board, 111, 113-14; and industrial rivalry, 58-59; during the Korean conflict, 52; and McNair, 35-37; and military reorganization, 44; and Mitchell, 24; and Operation Menu, 108-9; and the ordering of priorities, 14-15; during the post-World War II period, 45-52; and the psychology of technology, 62-64, 66; and the *raison d'être* of the Army, 38; and roles and missions conferences, 53-54; and top politics, 128-33; in Vietnam, 120, 123-24; and weapons procurement, 66-77, 100
Rivalry, intraservice: and air power, 21-24; among aviators, 95, 141; and decentralization, 102-3, 148; and interservice rivalry, 18-19; "Red" versus "expert," 109-10. *See also* Army aviation
Roles and missions: assignment of, 4-5; in a bureaucratic setting, 89-93; defined, 3-4; and domain controversy, 47-52; early Army-Air Force agreements on, 52-55, 72; and insurgency, 18; in the Johnson-McConnell Agreement, 117; the provision of air defense, 56; in top politics, 129-32; and universal military training, 56; the Vietnam War's impact on, 123, 128-31
Rogers, Gordon, 108
Rogers Board (Army Aircraft Requirements Review Board), 108
Root, Elihu, 21-26
Roosevelt, Franklin D., 25, 26, 27-28; death of, 41; and Marshall's drive for military reorganization, 43

Sagebrush, 72
Second Hoover Commission, 67
2nd Infantry Division, 115-16
Secretary of Defense, Office of, 47, 49, 59
Select Committee on Postwar Military Policy (Woodrum Committee), 43
Senate Armed Services Committee, 57
Senate Military Affairs Committee, 45
Separatists, 23, 25
Shenandoah, 24
Shils, Edward, 11
Sierva y Cordorina, Juan de la, 69
Sikorsky, Igor, 69, 70
Sikorsky Corporation, 75, 78
Sky Cav: at Fort Benning, 75-76; at Fort Rucker, 72-75; growth and accomplishments of, 76-78
Snedeker, Edward, 81
Snow, Sir Charles Percy, 4
Social change, 66
Social circles, theory of, 148-50
Soviet Union, 24, 41-43
Spaatz, Carl, 23
Sparkman, John, 106
Specialization, 141
Speer, Albert, 155
Stahr, Elvis, 111
Stimson, Henry, 25, 28, 30

Strategic aviation: and Air Force separatists, 17, 22-23; and the Navy, 52; role of tactical aircraft in, 51; in World War II, 33-37, 42
Structures of trust, 131-32
Support, intraservice, 146-47
Swenson, J. Elmore, 105
Symington, Stuart, 129, 134-35

Tactical aviation, 33-35, 51, 119. *See also* Army aviation; Close air support; Light aviation
Task, 4, 12, 14. *See also* Mission
Taylor, Maxwell, 71, 80, 104
Technological lag, 64
Technology: and the Army's outlook, 61; and doctrine, 64-66; and the federal budget, 51, 67-68; and the helicopter, 62-81; and invention, 68-78; and organization-sets, 41; psychology of, 62-64, 132, 138, 149; and public policy, 155-58; and technicians, 105, 109-10, 145, 155-56; and weapons procurement, 66-67
10th Transport Company, 114
Terminology, as a political weapon, 77, 89, 96, 136-37
Test boards, 98-99, 107. *See also* Airmobility, testing of
Theodicy, 13
Thompson, James D., 65
Thompson, Victor A., 92
Thor-Jupiter controversy, 4
Thurman, Strom, 134-35
Tolson, John J., 105
Top politics: Army aviation in, 93, 121-42, 149; Marshall's involvement in, 25-29; models of, 4; and the National Security Act of 1947, 48; and perspectives of the Joint Chiefs of Staff, 118
Tower, John, 133-35
Traditionalists, 24, 25
Trist, E. I., 40
Trueblood, Elton, 89
Truman, Harry S., 8, 41, 51, 57
Truman Doctrine, 42
T-37 jet fighter, 55

UH-1, 78
U.S. Army Aviation Digest, 79, 107
U.S. Military Academy. *See* West Point

Universal military training (UMT), 56
Utility tactical transport aircraft system (UTTAS), 141
Utility Tactical Transport (UTT) Helicopter Company, 78

Valian, Preston, 85
Values, 11-14, 153, 155-57
Vandenburg, Hoyt S., 100
Vanderpool, J. D., 72-73, 74
Van Karman, Theodore, 68
Vertol Corporation, 77
Vietnam: combat in, after the Johnson-McConnell Agreement, 119-20; impact of, on the Army's domain, 60-61; public relations and, 79; scope of Army aviation in, 1, 9, 120, 121; testing of helicopters in, 78
Vietnamization, 123
von Cholitz, Dietrich, 8
Von Kann, Clifton, 110

Wann, Henry, 30
War Department, 24, 26, 27
War Powers Act of 1918, 22
Watson, James McCord III, 29
Weapons allocation, 4
Weapons procurement: and McNamara, 149; politics of, 132-33; recent trends in, 139-41; and technology, 66-67
Weber, Max, 12, 13, 15
Wellington, Duke of, 75
Westmoreland, William, 121
West Point: and Adams, 103; and Gavin, 145; and Howze, 104; and Hutton, 110, 145; linked to Cub tradition, 107; and military outlook, 11-12; role of, in "Red" versus "expert" struggles, 109-10; as source of Army aviation "stars," 150; and Williams, 99, 107, 145; and World War II leaders, 8, 26
Wheeler, Earl, 114
White, William D., 130
Willer, David, 12, 13, 85
Williams, Robert R., 126, 139; and efforts for Army aviation, 32, 99-100, 107, 110, 114, 145
Wilson, Bryce, 69
Wilson, Charles, 54, 55, 90
Wilson Memorandum: exceptions to, 90; impact of, on Army missile pro-

Wilson Memorandum *(continued)*
grams, 55, 107; rescinded, 137; specifics of, 55
Wingate, Orde, 7
Woodrum, Clifton A., 43, 44
Works Progress Administration (WPA), 28
World War I, 22, 26
World War II, 25, 41; the Air Force's view of its role during, 5, 17; the Army's view of its role during, 17; Cub pilot veterans of, 109, 144-45; interservice rivalry during, 33-37; and origins of Army aviation, 69-70, 92-95, 144-45
Wright Brothers, 21, 26
Wyman, W. G., 73, 80

Zald, Meyer, 84

Library of Congress Cataloging in Publication Data

Bergerson, Frederic A.
  The Army gets an air force.

  Bibliography: pp. 195-207.
  Includes index.
  1. United States. Army—Aviation. 2. United States—Military policy.
  3. Sociology, Military—United States. 4. Bureaucracy. I. Title.

UG633.B434   301.5'93'0973   79-18191
ISBN 0-8018-2205-X